System Upgrade
v2.016

Solutions for a failing economy, wealth distribution, declining democracy, climate change, and robots that steal jobs

Gris Anik

SYSTEM UPGRADE V2.016

SOLUTIONS FOR A FAILING ECONOMY, WEALTH
DISTRIBUTION, DECLINING DEMOCRACY, CLIMATE
CHANGE, AND ROBOTS THAT STEAL JOBS

COPYRIGHT © 2016 GRIS ANIK
COVER DESIGN - GRIS ANIK
BOOK DESIGN - GRIS ANIK
CREATESPACE – NOVEMBER 11, 2016
ISBN (print): 978-0-9956750-0-1
ISBN (epub): 978-0-9956750-1-8

To my mother and father,
for giving me life – twice.

Contents

Preface

Many books with similar content usually start by listing problems first; I have a tendency to do the same, so, for this book, I would like to change that. In this book, I will first explain the solution, and then I will discuss the real world problems I am trying to solve with it, and why it is so important to solve those problems in that particular way.

The general principle of finding a solution has a parallel with the riddle "The Slowest Race," which is a part of Sheikh's heritage stories. If you've never heard of it, it goes like this:

> "A king had two sons. The king was getting very old, and he didn't know who to give his kingdom to. So, he got his sons together for a horse race. He said, "Whoever's horse crosses the finish line last gets my kingdom. So, they both started out very slow, until they came to an old man on the side of the road. He asked why they were riding so slow. They told him their story, and the old man gave them two words of advice. After hearing these words, they took off as fast as they could.
>
> What were the two words of advice old man gave them?"

* You can find answer in the Notes (note *[1]) at the end of the book.

The notion that **we can tweak the rules just a bit and yet achieve significant effects** can be applied to our world, as well, as many issues we have experienced are rooted just in the way we perceive the physical and social world around us.

This book is my humble attempt to find answers for the challenges we are experiencing now and will face in the future. At the same time, this is my response to the books "Robots Will Steal Your Job, But That's OK," by Federico Pistono, "Rise of the Robots: Technology and the Threat of a Jobless Future," by Martin Ford, and "The Moneyless Man," by Mark Boyle.

My long-time fascination with technology and our impact on nature, as well as the possibility that we may end up in a dystopian society, made me spend a quite a time thinking about the ways we could create a future with a good outcome.

I firmly believe that it is possible to live in a highly-automated society without the need to revert to the Stone Age, that technology, if done properly, can work with nature, not against it, and that we can have high standards of living without a future economic crisis.

It is important to stress that ideas you will find here are not panacea, and they do not represent definite cures for all societal illnesses we have or may experience; it is just a step toward paving the way for many solutions to come.

We live in really strange and exciting time in the human history. Our knowledge, science, and technology are offering solutions for huge numbers of issues that have pestered us since the dawn of humanity: food shortage, access to clean water, liberation from the drudgery of work, diseases, even aging can soon become things of the past. However, at the same time, we are experiencing issues like the end of fossil fuels, pollution, technological unemployment, democracy decline, overpopulation, hunger, climate change, the possibility of global nuclear war or worldwide pandemic, and many other issues that could wipe out our race or create a dystopian society.

More and more, it is becoming obvious that one planet will not be enough and that, in order to increase our chances of survival as a species, we cannot stay on only one planet; we will need to search for and populate other habitable worlds in the universe.

Our progress is shaping an amazing — but, at the same time, somewhat terrifying — world, where humans could become like the gods we once feared. We are becoming able to resurrect species but, at the same time, we are also becoming powerful enough to destroy planets, increasing the risk of destroying ourselves in the process.

A more pressing issue is that more and more jobs are and will be taken by robots, so it begs the question of whether these God-like powers are meant for everyone or just a privileged minority.

This book will not give a fix for climate change or how to travel to other stars, but it will show a way to organize ourselves better, so we can get there faster.

For me, writing this book took a bit longer than I would want, but, in order to save my sanity, it was something that needed to be done and something I have needed to share. This book is written in the way, that most people, regardless of their background, could understand or relate to. So, I hope you will enjoy the book, and you will find some of the writings useful.

Also, I would appreciate your feedback; feel free to ask me anything (ok, almost anything), send me advice, or leave positive or negative comments; they could help me to improve this book and make it better in future editions.

I would like to thank Ryan Smith (grammar_guy) a proofreading editor I found on Fiverr, who spent a significant amount of time keeping this book clean of spelling mistakes and grammatical errors.

Before beginning, I would also like to thank you for buying this book, as all the earnings will go toward developing the BTC platform and fighting climate change. How the money is spent will be posted on the official website www.basictaxcontrol.org, where you can find more information on how to join the movement and help the cause.

Part I
Solutions

Introduction

Almost all of the stories in this book were written in the context of necessary changes to the system from the perspective of solving unfair wealth distribution, technological unemployment, political systems, global warming, and many other issues that could push us into the dystopian society.

There are many technological solutions out there, and the best option would be if they could all work together. However, the biggest change that needs to happen must happen in the political and economical sphere. In order to make that change, we are lacking intermediate steps that would help us to avoid sudden disruption. We do not need another revolution that will start a new cycle, rising like a phoenix from the ashes, repeating the same thing all over again. We need a fix for the currently malfunctioning system, and we need steps that will work for everyone and will allow everyone to adjust and adapt to new requirements.

This solution can be considered as a small piece of the puzzle necessary to push us forward to a society based on direct democracy and basic income. Also, even when we get there, those are just temporary states; in the not-so-distant future, there will be no money (physical such as metal, paper, plastic; or digital, such bank transactions or crypto currencies); instead, our economy will look like something that no one has seen before.

How to get there?

Just ten years ago, direct democracy was not technically possible for any large community. Technologically, we have not had means that were good enough to allow us to communicate on a larger scale in a timely manner. Referendums, an essential tool of direct democracy, in the way we conduct them now are expensive and time-consuming. However, now we have online surveys that are cheap, quick, and easy. By using an online solution, properly designed, we could speed up debates by removing repetition of the same arguments. Nowadays, many existing online social platforms already have similar properties like those.

In the economic sense, crowd-funding platforms have the ability to join the resources of many people, in order to accomplish higher goals. In return, people who fund projects get some kind of reward.

Following the same logic, the government is one very large crowd-sourcing fund: it takes our money and invests it in things that are important for society (or, at least, it should).

What is wrong about this picture?

Similar to some of the crowd-funded projects, government can waste money. Sometimes, it happens because of corruption, but it is usually because they are not able to control everything in a way that would prevent misuse. Disproportion between the size of the government and the body they control can create a bottleneck, preventing them from carrying out positive changes they would like to do, thus creating unintentional issues. Most of the officials are not as bad as portrayed; instead, mainly, it is just a case of misguided intentions. That misguidance does not surface only because of human flaws, but it is a much larger problem, related to shortfalls of the system's design and its inner workings.

Thirdly, years of capitalism lead to the concentration of wealth into one small percentage of the population, basically jamming the system, and potentially risking large economic and political failures. The way to solve this is by using Basic Tax Control funds, supported and driven by online social networks.

Basic Tax Control

Basic Tax Control (BTC) *[2] is the schema in which a certain amount of money is given from the tax budget to each person of a certain age. Then, each person needs to invest the received money into the projects created by people, companies, or government for the public good. In return a portion of the project's profits are given back to the fund, either as a percent of the profit or as a share in company's ownership. Also, depending on the project type projects could be given to **public ownership** in their entirety.

The main idea of Basic Tax Control is identifying and fixing the real issues in the current system, instead of destroying the existing system completely and starting from scratch all over again. Especially, as starting anew does not guarantee that we will not repeat the same mistakes. We have already tried this approach many times but, as history has shown, it did not fix the things that were broken. What was broken back then is broken now, causing more issues than before.

A good analogy would be to imagine a car that has flaws. At some point, while driving those cars, we realize that there are flaws and that some of those flaws will appear only after we drive a certain amount of miles. Furthermore, the faster we drive, the more dangerous those flaws become, endangering our lives and safety. We get angry, and, instead of fixing the car, we get the revolutionary idea to stop, burn the old car down, and start from scratch building a completely new car. Now, building from scratch is a complete setback for our trip; we are not travelling, and we are wasting time repeating the same thing. Even worse, while building the new car, we use the same engineers who have the same mindset as the builders of the previous car, and even worse they use the same plans, at the end the only things they are changing are the colors, door knobs and driver. After driving the new car for a while, we will again realize that we have the same issues as before. However, it is even worse now, as we lost time building the new car, we decided to drive as fast as possible, but, the faster we drive, the more those flaws become noticeable, and the more dangerous they become for everyone.

Instead, we could decide that we do not need to stop; we could just slow down a bit and fix the flaws while driving. Although this looks impossible, we need to remember that we invented open heart surgery, and we have practiced it for quite some time. Cars are far simpler than the human body, and, although no one ever tried fixing them while they were running (as they do not have life and cannot die if they are disassembled), I am pretty sure that, if we needed, we could easily invent a similar procedure. Our socio-political structures have life, very much like our own bodies, but by their complexity they are more like cars. They are also far more resilient: they can withstand many changes without major society disruptions or breakings. We can replace many parts, and our society will still run as usual.

Basic Tax Control philosophy is fixing instead of rebuilding, evolution instead of revolution.

Ideally, what we want is to modify and fix without affecting normal life, without causing major negative disruptions, destruction, or wars. Similarly, people were not hugely disrupted by the mobile phone revolution; we just changed our habits and adapted to new.

What the Basic Tax Control (BTC) stands for?

Basic - stands for a small amount of money that is given back from taxes at the beginning. But, also it means a basic form of control of those taxes by the people who receive them.

Tax - each person will get small amount of money from the taxes collected, and each person will have the ability to decide where he/she wants to spend that money on projects that are of public and social interest.

Control - each person is controlling his/her own dedicated tax money, and the nature of control is basic, as the amount of money is very small; in the first phase, it will not largely impact the current tax budget.

A person cannot use the BTC funds for personal gains but can decide on her/his own how and where to "invest" those funds. This is a paradigm change; although it looks small, it can have a massive positive impact on the economy and on the welfare of the overall population.

How does Basic Tax Control work?

From the total tax revenue, the government dedicates a small amount of money (£5 or higher) that will be paid to each eligible citizen (age, cognitive ability etc.) through Basic Tax Control schema.

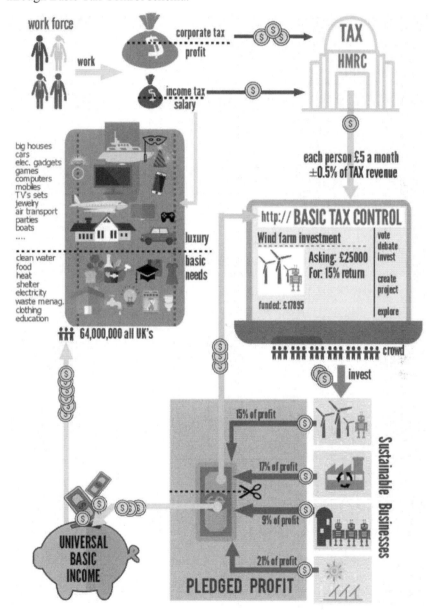

For the United Kingdom, the total amount (at £5 per person) would be around £3.4 billion or 0.5 % of total tax revenue. All people that are eligible would have an account on the Basic Tax Control platform, where they can create their own projects and business proposals for which they wish to get investment. Business creators need to describe the project as best as they can, in order to attract interest and get funds. In the process, they would need to specify a realistic amount they are requesting and also how much of the equity they are willing to give in return for that investment.

The quality of the business idea, rationality of funding, and portion of the profit someone is ready to give back will determine whether people (users) will be willing to support the idea.

Not everyone will want to create a project, and not everyone will succeed in securing funding, but some of those who do will one day start generating profit. When they start generating profit, each month, a pledged portion of the profit will be returned to the Basic Tax Control fund.

A certain percent of the "profit" money will be spread across all people inside of the platform, ready to be invested again. The second part will be transferred to the Universal Basic Income (or Citizen Income) fund, ready to be equally divided among the entire population of that country, according previously-agreed Basic Income rules.

The goal of the Basic Tax Control scheme is to create enough sustainable, automated businesses that they will one day generate enough profit/funds to cover all basic human needs.

Until we create a fully-automated, AI-driven society, there will be a need for some people to do these jobs; until we get there, Universal Basic Income must be such to cover only basic needs: access to clean water, healthy food, basic housing, clothing and heating, decent amount of electricity, secure waste management, and enough education to allow someone to find a job that will cover all other needs someone may have.

Who should receive Basic Tax Control funds?

Almost every person should receive Basic Tax Control funds.

Every person who is a citizen of a certain area and is literate enough to know how to read and write, has basic knowledge of how to use computers and the internet, and has the minimum necessary cognitive abilities — should receive funds.

In other words: every person older than 9 years who does not have any cognitive disorders that would prevent him/her from thinking or using the system.

How much money do we need?

Not much. For a country the size of the United Kingdom, for instance, with 64 million people, we would need as little as £5 per person for the initial phase, which would total £285 million per month. [i]

Calculation

 64 million (population)
  – 3.5 million (under age of 9 *[3])
  – 3.2 million (mentally not capable *[4])
 = ~ 57 million people

 57 million people * £5 for each person = £ 285 million

 For one year, that is £ 3.4 billion or 0.13% of UK's GDP.

For the year 2014-2015, the projected tax revenue in the UK was £648.1 billion *[5]; therefore, for the Basic Tax Control, we would need to set aside 0.5% of total collected taxes. This is miniscule, especially if we consider the good things that BTC can accomplish. Think about one more number: the UK's military expenditure for the year 2014 was £60.5 billion. Now, ask yourself: if we can find money for wars, can we find 20 times less money to create peace and welfare for everyone?

If you still think that neither of these things is an option, think about one more number — one important number that must not be forgotten: the amount of tax avoidance. In the UK, just for the tax year 2012/2013, the price tag of tax avoidance damage was £34bn. *[6] It is a huge number and also the reason why it is important that everyone pays a fair amount of taxes. Movements like "Fair Tax Town" have brought this issue to national attention, especially bringing to attention that tax evasion is available for any business, and it is very easy to setup.

---

[i] Total yearly amount would be a five times smaller than the advertised £350 million a week during the Brexit campaign.

For Basic Tax Control, it would be possible to take the money without any significant pressure to other services, but, if we could retrieve money dodged by big corporations, we could get significantly more money — more than enough to do the trial test of a Basic Tax Control system.

Basic Tax Control should be funded from collected taxes. While, for the early implementation and test runs, it would be possible to use private (our own) money, but that should not be continued as a practice. This voluntary approach means that, similar to giving a monthly donation to charities, people can organize in some region and give £5 each month, or more, to jump start the schema. However, regardless of the fact that the voluntary approach would be a good option for a quick start of the schema, it should not be run indefinitely, as there would be additional costs for processing transactions, and, also, by this voluntary, self-organization, the crucial aspect of schema where citizens have the ability to actually control a small portion of tax expenditures would be lost. The end goal is to take money from the already-existing means of socially-collected funds ("**taxes**") we collect for public purpose and put the control in the hands of common people, so they will have basic control.

Should the Basic Tax Control amount always be the same?

Every country or community (if privately funded) should decide the amount of money they want to dedicate for BTC, but, whatever amount is decided, it must be the same for all members of the group.

The BTC amount per person should not be fixed. Potentially, it should increase over time, until it gets to the proportion that is equally comfortable for the government and for the public. The more direct a democratic society is, the more taxes will be controlled by the people. The idea is to shift/disperse a portion of responsibility from the government to each person in society.

Increasing the funds controlled by the people should happen gradually. Based on the feedback metric (success rate) obtained from the real-world BTC system, the government could (using standard means, such as passing bills or taking a vote on) increase or decrease Basic Tax Control funds. This can be done at the same time budget expenditures are determined or more frequent if required or found fruitful.

For instance, if the trial has been successful after 3 months or so, the amount should be increased, relative to the size and amount of success. Ideally, the increase should be calculated in a way that would achieve optimum efficiency for the next step. Deciding the BTC rate should be one of the major influences of the government on this system, along with providing regulatory framework against fraudulent activities; otherwise, the government should refrain from any other type of control or influence on the system.

In theory, the public could control 100% of the tax revenue, but that would require a high level of understanding about public services and public needs, like welfare, healthcare, state pension, defense, justice, etc. Any disproportional funding could cause disruptions and issues. Although 100% is very difficult to achieve, it is possible with the proper level of knowledge of people who are involved.

Shouldn't we move from taxes?

There is an argument that taxes, as they are mandatory and not voluntary, are a tool of oppressive governments. In this view, taxes should be abolished.

Why is that a wrong assumption?

There are two parts of our lives: one is personal, and the other is social.

In the same way as we have personal needs defined by Maslow's hierarchy, we have our societal needs. We collect taxes, in order to satisfy those needs. Roads, electricity, gas, communication, law, justice, healthcare (in many countries), and many other things are there because of tax collection. Tax collection is helping us to move our society forward, build infrastructure, and increase overall wealth.

A voluntary approach to taxes would raise many other issues, like protection of community property from the members who wished to be excluded. Or questions like following: if people who choose not to pay taxes are invaded by another country, does the military come to their defense?

In order to simplify things, at some point, we decided that we all must pay a share, and I agree with this. Taxes are important, but, also, it is important what we do with them — are we using them for good or bad things — and that is something that should be everyone's moral decision, not just the burden of our governments.

Why Basic Tax Control?

Basic Tax Control is cheap and easy to implement. The amount of money necessary to implement Basic Tax Control is significantly smaller than the amount of money needed for full Unconditional Basic Income. Although Basic Tax Control is not private/personal and unconditional like the Basic Income, Basic Tax Control's purpose is implementation of Universal Basic Income and pure (full) democracy.

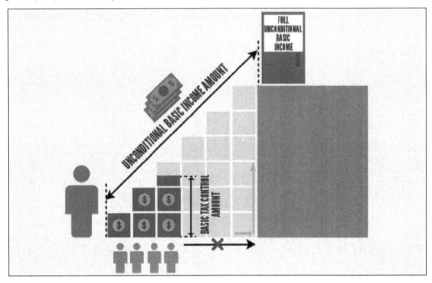

We can think about Basic Tax Control as a staircase to the door on the first floor. Doors on the first floor represent the minimal amount needed to be able to give Universal Basic Income (UBI) to everyone. Each step represents a portion of money dedicated for Basic Tax Control, and the height of the step represents the amount of money that was returned to the UBI fund from investments. The number of steps we all need to build and the path we need to travel are not known at the beginning, but it would be possible to estimate what it would take to get there. Every step we build will lift us higher, but only if it's done in the correct way. If we build stairs aligned like floor tiles, we will never get there.

Basic Tax Control can be implemented gradually, and every country can set its own amount of money controlled by the public. It can be adjusted per GDP or per amount of taxes that are collected. Basic Tax Control can be a much easier step forward than the immediate implementation of Basic Income, especially for those countries which do not have enough money for Basic Income.

Basic Tax Control can build entrepreneurship, collaboration, a sense of being a part of and belonging to the community. Basic Tax Control counters the sense that your government is some ruling entity somewhere above you and that it must do something for you or that you have to do something for your government. Instead, Basic Tax Control gives the sense of being a part of that government, being a part of that society, being part of change — instead of dreams, wishes, and hopes — the role is shifted, and everyone has the ability to decide, create, or take action in creating a future society.

As Basic Tax Control is transparent for the public and for the companies involved, it builds a sense of trust and decreases the chances of fraudulent activities and manipulations.

Basic Tax Control will be an online platform, which increases efficiency and our ability to communicate, regardless of distance, and, as the prices of smart phones and computers are constantly dropping, there is no reason why any member of our society should not have access to it, unless he or she deliberately does not want it.

How is Basic Tax Control a step toward direct democracy?

Government primarily rules by two means: by managing tax collection resources and by creating laws and policies. By shifting a small portion of money back to the public, and allowing the public to be more involved in affairs for public welfare, gives a small amount of government responsibility back to the public.

By direct involvement, the public learns how to be more socially and democratically active, learning how to think in the sense of the community and what is good for others — not just what is good for single person. Therefore, Basic Tax Control is a way to allow society to achieve fairer and more direct democracy.

Usual argument on "why power cannot be transferred to a wide population" is the mob behavior. However, the reason why some societies become more liberal toward minorities and different races is due to advances in technology, communication, change of generations, shift in thinking, but also because the power was in the hands of a few who were enlightened enough to see the benefit in those changes. Increasing the rights of minorities is a very good example that not everything the government does is bad. We can argue that there were always opposite currents in government, and that explained is not a rule but the exception, still, we must ask what would happen if those decisions were left to uneducated masses of people. Many things would never happen, and we would still have widespread racism, gender inequality and oppression of different sexes.

A major hurdle to direct democracy ideas can be a mob behavior, so, meritocracy in some sense is still necessary, in some sense. In order to find a solution, society still needs the most skillful people for certain subjects and needs people that have multidisciplinary knowledge. Those most skillful people, top scientists, and experts in their own fields need to present solutions in simple, understandable ways and be open to discussion or scrutiny by peer reviews. From that point onward, the public would decide what is the best solution or approach.

This is similar to daily life: if we need to design a building, we would find an architect; if we need complex calculations, we would find a mathematician; if we need to examine material for certain properties, we would find a chemist – and probably we will try to find a good one. Every field has people with certain knowledge, and each type of knowledge can help in finding solution. No one can deny that science has become an integral part of our lives, and on its own science is neither good nor bad. It is a tool to be used, and way we use it defines its nature. If we have moral questions, we would ask a theologian, philosopher, ethicist, or psychologist, or maybe even a religious monk — point being that every subject has people who have domain knowledge and who can help us when we get stuck with difficult questions.

Having experts proposing solutions does not mean that society is meritocratic; it only means that we will find solutions faster, and, whatever they find, the final decision will still lie in the hands of the general population.

What are the benefits of a Basic Tax Control system?

Listed here are some of the most important benefits, but along those there will be few as a byproduct or consequence of the main benefits such better health, longer and happier life, smaller crime rate… but I will not write about those in details, as mainly those benefits can be attributed to Universal Basic Income data.

Education

> Basic Tax Control educates, in a practical way, what democracy is all about. Through the platform, people learn in practical ways about responsibility, what social life means, and that their own actions can impact their own future. They learn how to be responsible, and, by taking that responsibility, they switch from a "vote, hope, and forget" system to active involvement in the making of our society — the society we need.

> Basic Tax Control is, in some way, like a driving license for democracy, teaching us that driving is not about ourselves but also about other people in traffic. It also teaches us that, whatever destination we are trying to reach, we will get there only by respecting the rules and those other drivers around us.

> Through active involvement inside of the platform, the general population learns how to be open to each other and how to communicate in an open, non-violent way, respecting others and their needs.

14

By using Basic Tax Control platform, democracy is not just learned, it is exercised on a daily bases. The person has to think, be involved, and make decisions. Although those decisions look small and insignificant, because of the small amount of money we need to manage, when combined, those "insignificant" amounts (by the law of large numbers) can make a significant impact on society.

More prominent and altruistic members will spend more time on the platform. They will read more and learn more about different subjects, in order to help the community by enhancing social entrepreneurship; that will lead to change. Think about it: if we can spend hours inside virtual worlds, why not spend time inside of the "game" that will actually change our own world to become something better.

Involvement does not need to be mandatory, and there should not be any type of fine or punishment for those who miss the opportunity to engage in or support community projects. However, accounts that are dormant for some time could be temporarily disabled, and their BTC account will be zeroed out, and their dedicated funds can be spread to others members. Before disabling the account, system administrators will try to message the person in different ways in order to find the reason behind the inactivity; if the same habit continues without a valid reason (inadequate projects, disability, illness, etc.) then the account will be disabled, but it could be activated again (with predefined delay period) if the user expresses a wish to activate his/her account again. At the end of the day, money must flow in order to create a change – dormant accounts should not prevent that flow.

Not just adults but children from the early age would learn about society, democracy, investment, and cooperation. By creating projects, people would learn about entrepreneurship and what it takes to make a change in society. Those who pledge their BTC money would get firsthand experience on how democracy works and how each vote matters.

Any member of the platform could voice his or her own opinion, point out the issue, or speak on behalf of those who do not have their own voices, in the same way people may gradually learn to become more solution- than problem-oriented.

Economy

The best way to explain economic benefit would be by giving a few examples:
- The company "West Wind Acme Ltd" needs £200K, in order to start production of a new type of wind electric generators with

10KW capacity. In return, it will give 10% of each year's profit back to the Basic Tax Control fund and 5% to the Universal Basic Income public fund.

- The company "Veggie Robotics Ltd" needs £500K, in order to produce 5 lines of fully-automated vegetable farms. In return, the company is offering 30% of its shares to the Universal Basic Income public fund.

The Basic Tax Control platform can boost fresh ideas and the economy; also, it could be used to tackle difficult issues, like global warming, for instance. If the idea is good, it can be funded by the public, instead of waiting for investors or grants that usually favors high yields with technologies that are part of the problem, instead of the solution, such as oil companies for instance.

Each person from the crowd has a small amount of money to share across the projects or people she/he loves and wants to support. Those projects should be for the good of the entire society. In return, projects need to satisfy two principles: either they will be made exclusively for the public good (fixing the roads, building public libraries, etc.), or they are companies that are funded to return equal or greater amounts of money into the BTC funds over time, by sharing their equity with the public through Basic Tax Control fund or Universal Basic Income fund.

Basic Tax Control investment in exchange for the business equity share is an alternative approach for one country to achieve Universal Basic Income, which is especially convenient for countries that are less developed and do not have a high GDP. This approach should not be used to undermine implementation of Unconditional Basic Income as a basic right. Bearing in mind increasing automation and technical unemployment, Unconditional Basic Income should be implemented regardless of the path we choose in the near future.

When shares are equally dispersed, instead of giving them back to the BTC "investors," those shares could work for everyone equally. In order to keep things interesting, some kind of reward system should be considered for those "investors" who are more successful and more active. By investing in projects and companies, money will circulate more, new jobs will be created, and new solutions will emerge, as a result of that process, creating a generally positive effect on the job market and the economy. That would significantly boost GDP, and, more importantly, it would direct people to work together and form solutions to fight difficult challenges, like climate change, for example.

Additionally, the idea is for any company that achieves a high level of automation is that it has to pledge most of its earnings to the public funds.

Once a company is 100% automated, it has to become a public service, giving its owner lifetime benefits, similar to what we do for former presidents. *[7]

Wealth dispersion

Basic Tax Control would create and finance companies that give money from profits back to the public. As this system permits big investors in those companies, money would not go to the top 1%. By dispersing wealth, we would avoid the accumulation of wealth and dangers that go with it. When everything becomes owned by the public, we will think twice before investing in technologies that can harm the planet or us.

Also, this type of ownership is neither government nor private ownership — it is "Public" or rather **"Social-private" ownership**. "Social-private" ownership in those companies is not transferable and not inheritable. Upon death, everything that has been under the control of that person should return to the BTC public fund and dispersed to other members of society.

This type of ownership should not be confused with the government model of ownership usually seen in socialistic countries; the government in this instance should not have any type of ownership or control over those shares.

This is very much like what nature does with the atoms of our bodies when we die, spreading them around. Think about it: no one complains because he did not get all the atoms of his grandfather when he died. In the same way, we should not complain about where our money goes when we or our relatives die. We should be like the sun, shining equally on "good" and "bad" people alike.

Support for the implementation of Basic Income

Universal Basic Income can be implemented from return on investment in Basic Tax Control projects. Dividends and profits from projects funded by the public through Basic Tax Control can be the foundation for Basic Income. Gradually, more projects and more automation will increase global wealth and bring people out of poverty and beyond what is considered the Basic Income level.

Wealth is nothing more than an amount of commodities we can provide to the population, in order to satisfy their wants or needs. Therefore, using this model to increase the overall wealth of the population would be a natural, evolutionary step in our economic development.

Basic Tax Control and automation

This is an important thing you need to remember: automation is only a problem within the current system, as automation means less jobs, and, therefore, a problem for the economy.

Basic Tax Control reverses that image by dedicating ownership of automated companies to "Social-private" ownership by the level of their automation (if 20% automated, 20% will go to funds for Basic Tax Control and Basic Income). Suddenly, what was a problem becomes a goal. Therefore, if machines are working for everyone, of course, we would like more machines and more automation. More automation means less work and less drudgery, especially while doing those repetitive, physically-demanding, boring jobs. Machines can do all that while providing an excessive amount of wealth for any person on the planet.

This will literally liberate our time, so we can purse higher goals, so we can explore our physical universe, or the universe that resides within us, allowing us to set free our creative nature.

So, while reading this book further on, whenever you come across an industry that will lose jobs because of automation, just try to remember Basic Tax Control and Societal-private ownership – and that, having less jobs, companies which require less material or people will save energy and optimize our business processes – are what we should consider to be our new primary goals.

Basic Income

Before explaining what the Basic Income is, first ask yourself following:

- If basic existence was not an issue, what would you do in your life?
- If someone would give you each month enough money to cover basic needs what would you do?
- What do you want to do with your life?
- How happy are you with your life, and what do you think would make you happy?
- What do you think what is your contribution to society?

Basic Income, also called "unconditional basic income" or "universal basic income" (UBI) *[8], and sometimes "citizen's income," is a form of social security system in which all people of one country receive a certain amount of money unconditionally, and the amount must be large enough to cover the basic existential needs of one person.

If the amount of money is not enough to satisfy all basic needs, it is called "partial basic income."

The idea of a minimum income first appeared at the beginning of the 16th Century, theorized by Thomas More (1516) and Johannes Ludovicus Vives (1526) as a means of providing welfare for poor people or as more astute way of fighting theft than sentencing thieves to death. *[9] Towards the end of the 18th century, Marquis de Condorcet and Thomas Paine (Founding Father of the United States) similar ideas emerged that had a great role in the easement of poverty throughout Europe. Trough 19th and 20th century, many famous people like John Stuart Mill (English philosopher), Charles Fourier (French writer), Bertrand Russell (Nobel laureate in literature), James Meade (Nobel Prize-winning economist), Richard Nixon (37th U.S. President), Martin Luther King Jr. and many others supported and advocated idea of Universal Basic Income in one form or another.

Basic Income is a simple and yet very powerful and effective system that has the potential to solve many social issues we are experiencing now and will experience in the future, and, although it is gaining more and more traction lately, there are some fears and issues preventing wider implementation.

What are the major fears?

The largest fear is that, if we get Universal Basic Income, we will just turn to watching TV and play video games — basically not doing anything and crippling future society.

In order to tackle this problem, in several studies following question has been asked: if basic income is enough just for basic needs, would you still work?

When people are the one presented with the question, usually 99% them answer, "Yes, we will continue with some type of work." They list reasons for that answer, such as ambition, socializing with other people, having access to more things, etc.

However, if same people were asked whether they think others will continue to work if they get basic income, they tend to answer in the negative, saying that they won't do anything and that they will be lazy most of the time!

As you may notice, this is an obvious paradox, created as a consequence of biased thinking. If we really want a better society, it is necessary to shift from any similar attitude – we need to start trusting our neighbors the same as if they were our own reflection in the mirror.

Many people who traveled around the world by foot or bike, despite experiencing a few bad things along the way, have a similar stories saying that – the majority of people are good. One of these people is Mike Carter, who wrote the book, "One Man and His Bike," *[10] explaining his 5,000 mile cycling adventure around the entire United Kingdom coastline and experiencing innumerable random acts of kindness, he made the same conclusion. Furthermore, in support of this argument, some scientific studies which have tried to answer the ultimate question, "Are we naturally good or bad?" say that a basic human instinct is to prefer friendly intentions over malicious ones. *[11]

The same goes for the basic income question and whether we would work while receiving free money. Survival is not the only thing that drives us as human beings. There are many other reasons why we do what we do: love, ambition, competition, curiosity, knowledge, compassion, altruism, and many others.

What can be the issues of Basic Income implementation?

Introducing Basic income can backfire, and there are multiple issues that can happen, but, also, there are many ways to deal with those issues.

Job side-effect

Introducing UBI in the current economic system could create a more competitive job market; therefore, it would be more difficult to find a working force for those jobs that need to done but which no one wants to do, as they are either low-paying, hard, or boring.

That is not necessarily a bad thing, although it looks like a catastrophic economic chain reaction waiting to happen.

Another issue is that it can create an economically unsustainable situation for some companies or public services, as it would affect profit so much that it would not be economically viable for the company to exist.

How do we deal with this?
The answer is simple: either automate/innovate or do not do the job.
If you cannot automate, innovate, or increase the price of the product or service, in order to achieve economic viability, then that product/service should not exist.

Take, for example, McDonald's or Walmart. Thanks to the currently-existing "social contract," these companies have huge revenues; sometimes, they even avoid paying taxes, and, despite the size of their revenues, they do not care about their workers, usually putting them on minimum wage.

Now, the question is how would they find workers, if Basic Income is implemented?
They could increase salaries (reducing those huge revenues), they could automate/innovate, or they would just stop working.

Now, is it bad if those giants stop working?
No. Actually, those giants are responsible for the destruction of countless small shops and businesses, so destroying McDonald's and Walmart would just open (or reopen) some new small local shops, allowing for a more even distribution of the wealth by supporting the local economy in the process.

Now, one may ask, "But, if someone receives Basic Income, why would he or open the small shop again?"
Because Basic Income covers only basic needs. So, it is very likely that people would like to do something, in order to earn more. The second reason is just because they like to do it.

Price side-effect

The one more serious issue is that the introduction of UBI can cause a pricing bubble.

If we give free money to everyone suddenly, excess money on the market can cause a price hike. For example: rent can jump by an amount equal to what we have distributed for basic income, siphoning money into the pocket of a few and again creating the same poverty issue we had at the beginning. Eventually, this can cause an inflationary bubble that can collapse the economy.

How do we prevent UBI from causing an inflationary bubble?

In order to avoid this, we would need to either create policies that would not allow products or services to increase prices over the typical inflation rate, or we would need to rethink that type of industry.

One glaring example of something that needs rethought is housing.

Simply said, housing is not a thing anymore; it is not innovative, it is the most expensive investment people make, and, by and large, it is a major economic problem. It can be resolved entirely, if we start thinking in a different way.

The only reason why housing has existed in its unmodified form for so long is because it is one of the biggest tools of enslavement and control of the masses. How does housing do that?

To buy a house is one of the largest investments in someone's life and, if that person takes a mortgage, over time he or she will repay double of the money they initially borrowed – despite the fact that a bank created that money from thin air. They will spend most of the time working for the bricks or wooden beams. The higher on the social ladder they are, they will be chained with higher property values. If they do not take on a mortgage, most of their earnings would go into paying rent. By calculating, you will find that, for the majority of people, more than 4 working hours a day will go into paying rent or mortgage. That means that, during their 40-year professional life, they will spend 20 years or more on – bricks.

Housing can be solved in different ways for the future society, and there are many ideas on how to disrupt housing market by making it more affordable while keeping or increasing the level of quality. Although solutions for housing can be a book on their own, here, I will hint just a few. One of the solutions could be an accumulation of Basic Income for kids, which could give a head start to future generations (explained in the following subchapter as part of the solution for the issue of "Age exploitation"). Next is creating cheaper, eco-friendly materials, decreasing the price of building. Simplifying the administration needed for building permits and, in the process, decreasing the prices of documentation. Open sourcing is also an option; designs, planning, and engineering of simple, template-houses can be done online. Last but not least, it could be possible to decrease prices by automating the building process, using industrial 3D printers and robot brick layers that can build houses in a matter of days.

Age exploit

As every person receives universal basic income, this can create issues where parents or guardians are attracted to the idea of having multiple children, in order to gain more money.

This can either promote a baby boom behavior, like it already happen with young UK teen mothers, or it can create "Oliver Twist" type of frauds, where children in foster homes or orphanages are kept in terrible conditions, so that their "patrons" could enjoy a wealthy life.

Population explosion on a finite planet with finite resources is a huge issue, and, in some sense, basic income can be used effectively as a tool for "controlling" population numbers.

Limiting the age for receiving basic income would violate the basic premises and simplicity, which says that everyone should receive it, regardless of age, gender, or origin. The work around of this problem would be that children can be given access to their compounded basic income funds only when they become adults, so they can decide what to do with that money.

That approach could resolve one more issue, by the time they become adults they would have enough funds to buy their own homes and continue living on their own basic income independently.

The other way to solve this is to give smaller Basic Income to children or divide it by providing different amounts by age group. The proposal goes beyond this by giving less income to any subsequent child (RSA model); although that could slightly increase the administration necessary to handle those exceptions, it would probably achieve the desired result.

Behavior side-effect

Although, in trial runs, Basic Income had positive effects on people's behavior, showing that the majority people are not lazy, let's consider the hypothetical possibility that this is exactly what will happen — that for some group of people, adapted to poverty conditions and high crime, basic income will do an ill favor and enhance their bad behavior.

How do we solve that possibility of a bad behavioral side-effect?
It would be wrong to introduce basic income, expect that everything will resolve on its own, and then judge the idea based on a group of people who failed without looking into the reasons for that failure.

It is very much like giving a winning lottery ticket to everyone: of course, there are those who will not know how to handle it, but the good thing is that the majority will know. Those who had working habits, knowledge, or are naturally self-driven will manage, but a certain portion of people will not live better – just like those stories about those lottery winners who blew it all. *[12]

It is similar to giving money to an alcoholic; of course the person will buy more alcohol, because his biggest problem in the first place was not the lack of money but his addiction.

Although Basic Income can reduce crime rate, it will not prevent or stop crime completely; same as people who have problems with addiction will still have issues. Murder, theft, and gambling will still continue to exist. Basic income also does not tackle issue of greedy people, and they also will continue to exist People who are terrible with money management will still spend it all at once. However, although it will not help criminally inclined people, it will help those who are caught in bad neighborhoods without a chance to move forward; it will help many who are willing to make a change and improve their lives.

In order to combat crime and anti-social behavior, society would need to create more support groups and free learning help groups. Similarly, just as we are taking care of childhood boredom, we would need to find a way to educate and animate those groups toward positive change. Education is the key; if we do not want to let people slide into boredom, we need to open those people's minds and expand their horizons through continued, voluntary education.

When we teach people to dream better dreams, they will rise to grab them.

The new structure of society would require psychological help for every member of society, but not in the specific sense of psychotherapy; instead, it would be more like orientation-therapy — basically, helping people to find what they love, especially if they lived in such circumstances that they cannot remember on their own.

We always have a choice; we can continue dealing with crime and anti-social behavior with the existing punitive approach, like we have done before. Or, maybe we can find a better way and help each member of society to find its own way?

The argument that "It is wrong to give something for nothing"

To begin with, everything we have and nearly all infrastructure that surrounds us has been created by other people. In many ways, we are using it for free or almost free. Countless generations before us created knowledge, roads, the electric grid, underground tunnels, ships, cars, etc. Regardless of how big we may think our contributions to society are, we have done these things only because of those who came before us.

In order to address ownership of capital, we may argue that our social contract was wrong from the beginning. If our ancestors had a better social contract, we would not need to argue this question at all. If they had a proper social contract, they would have had shares in each company for which they have worked, proportional to the contribution they have made to that company. In this way, when everything becomes automated, they would have if not equal then at least enough access to resources that would allow them and their descendants to survive...

Try imagining a scenario where a couple of people worked toward a similar goal. For instance, the goal was to build a machine that mills wheat seeds into flour. At the beginning, the job was done manually, and it was tiring and time-consuming, as everyone needed to work, in order to produce enough. Someone had the idea to harness river stream and build a waterwheel to roll the milling stone. In the process of making the machine, everyone had some job. It was not just building the waterwheel but also creating the stone, the hut, the road to the river, cutting trees, preparing food, etc. When the job was done, it was not reserved only for the one who invented the waterwheel; it was accessible and available for everyone who was involved in making the project possible. Everyone could use it for free. With time, the waterwheel would need just a bit of maintenance, now and then, and that is all. It is there for everyone to use, for everyone to share.

This idea is not socialism. It is not communism or any other –ism. It is common sense. It is collaboration, instead of competition. It is giving and sharing, instead of guarding and hoarding. It is what society really means — creating a better life for everyone.

Master and puppet issue

One more issue that can arise is the active control of the public through price manipulation and income control. In a democratic society, there is a huge difference between having the ability to decide and being controlled.

One possible danger is that in fully automated system, basic income can become a tool of keeping the masses deliberately very close to the poverty level, not giving them access to resources. The decision of controlling the amount of funds that are dispersed could fall to the government, giving it the ability to control and manipulate the market through inflation and price increases, in order to siphon all the funds into the pockets of a few who are at the top effectively crating dictatorship.

In order to avoid possibility of master and puppet issue in the society with basic income, it would be necessary for that society to become a pure democratic society (also known as direct democracy *[13]), where all people will be involved and work for the benefit of the society.

Cost

A frequently asked question is:"How much would it cost to implement Basic Income?"

Let's consider the following numbers for the United Kingdom:

- The population in the year 2015 was 65 million people *[14]

- The Gross Domestic Product (GDP) for the year 2015 was £1.834 trillion *[15]

- The total amount of Tax Collected for the year 2014/2015 was £648 billion *[16]

If we suppose that, in order to cover the basic needs of each citizen in the UK, we would need to secure between £450 and £1000 a month per each person, that would mean that we need to secure (£450 to £1000 a month * 65,110,000 people * 12 months) between £351.6 billion and £781.3 billion.

That is 19.2% to 42.6% of the UK's total GDP or **54.3%** to **120.6%** of total collected tax money, which looks unacceptably high.

But, according to The Royal Society for the Encouragement of Arts, Manufactures, and Commerce (RSA), we could accomplish the same goal with an amount that will be more acceptable. Their Basic Income model calculation says that the needed amount would be around £284 billion. They made this possible by dividing people into age groups, where each group had a different income. *[17]

A Joseph Rowntree Foundation (JRF)-supported publication calculated that the necessary Basic Income amount for the entire UK population would be between £176.9 and £209.5 billion. Similar to the RSA they used different amounts for different age groups. *[18]

If we round the needed amount to £290 billion, the question is where to get that money from, as amount still accounts for almost 45% of total tax revenue.

Tax summary description	Description of PESA source (See PESA Table 5.2)	Public Sector Expenditure (£ billion)	%
Welfare [*]	'Social Protection' excluding state pensions	171.1	25.3
Health	Health	134.1	19.9
State Pensions [*]	Within 'Social Protection' 1	86.5	12.8
Education	Education	84.3	12.5
Defense	Defense	36.5	5.4
National Debt Interest	Within General Public Services, but shown in more detail in table 5.2	33.5	5
Public Order & Safety	Public Order & Safety	29.9	4.4
Transport	Economic Affairs, without Business and Industry but shown in more detail in table 5.2	20.5	3
Business & Industry	Economic Affairs, without Transport	17.9	2.7
Government Administration [*]	Captured under General Public Services, but shown in more detail in table 5.2	13.7	2
Culture (e.g. sports, libraries, museums)	Recreation, Culture & Religion	11.9	1.8
Environment	Environment protection	11.7	1.7
Housing and utilities (eg street lights)	Housing & Community Amenities	10.9	1.6
Overseas Aid	Captured under General Public Services, but shown in more detail in table 5.2	8.8	1.3
UK Contributions to EU budget	EU Transactions	3.7	0.6
	Total:	675	100

Table 1: Public Expenditure Statistical Analyses 2015- PESA Table 5.2 [*19]

If we take a look at the Public Expenditure table, we can immediately spot areas where we could save money or that would be completely replaced by the Basic Income schema.

If we could replace all the Welfares, State Pension, and, at the same time, reduce expenditures on government administration, we could spare £261.7 billion (171.1 + 86.5 + (30% of 13.7 =4.1)), which still makes the needed amount run short by about £28 billion.

Both the RSA and the JRF paper are proposing that it would be necessary to slightly increase (3%) income tax for basic and higher rates.[*20] Other proposals are to increase taxation on inheritance and capital gains and/or the introduction of a land value tax. However, both papers conclude that finding the missing part of the cost of a UBI should come from the capital gains, rather than from additional taxes on labor income.

One more thing worth considering: in the past 20 years, the use of drugs like antidepressants has soared by 500%. *[21] From 1997 to this day, health care costs have almost tripled, from £54 billion to £134 billion. *[22] Professor Evelyn Forget from the University of Manitoba, cross-referencing data from different sources, has found that, when a family received basic income, people had fewer doctor visits; the hospitalization rate dropped by 8.5%, and there were even fewer accidents. *[23]

By improving food nutrition and hygiene conditions among those below the poverty line, it could be possible to further reduce health costs even more.

Reasons for supporting Basic Income

Reasons why people with different backgrounds support Basic Income are due the following benefits it can provide for society:

- **It is unconditional** - Basic Income does not discriminate; it is a fairer system, where everyone receives income as a birthright. Although some of the models envision separation by age groups, in the end, everyone should receive the amount necessary to cover all basic needs.

- **Simplifies administration** – necessary to handle distribution of the income. In many countries, welfare systems have become increasingly complex, intrusive, and administration-intensive. As the only requirement needed for Basic Income is to have a citizenship and a bank account, additional checks are not necessary, which makes the number of people and administrative processes needed to handle the schema close to none. It is considered to be the simplest tax benefit schema.

- **Removes the need for other types of welfare** – when fully implemented, as people have enough resources to cover basic needs, all other welfares are discontinued. By replacing other welfare systems, a significant amount of money is redirected into the Basic Income fund, and, by that, **reduces overall costs** or possible pressures on the budget. Also, removing other welfares would mean that there is no need for expensive administration and mechanisms necessary to run those programs, which is already mentioned in previous bullet. During the transition phase, some of the welfare forms like housing benefits will need to stay until the effects of the schema kick in.

- **Saves money** – as the result of the previous two. Simplified administration removes unnecessary expenses connected with additional administration needed to handle welfare systems and the government apparatus needed for preventing, detecting, and fighting frauds.

- **Reduces welfare benefit frauds** – false reporting on income or size of household does not give any advantage, as it does not have any impact on Basic Income payments.

- **Distributes the wealth more fairly** – instead of supporting banks and stock market gambling, money is distributed directly to consumers. This is beneficial in multiple ways. Many studies are pointing out that the middle class, immensely important for a stable economy, is in constant decline, experiencing a long time of stagnation of salaries while the GDP is constantly growing. By distributing money to everyone, it would be possible to stop the financial decline of the majority caused as the consequence of wealth accumulation by a few. Additionally, Basic

Income can serve as a safety net that can potentially increase salaries by putting the average worker in a better negotiating position.

- **Reduces inequality** – by sharing wealth. Instead concentrating wealth in the top of the pyramid, Basic Income can reduce the growing wealth gap between classes, and also has the ability to reduce income inequality between genders, creating a significant emancipating effect.
- **Eradicating extreme poverty** – by giving money as a right, without any obligation directly to the people, Basic Income can end the suffering that is part of almost every developing country and return dignity to those people roaming on the streets, begging for change, just to survive.
- **Economic safeguard** – as people have their "survival" guaranteed through income by default, the stress of finding a new job, taking maternity leave, or having a longer professional break does not create stress and suffering. Basic Income can provide a safety net that is especially valuable in times of economic and social insecurity, followed by unpredictable work patterns.
- **Professional orientation** - Basic Income can help people rethink what they truly want to do in their lives. It allows them to take more time learning new skills while maintaining a decent standard of living.
- **Improving working conditions** – with Basic Income in place, workers will have more courage to challenge their employers, if working conditions are unfair or degrading. Mandatory unpaid overtime hours, bullying, and harassment could become things of the past.
- **Freedom and independence** – the current system in place can be described as wage slavery, where many must work low-paying jobs, in order to survive. More workforce supply than demand creates a job market with low-paying jobs, where a single job is not enough to support the basic needs of one person. With Basic Income in place, people will have the financial independence necessary to survive, and they will have freedom to choose where they want to work or whether they want to work at all. On the other hand, employers will need to increase salaries, on the account of their profits, in order to attract a working force, or they will need investment into automating those jobs. Furthermore, this will increase personal autonomy and oppose domination by allowing people to escape abusive relationships, giving them the opportunity to pursue education, find better jobs, and live happier lives. Basic Income will give people more time to care about their children (especially single mothers and fathers) or relatives — elderly, disabled, or otherwise vulnerable persons — and give people more time for other community responsibilities.

- **Acknowledging unpaid work** – housewives/househusbands, parents and grandparents, open source contributors, and many others have done immeasurable amounts of work by caring for family, doing housework, creating software or hardware, and many other things that our world relies on. Today, it would be hard to imagine the world without Wikipedia or Linux, and, yet, society has not recognized those as economic contributions. Basic Income can be considered as recognition and "salary" for those activities, additionally paving the way for new generations to come that will give their knowledge and time creating a better society.

- **Working hours decrease** – being financially secured, people will have the option to reduce their working hours or more easily take time off. They will be able to spend more time caring for their kids or family members, learning, or doing any other things they find meaningful. On the other hand, employers will need to find more people to compensate for those hours, which can create a better distribution of jobs in the labor market, allowing those struggling to find a job to become productive members of society.

- **Health impact** – with Basic Income, people will have access to more nutritious food, without the stress of survival or job loss. People may become happier and reduce stress-related health issues, therefore improving overall health and extending life. A healthier society will save more money on health expenditures (currently, in the UK, £134.1 billion of tax money is spent each year on health).

- **Crime rate impact** – although crime will not disappear, in some countries, where tests were conducted, studies showed that crime rates went down, reducing the expenses of the police and justice systems (Police statistics showed a 36.5% drop in crime since the introduction of the Basic Income pilot project in Namibia).*[24]

- **Employment and business impact** – although it looks counterintuitive, when Basic Income is implemented, employment rates usually go up, as people start working more for the betterment of themselves and society. In pilot Basic Income projects, people have shown the ability to self-organize and pursue higher goals, such as education, training, creative work, or personal projects or startups, creating a more vibrant, entrepreneurial, and economically more valuable society. Women, becoming more independent, will start looking for work, contributing to an increase in overall GDP.

  Geneva-based International Labor Organization has shown that nearly all large economies — including the UK and the USA — are "wage-led," not "profit-led;" they will experience slower growth when an excessive share of profits end up in the hands of investors, with less going into wages.

- **Overcoming the "rat race"** – people struggling to satisfy existential needs waste most of their time trying to find a better job while already working one or more jobs. In order to overcome that struggle, a person needs to find a better job. For a better job, the usual requirement is better education. For better education, a person needs free time and money. As most of the time and money are spent on basic survival needs, freeing up the time and finding the money for better education becomes an example of a "Catch 22" problem (impossible task). With Basic Income provided, people become masters of their own time. By overcoming that struggle, a person can dedicate his/her time to education, personal projects, volunteering, or creative work that can actually benefit something or someone. By removing the worry about existential needs, this will reduce economic inequality, which can otherwise hinder a person's development.

- **Alternative social contract** – Basic Income gives an alternative to the currently-existing "stick and the carrot" approach. People will stay in a workplace not because they "must," but because they "want to" be there. This motivation effect builds employees' self respect and creates a higher quality working force that can increase the overall productivity of the company while creating a healthier company culture and environment.

- **Solution to problem of technological unemployment** – as a consequence of the Fourth Industrial Revolution, *[25] with the advance of computer science, technologies, and Artificial Intelligence, increasing numbers of jobs will be automated (drivers, call centre workers, assembly line jobs, radiology diagnostics…), in the process disrupting entire industries and an already fragile labor market. Largely, our society is wealthier as a result of the efforts of our ancestors; therefore, it would be logical and morally right to fairly redistribute wealth created as a product of that technological advancement. Basic Income is one way to do that.

- **Reinforcing Democracy** – by having more time and worrying less about work, people will dedicate more time and be more actively involved in things they care about; this will result in innovation in political and social spheres, improving the relationship between the state and the individual.

- **Tackling the problem of population growth**– raising people above the poverty line can, among other things, effectively prevent population explosions, as wealthier societies tend to have fewer children per woman. *[26]

- **Ecological effect** –shifting to less work could encourage people to fulfill their lives with things other than consumerism. Without cheap labor, companies that make products no one needs could gradually disappear.

The planet cannot sustain the current rates of consumption, waste and growth. Having enough resources to support themselves, people could turn to more sustainable lives and could dedicate more time to volunteering or finding creative solutions to tackling the imminent dangers of climate change.

Among many positive things Basic Income is and can-do, it is not a utopian system. Although it can lead to better society it is not a solution for all of our problems.

How do we get there?

Although Basic Income is probably the most logical step we can think of at this point, it seems that many people are still reluctant, and they still do not know how to manage the transfer of the current system toward basic income society.

One of the approaches would be to vote (maybe by having a referendum), switch, and see what is going to happen.

A more cautious, infrastructural approach would be to prepare systems and institutions (education, consulting, volunteering, charities, group therapies, art, etc.), making a campaign to educate people, and outlining the goals and ways how to move toward the future.

One good example of already built infrastructural approach is charity in the United Kingdom. Charity there is part of the culture, and it has quite a developed infrastructure. I won't go into a discussion on how effective they are, as my only point is that people are keen to give away money to charities and different causes and that, for them, that act of giving is as natural as breathing. The same can be done with supporting infrastructure for basic income.

Although Universal Basic Income is gaining traction, progress is still quite slow. Basic Tax Control could help in speeding this process and reinforcing our democratic society, which could one day transform our society in a fully-functional, direct democracy, technically-advanced, moneyless world.

Basic Tax Control vs. Universal Basic Income

The main purpose of the Basic Tax Control online platform is to make a gradual transfer from our current society to one that is not moneyless but is organized in a way in which no one needs to worry about basic needs.

Actually, there is no versus here. Basic Tax Control is just different side of the same coin; it is a possible step that will move society into a new political and economic system, without need for a revolution and everything that comes with it.

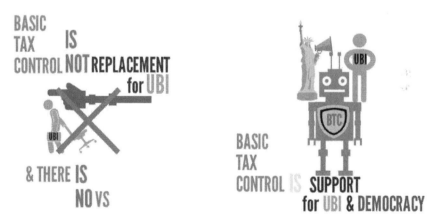

There are two natures of our being one is personal and the other is social. Each has its own needs to be satisfied, in order to survive. So, there are physical and social requirements. Universal Basic Income is envisioned as a system that will satisfy our personal needs; the Basic Tax Control is there to satisfy the needs of our society and, through those needs, build the path toward satisfying our basic personal needs.

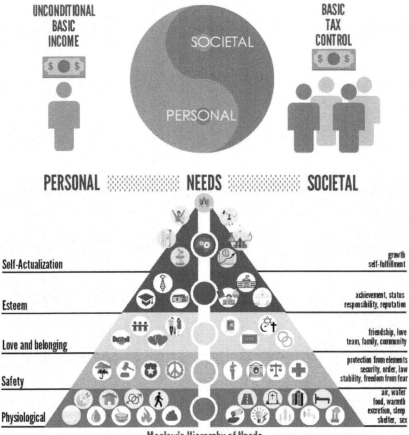

Maslow's Hierarchy of Needs

In that context:

- **Basic Tax Control** is a societal income dedicated to individual people, so they can spend it investing in companies that give back portions of profits into a public fund.
  Universal Basic Income is personal income.

- **Basic Tax Control** does not exclude the existence of Universal Basic Income; in fact, BTC makes it possible to implement UBI sooner.

- **Both systems** are funded from taxes (money collected from the public for public purposes).

- **Basic Tax Control** has rules.
  Unconditional Basic Income is unconditional, no rules and no strings attached.

- **Basic Tax Control** includes only people who are literate enough to participate in it.
  Unconditional Basic Income does not discriminated and is given as a birthright regardless of age, sex, knowledge, race, mental condition etc.

- **Basic Tax Control** can be implemented with a very small amount of money.
  (For BTC, we would need as little as **0.5% of total collected taxes in UK** for ~57 million people)

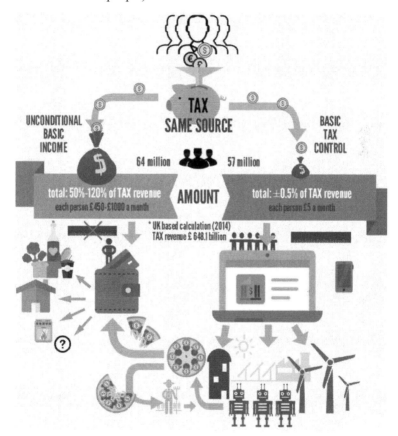

- **Unconditional Basic Income** requires enough money to cover basic survival needs of all people.
  (If we take ~£1000 per month for each of the 64 million people **in the UK, we would need roughly 119% of total collected taxes** [ii]). *[27]

---

ii   Calculation made for total taxes of £ 648.1 billion in UK for 2014

- **Basic Tax Control** – everyone invests and works together. However, each person can manage his/her own funds in whatever way he/she likes (just like they would use their votes during elections).
  Unconditional Basic Income - you mange on your own money in whatever way you like.

- **Basic Tax Control** – funds should not be used for charity. Charity is something you would finance from your personal funds. Basic Tax Control has a well-defined purpose.
  Unconditional Basic Income – does not limit how you spend your money. You can spend it on charity or alcohol or whatever else you want; it is your choice.

- **Basic Tax Control** – is the way to democratically influence positive changes with dedicated funds or by participating in online debates.
  Unconditional Basic Income – gives you enough time to become whatever you want. You can become an activist or volunteer for causes and help to create a better society. It is completely yours to choose.

- **Basic Tax Control** – the platform is technologically supported and relies on online and mobile technologies.
  Unconditional Basic Income – is paid to your bank account; from there, you do with it whatever you want.

- **Basic Tax Control** – does not require extra fees or taxes per transaction, because funds can be virtually managed until the point they were transferred to the companies.

- **Basic Tax Control** – can be used as a tool for increasing wealth by investing in sustainable technologies that can help us fix both global and local issues.

- **Basic Tax Control** – the best way to use it would be investing in the projects and companies that give back the highest guaranteed portion of investment returns.

Lastly, **Basic Tax Control** can be boosted by wealthy people; they can pledge their companies to public fund like a form of inheritance or legacy. They can also directly donate a portion of their company's shares into the fund. However, not every company should be allowed to participate. If a public committee decides that the company worked fraudulently or has a previous bad track record showing a detrimental impact on people or the environment, those companies should be banned from any type of participation in the BTC schema.

Politics - the next system

In the game of "Monopoly," it is common to hear "elite" saying:

"We need to encourage people to work, and work hard, to keep the old winning dream alive and to keep the country going forward". *[28]

There, one has to ask: "If work is so important, why do they not work? Also, why do they not work hard?"

Even more contradictory about that particular sentence is the fact that you cannot work if there are no any jobs. If a job is the only thing that separates you from necessary resources in order to survive, and those who hold the resources do not have any jobs for you, how exactly are you supposed to get those resources?

If you consider that more and more jobs are automated, it follows that fewer jobs will be there on the market; it is simple math. If that is true, and it is, there is one important question we have to consider:

In the fully-automated system, who is the one who decides who has access to resources?

Who are the people who will get food when all production is automated and no one needs to work anymore?

What are the criteria for accessing food or clean water, when jobs do not exist?

How are you going to get food, if everything is in the hands of few?

Maybe you think you will reach for weapons, in order to fight for your right? But, do not forget that those who have ownership have resources, military, and the industry capable of producing those guns. Then, maybe option is to become their protection, as they will need someone to protect them, and we will become a soldier or policeman, in order to get food. But, what if they do not need military? What if they have an army of intelligent robots that are a thousand times faster, more capable, and thousands of times more deadly than any human?

To answer those questions, we have to find a solution for the game of "Monopoly." We have to find a better replacement for the historically pyramidal structure of the system.

Structure

The most dangerous thing about the pyramid is the concentration of power in only one point. That makes this type of system very vulnerable. The danger of concentrating power to one point is the same as with achieving critical mass in a nuclear reaction: once critical mass has been reached, the system explodes violently.

Imagine what would happen if your brain functions depended on a single or just a few neurons?

How efficient, creative, and capable would your brain be in that case?

What would happen if those cells stop working properly?

It has been said that a pyramid is the most stable body, but, in terms of politics, that is not true, because our system is actually a pyramid that stands upside down.

By replacing the pyramid type of system with the trapezoid — by increasing the number of the people in the very top — the system becomes more robust and more prone to error and mishaps. This is what was going on for quite some time, as there are political bodies that serve this purpose. We have the Parliament and its members. The only question is what the optimal number of people for the Parliament is.

Currently, there are 640 people in the UK's Parliament. If we compare that with the population of 64 million that is 0.001% — a number so insignificant that we can still call the structure a pyramid. In the US, that difference is even more significant, as there are only 535 voting members in Congress – that is 0.0002% of total US population of 320 million people.

The question is whether it be possible to flatten the pyramid/trapezoid further, increasing the number of people in the top layer, and would that be feasible from the ruling/governing perspective?

Turning the trapezoid system upside-down would make it more stable than the pyramid, at least metaphorically speaking.

In terms of social affairs, more people may mean an additional controlling effect, which could potentially create a better balancing of the system; from this, bogus actions could become less frequent. On the other hand, if done in the same way as it is now, it can create additional bureaucratic apparatus, making things even more difficult to accomplish.

What would happen if we flatten the trapezoid further, allowing even more people to rule or make decisions?

In nature, a group of not very intelligent beings organized around pyramidal structures, like bees or ants, can show behavior that exceeds expectation of what is possible for a single member of that society. But also, groups of very intelligent beings can show group behaviors that are less than the sum of its members.

Ideally, what we want is not a trapezoid or a flat surface; ideally, what we want already exists, and it is called a topological network. In our case, it is a network without end or beginning, where each of its nodes has a connection to his neighbor/friend on the three-dimension body, shaped like a ball. The beauty of networks is that they can have different topologies and that, regardless of their topologies, they can seamlessly connect.

What are the issues with democracy as a system?

At the beginning of democracy, only a handful of people had the right to vote. Gradually, the group who had voting rights expanded, allowing every citizen of adult age to vote. Nowadays, the concept of voting has changed its original meaning it had in the past. Before, to vote meant the individual right to decide on various matters of the state, but now unlike it was imagined at the beginning to vote mean electing officials that will decide about those matters instead of us, basically those officials "represent" our right to vote.

Mostly, current democracies are "representative," where elected officials represent a group of people, and rarely they are "direct" or pure democracies, where as the name says, "demos" (people) have the right to "kratos" (rule).

The problem with representative democracy is exactly what the name says: it is representative. Officials elected to be representatives of the people often do not represent the will, ideas, or the interests of the people who elected them, and, very often, they work only for their own interest, thus becoming misrepresentative democracy. Another issue is that most of the people who vote do not have enough knowledge about the people for whom they vote, allowing the entire electoral process to be very prone to different types of manipulations. Even when people know a bit about them, voters vote more from a politician's performance on the stage and the ability to promise as many believable things as people can fall for, rather than voting for ideas and the politician's ability to put these ideas forward in a realistic manner that can actually be implemented.

On the other hand, the problem addressed by "direct" democracy is that most people do not have enough knowledge in order to make reasonable decisions on certain policies or subjects. Large masses of people are prone to lynch-mob behavior. Thus, not everything is bad with a ruling minority; in fact, many positive changes — such as fighting prejudice, racism, sexism and many others — we have won only due the fact that those decisions were made by minorities.

Additionally, the "direct" democracy approach was not very practical for much of human history, at least not from the standpoint of creating policies, making decisions, or voting. Even the simplest act with a large group of people would need a humongous effort to get to the final decision; debates and discussions could last forever.

Although not very efficient, we use direct democracy when we need to decide difficult public matters by using a referendum.

Referendums historically weren't very efficient: they require a lot of time to organize and discuss, and they come with similar costs to elections. Although this statement is true, we have neglected many ideas, technologies, and the level of development that currently exist.

We have many technologies and products that never before existed, but, in terms of politics, nothing has changed; we still have the same type of system. We have advanced our technology, but some of our systems are in the same state they have been for hundreds — if not thousands — of years. We are completely neglecting ideas that have been with us for quite some time.

When we say "ruling," we tend to think about the people on the top of the pyramid, but ruling is nothing more than making decisions around tasks/problems we are experiencing and need to solve.

New system basic requirement

In order to implement a direct democracy, one prerequisite has to be satisfied: political and social literacy. In order to read, we need to know letters; in order to use computers and smart phones, we need to know basic operations. It is the same with politics and social affairs: we need to be literate and active. We have to exercise our democratic abilities.

In order to move towards a more direct democratic society, we would need to stop with the "vote and forget" practice. Our political activity must be constant and frequent. By saying this, it already looks like a full-time job, but what I have in mind is more of a usual activity that everyone does, similar to reading the news, eating your breakfast, or checking your Facebook wall — even 5 to 10 minutes a day would be enough and would make a significant difference.

Every citizen who knows how to read, can use modern tools of communication, and has a sound mind is a good candidate to make a positive change. If a child or very old person can contribute with good ideas and/or actions, why should we prevent that?

Political activity should be thought of and carried out the same as any other social activity (shopping, meeting people, talking, etc.); it should come naturally, like our breathing. It would be valuable to have society composed of such of individuals.

We may be afraid, though, that this can be dangerous, as large masses were not, historically, very good at making decisions. However, I would argue at this point that this was due to a lack of education. Nowadays, at a time when education, for the most part, is freely accessible and available via the Internet, I believe we can change that.

What has changed in the world that can allow us a more "direct" democracy?

Many new ideas and invention are literally popping into existence on a daily basis. We are connected like never before. We have our "Star Trek" like communication devices, and we can speak with each other, regardless of the fact that we are on different sides of the planet.

Communication and connectivity has changed. If we wanted, we could be connected with an unimaginable number of people; we can exchange our ideas, chat, talk, or have video conferences. We can speak to many people, and we can read what many other people say.

Communication, connectivity, the Internet, networks, phones, and computers are tools that give us the ability to be connected like never before, and those tools can make direct democracy come true.

Can the same technology work as a governance tool? Again, politics can look quite complex...

Internet communication and computerization are great tools, but they are almost completely neglected as tools for making top decisions that affect all of us. Although, decision systems can function simple as aggregating massive amount of surveys into single report, this never came alive on larger scale.

Imagine what would happen if we could legally take political decisions or/and the creation of policies into our own hands. Imagine a world where each voice would really matter, and where you would be morally responsible for your own decisions — a world where your voice, combined with everyone else's, could make a political decision by using electronic devices instantly. Would that be possible?

Currently, we are making day-to-day decisions with our electronic devices by making online purchases and managing our internet bank accounts. We are making decisions on how we are going to spend our money. As the shopping and banking systems are computerized and connected, all of our decisions can be processed in a matter of seconds. The system is secure, and all transactions are done in a manner that does not interfere with our shopping experience.

Making political decisions can be the same. Imagine a web site where you could discuss different political subjects, policies, make amendments, and suggest improvements. People could read the discussions, comment, and vote on a daily basis. Such a system would be almost inexpensive, but, yet again, very efficient, and that is something **Basic Tax Control** is trying to provide.

Of course, there will be a price for hardware, software, and maintenance, but that price would be miniscule in comparison with organizing just one referendum. The benefits would be significantly higher than the cost we would need to pay.

For example, the Scottish independence referendum *[29] had a price tag of £13.3 million (around $19.3 million), and Scotland is a small country with population of just 5.3 million people. A similar amount would be sufficient to support electronic system for a much larger country for several years with almost unlimited numbers of "votes" and "referendums."

Also consider this: if someone would give you the moral burden of a decision to send military troops into war, where thousands would die and millions would be affected, would you decide any differently than your government?

Moral question of tax control

The moral dilemma is whether you, as a taxpayer, are responsible for the evil deeds your government committed in your name?

As a good, law-abiding citizen, you pay your taxes each month, and your vote was cast for the elected government. If your government uses those taxes for evil means, like guns and bombs, you are partly responsible for their actions, and, in case some innocent soul dies from those arms, you are directly responsible for that death.

Using the Basic Tax Control platform should tackle that problem. You would use Basic Tax Control like you would otherwise use any online shop: you would log in securely, and, instead of letting someone else decide how your tax dollars are going to be spent, you could do it on your own.

For the portion of money you do not control, you could make recommendations to your government on how you wish they should spend your money. This could be created like a "wish list" from Amazon. Sometimes your friends will grant those wishes, and sometime they won't; at least the government will know where your heart was.

You will have the ability to dedicate your tax dollars to whatever you think is the best thing for your society. If this already works for all the banks and businesses, there is no reason it would not work for taxes, as well.

Using the Basic Tax Control to manage small amounts of money and express their opinions about different country/area functions is a great way to help the government understand how their people really think and feel.

Someone would invest his tax dollars into education, green energy, infrastructure, space exploration, science, and healthcare. On the other hand, maybe he/she would never invest in offensive military actions, because I personally feel that we have already reached a stage in destructive power where we could wipe ourselves from the planet in matter of minutes, and, instead of finding money for wars and destruction, we should find money for sustainable coexistence. Regardless of what I feel, maybe someone else does not feel the same way, and I do not have anything against other people's choices; whatever you decide, it will be on your conscience.

Think about it: where would you invest your tax dollars?

Wouldn't direct democracy just jam the system completely?

It would not, if it is done correctly. Networks can have different topologies, and they can connect with each other. If they are balanced properly, similar to current internet or road traffic, it would be possible to avoid congestions and points of failure.

It is obvious that our current social and political systems do not keep pace with the current level of technology we have. We use the name "democracy" as a notion of ruling of the people by the people, but, instead, we have ruling by the elected elite. We could argue that the elite are also people, but democracy does not mean that. By the same analogy, we could argue that all other systems — monarchy, socialism, or/and communism — are also democracies, because they are ruled by the people.

Topological networks gravitate around certain nodes; some nodes have more connections than others. Similar like in social networks, some people have more friends than others, and they can be "followed" by more people than others. Some of them can be more influential than others.

Although a self-balancing system looks uncontrollable and can sound almost anarchistic to people who are control freaks, it is not. Each of us already has a self-balancing network in our heads, and that network (brain) works just fine.

Imagine if you were one of the nodes of the network; what kind of decisions would you make?

Would you make good or bad decision for others?

If your decisions had an equal impact on you as they would on everyone else, would you decide differently?

Are officials required in the new system?

Yes, they are required. Their role would be more administrative than anything else. Also, in order to avoid mob behavior, we would need some kind of rules, and those rules would need to be applied by officials. Just as online shops or banks have their own personal, and just as web sites have moderators, a political system management would need to have some type of personnel to maintain the system. Scientists, sociologists, psychologists, judges, lawyers, and any other person who has expertise in a certain field can be helpful, in order to give necessary knowledge or to resolve difficult matters. Later on, in order to achieve an unbiased, corruption-resistant approach, it would be possible to put AI in charge of this role.

Implementation

Direct democracy or electronically-supported democracy is not a new idea; it just happens that it has not been used or implemented on a larger scale. *[30]

First, let's consider similar networks that already exist and are widely used:

"Facebook" and "Twitter" are the largest social networks at present, and they are good examples of social connectivity. They provide tools for a large number of people to organize, communicate, and share digital content. The bad thing about these networks is that they are corporately held, not very transparent, and they have their own technical limitations.

"Kickstarter" and "Indiegogo" are examples of cofounding sites, where people can organize, without any special governance or monitoring, in order to raise funds and fund a variety of different projects, in return for some type of rewards or finished products. Also, they are in the hands of corporations and not very transparent.

"Paypal" and many bank portals are good examples of secure payment processing on a large scale by using Internet communication.

"Wikipedia" is a good example of an online collaboration project. It is an online encyclopedia with a remarkable amount of content and an even more remarkable ability to correct itself; it also withstands malicious attacks. Many people are involved in constantly making improvements. Sources are backed with references, and tracking down malicious edits can be an easy job to do.

All of above are examples of worldwide online collaborative decision-making systems. Every time we click on a like or dislike button, we are making small decisions. Every time something is "trending," regardless of whether it is a "funny cat video" or "Cancer research funding project," we are deciding, either with our money or with our votes, to show whether we support something or not.

Transparency

A very important aspect in the future system should be transparency. Web-based democracy networks would need to be highly transparent; every monetary transaction, every vote, everything we discus or comment on should be visible to everyone. This idea can make many people feel uncomfortable, afraid that this can be misused; but in a fully transparent political system, everything is known — even the fact that someone was trying to influence someone else's decisions.

What is lacking in the current system is full transparency; people should have the ability to monitor the actions of their governments very much like with the Wikipedia.

Besides, we are already transparent to our governments, to spy agencies, even to corporations. While this is something you would rather not like to think about, you are already monitored, and you are monitored 24/7: your browsing history, your emails, your phone calls, movies you watch, your professional career, even changes to your health condition, and much, much more. You are monitored, but you do not have access to that data or to anyone else's data. Basically, if they want to, those agencies can know more about you than you know about yourself.

Ask yourself what would happen if we could access all information about everyone else's activities?

What if you could watch those who watch you?

Politically, the gradual adoption of direct democracy is the way to go forward. Crowd-sourced political activity can bring us closer to the solutions we badly need for the problems we are facing now and we will face in the future.

While transparency is solved in the Basic Tax Control platform by allowing anyone to fully download the BTC database (except for the part that concerns user security permissions), BTC — like any other electronically-supported direct democracy solution — will be susceptible to mass behavior.

Uneducated people will make their decisions from an emotional state, rather than being driven by rational decisions. As emotions can be manipulated in various ways, irrational behavior can endanger the existence of the system.

The way to deal with this at the beginning is to give limited decision-making responsibility, until the democratic body shows overall progress and the ability to act intelligently and rationally. Another option is to have educated officials or even AI who would act as "conscience" advisors, with the ability to put a veto on a certain type of morally-unacceptable votes; although this is not democratic, it is necessary, in order to avoid malicious or trolling behavior. Malicious behavior, in this instance, refers to the usage of the platform for any type of malicious deed or type of communication that can promote attacks on a person or a group on the basis of gender, ethnic origin, religion, race, disability, or sexual orientation. Trolling is any behavior can be considered as any type posting of inflammatory, off-topic messages with the deliberate intent of provoking readers into an emotional response, disrupting normal, on-topic, democratic discussion.

As the system is fully transparent, and there won't be any anonymous users, it is important to stress that all users' actions are going to reflect their permanent user profiles, so all users will be advised to refrain from inadequate, overly-emotional, or malicious reactions while using the BTC platform.

Economics - the next system

Bearing in mind that more and more jobs are automated every day, it follows that fewer jobs will be available on the market. If that is true, and it is, there is one important question we have to consider: in the fully-automated world, who decides who has access to resources?

Who are the people who will get food, when all production is automated, and no one needs to work anymore?

What are the criteria for accessing food or clean water, when jobs do not exist?

How are you going to get food, if everything is in the hands of those few wealthy people?

Ultimately, who will have the right to decide who lives or dies?

This is the coming reality, and it will be mentioned a number of times throughout this book, as it is a serious problem for which we need to find a solution as soon as possible.

While discussing new systems, some people are hasty to use the "utopian card" as a dismissive argument, (** check chapter "Utopia semantics") and that argument is neither valid nor beneficial for either the discussions or the attempt to find a solution. Every idea on social structure, regardless how carefully it is thought through, will have pros and cons, and **humans, being humans, we will always have some kind of problems**. The rich people or celebrities are the perfect example this, regardless of the amount of money they have and the fame that follows, they have their own serious problems (health, addiction, identity etc.), and they can still end up being unhappy.

It is necessary to emphasize that this is not a discussion on how to make some utopian, futuristic system. Knowing what kind future awaits us, we can conclude — from the way things are going currently (with a degree of certainty) — that there is high probability of ending up in dystopian world.

As we already know, perfect solutions and utopian systems are more or less impossible, that they do not and cannot exist, and we do not want to end up in a dystopian system.

Therefore, the questions we need to answer are: What are our options? What is the solution?

Although, we cannot find the perfect solution, we can try to find an optimal solution — the solution that will be the best intersection between good and bad traits.

Whatever we choose, we have to realize that it will not represent the final system, and, wherever we decide to go, we will carry some of our problems with us, but the good thing is that, along the way, we can always change and improve things that do not work as we expected them to.

Prerequisites

The good thing is that we already have all the necessary technology that can allow us to do many things that were impossible before. With every passing day, we have even more new, amazing technologies that can allow us to resolve our problems much quicker.

Over the period of time many mathematicians, philosophers, thinkers, scientists gathered vast collection of knowledge, and, there are many theories and many experiments that can shows us how to continue further without causing major disruption of our society and creating a dystopian world. With designing Basic Tax Control I have chosen one path that looks like the most logical move from the position where we are currently.

Why we do things we do?

Ask yourself the following questions:

- As a species, do we know the reasons behind the things we do?
- Is it knowledge? If it is knowledge, what is the purpose of that knowledge?
- Is it curiosity?

- Is it laziness?
- Is it life preservation?
- Is it immortality?
- Is it preservation of conciseness and culture?
- What is our goal?

Sometimes, it looks like we are not sure why we do some of the things we do. It is important to verbalize answers on those questions. When we ask, "What is the goal?" we should not be necessarily asking, "What is the end goal?" Goals can change over time, and most of us understand that. We do not have the same goals now as we did when we were children. We need to clarify our goals. Just like driving a car, if you do not know where are you going, there are very good chances you will never get there, at least not in a foreseeable time. Clarifying what the long-term goals of civilization are will give us better odds of getting there quicker.

If we can define "why we do what we do" and "what are we trying to do?," it would make it much easier to find the fastest solution to get there — the optimal solution — while taking into account all necessary points of view related to it.

Let's assume that our primary goal is to use technology or modify our bodies, in order to make our lives easier and more enjoyable, and to promote learning, curiosity, exploration, creativity and invention, and by it fulfill our human potential and enhance our abilities.

In the process of getting there, maybe we will hand over manual jobs to AI or use it as knowledge support, but, surely, we would like to keep something for ourselves, such as decision-making or creativity. Also, there is a high probability that we do not want a perfect solution instantly, but we would like to get there gradually, because we intuitively know that this perfect solution will make us obsolete, or it will make our existence a very boring experience. Gradual change will allow us to adapt while moving to those long-term goals.

The only thing left is to identify feasible middle steps to that long-term goal we have defined.

From an economical standpoint, we know we will need to get rid of the current system, as technological unemployment will make it impossible to work, anyway. That being said, let's presume that our goal is a moneyless society while having more existential security for every member of society. The next thing we need to find is the middle step: how to provide some kind of income for people in the currently existing system while trying to find something new that will make the entire thing obsolete.

The good thing is that a natural step in that direction was already invented about 500 years ago, and its name is Universal Basic Income. Nowadays it is a system that is already a widely discussed topic in the media and in a previous chapter it is explained in more details.

The new idea here is the Basic Tax Control schema that will allow us to get there faster, without economic and psychological pressures that come with any large societal change, or, as someone once commented, it is a revolution but without pitchforks.

Basic Tax Control platform

What should the BTC platform look like?

If you ever used platforms like Twitter, Facebook, reddit, online banking, IndiGoGo, KickStarter, or something similar, the Basic Tax Control platform will not be significantly different. However, there are some specific things we need to mention:

The BTC platform must be transparent

Every transaction, every discussion, every comment, must be publically visible. Companies seeking investments would need to open their books and show how they do business. They would need to disclose all accounts and everything that is connected to that investment — every single expenditure and transaction must be visible to their "minority share holders" or "public patrons".

In this way, every transaction can be a part of public scrutiny and open for discussion. If the "project owner" is spending too much and not accomplishing what he has promised, that should be visible to the public, along with the reason why that happened. It is a form of "public shaming" and provides security and assurance against future fraudulent attempts from the same individuals or companies. Rogue companies and bogus projects, as well as people connected to those, should be stopped by this type of full transparency and by existing laws.

Companies must give regular updates reports on progress and how money is spent; all information must be standardized and easy to understand.

Bad money management by the company/project owner or fraudulent activities will impact ratings of the company and people involved. If someone does not fulfill the promises he made for instance, no one will invest in him in the future, as his ratings will be downgraded. Bad ratings will mean an inability to apply for future investments, and, in more severe cases, can have legal implications. If track records and ratings are good, the public will be willing to invest in the same company/people again.

The system is designed to balance itself. Those who are not successful in meeting their funding goals will not be treated as failures, and negative rankings would not be applicable to them. Negative rankings would be reserved only for those who get full funding but do not complete what they said they will do or do not execute the project in satisfactory (legal) way.

Both government officials and public investors could check the validity of operations at any moment, since the platform is open. Anyone would have ability to check, monitor, and react, in the case of suspicious activity.

Transparency is one of the key requirements; if someone wants to ask for money, then he/she has to show how it is being spent. At the end of the day, we want to avoid situations where someone is pleading for money to save whales, but spends it in a casino in Hawaii while drinking Piña Coladas.

The BTC platform allows anyone to create projects

Anyone can create a project, but that project must adhere to the existing rules. If a project is good, and it can benefit society, there is no reason why anyone who has a good idea cannot create project.

The BTC platform rewards success and talent

Successful projects and good ideas should be rewarded. A reward system, if done right, could additionally enhance entrepreneurship, innovation, and altruistic spirit, uplifting and empowering people to do more by putting additional effort into learning and doing more.

The BTC platform must be publically owned

The same public that gets BTC funds should also own the platform in equal proportion. The BTC platform, must not wind up in the hands of the government, private owners, or corporations — especially not giant corporations, like Google, Facebook, Apple, etc.

Although the public type of ownership does not currently exist legally, it could be created for this purpose. So, "public ownership" would need to be created as a third type of ownership that would be distinct from private and state or government ownership.
This type of **public ownership** should not be confused with the **public domain**, where belongings are available to the public as a whole, especially through not being subject to copyright or other legal

restrictions. Although public ownership of the BTC platform should allow anyone to suggest improvements, adding these improvements should be considered within the organization that will be responsible to the public, as the main objective of the BTC organization should be to protect its main purpose. The reason for this is to shield the BTC platform from outside influences, like corporations, government, or government agencies.

In that way, the main characteristic of the systems, like transparency and openness, would be secure from possible attempt of change, and, if those attempts come from within, the public can always decide to replace the board of directors responsible for the BTC platform.

Government or private entities would not have the ability to control "publicly owned" shares; only the public, as an entity, with electronic referendum decisions, could decide changes in very rare cases.

Public ownership, unlike private ownership, would not be inheritable or transferable; public ownership is always dispersed over the members of the group equally. Only in this way it would be possible to keep the level of transparency and independency need for a truly democratic operation of the BTC platform.

The BTC platform should respect the open/close principle

Open to connect and open to communicate. Closed to outside influence and control.

The end goal is to have BTC that has multiple levels: local, constituency, country, and world. Levels or nodes can open to each other, but not everyone is connected to everyone. Nodes should be connected as balanced topological networks.

Connections should be either based on the principle of geographical relations or communities similar to those of "twin towns" ("friendship towns").

The BTC platform must have a discussion section

This discussion section, if designed properly, should help people discuss and debate, in a constructive way, current and future projects, but not just projects, any matter of public interest can be discussed there. The goal is to reduce clutter but give everyone a chance to speak and express opinions in a non-violent manner. Ideas, discussions, and arguments should not be repeated; they should be brainstormed and then narrowed down to the most optimal ones.

BTC control should be more by design than by people and rules

Users decide how to use the platform; there should be general rules, but fewer the better.

Rules should be imposed, like in any other online system, more through functionality than through the wider set of regulations one needs to follow. Basic Tax Control has some integral parts: funding model, reward system, and a discussion platform – and those are good examples of control by design. One can only do actions inside the platform that the platform allows them to do.

The general rules of debating should be applied, in order to avoid inappropriate or spam behavior. The idea is to enhance cooperation, efficiency, and the level of public service needed for the wellbeing of all members of society.

The BTC should serve as a knowledge base for success

Individual success stories of people and companies, and especially stories on how to avoid challenges and overcome the problems, are an important part of the knowledge that should be freely available and shared openly. Those communities that succeeded and became self-sustaining should share their success stories and help others.

It is illusory to talk about real cooperation by excluding some areas, countries, or races; if we really want change, we will bring that change to everyone, regardless of their origin or religious beliefs. The success stories should be there for everyone to learn from and for everyone to share. We live on one finite planet, and the issues we experiencing do not know about borders or differences; therefore, solutions should not know borders, either.

BTC ratings

Both companies and people should have ratings. Individual ratings are reserved for members that support platforms with their expert knowledge or are involved in debates.

All projects will have several types of ratings: efficiency, execution, quality, ethics, impact, and similar. Negative ratings are applied only for deceitful and fraudulent actions.

The ratings for companies are a cumulative sum of not only their projects but also the people involved.

Those who have ideas that can achieve a great impact and can benefit society the most, along with a delivery that was within the boundaries of what was promised, are rated the best.

BTC is dynamic

The core rules must be kept, but the platform will change over time, in order to improve performance, user experience, or functionality. Basic Tax Control can be adjusted to better suit a certain environment, but it must not lose the main purpose and core rules from its sight, and that is moving toward a direct democracy and a society where none of its members need to struggle for survival.

Alternative social contract

The currently-existing "social contract" [iii] has allowed the top 1% of the richest people in the world an unprecedented accumulation of wealth. At the same time, the middle class has shrunk, and an increasing number of jobs have been replaced by machines, while not nearly enough new jobs have been created.

Because of the discrepancy between the small number of jobs on offer and the huge number of people who are looking for work, by the rules of market economy, middle class wages have stagnated for a long period of time, and, in some cases, income has reduced, pushing some members of the middle class below the poverty line.

The current system, by demanding exponential growth, is causing an increase in population and consumption of nature's resources. In this vicious circle of striving for more, we are creating unsustainable environmental pressures. It is evident that we cannot continue in this way any longer. The current economy is failing the working class, and the only one who is benefiting out of this is the richest 1%.

Having in mind that this is a persistent trend for the last 50 years, we have to consider the possibility that the same trend will continue in the future. With increasing levels of automation and drastically-improving Artificial Intelligence, if nothing changes, will lead to a denial of resources to those in need.

One solution would be to give everyone Universal Basic Income, an amount of money that would be enough for basic needs, reliving people of the stress of not having a job. This type of scheme would significantly change the social contract, allowing people to spend more time on education, and it would allow them to negotiate better salaries. For any company that relies on human labor for

---

iii   **Social contract** - is the idea that individuals have consented, either explicitly or tacitly, to surrender some of their freedoms and submit to the authority of the ruler or magistrate, in exchange for protection of their remaining rights. In this text it is used more as a synonym for the "nature of the current system."

providing goods or services, this would cause a better distribution of wealth, as more of the profit would be distributed to wages, instead going into the pockets of a few investors, significantly slowing down the snowballing effect.

Currently, for low paying jobs people usually pick any type of job that is on offer, as they do not have a choice. They will put aside any moral complaints they would otherwise have in regards to the nature of the business or the people who lead the company. With Basic Income in place, people do not have to worry about survival; they would choose more carefully and would demand higher salaries. As the end result, companies that work unethically would gradually cease to exist.

In the 14th century, during the great Bubonic Plague outbreak, the epidemic diminished 30-60% of Europe's total population. In the market, where it was not possible to find enough workers for all the necessary jobs, the wages of those who survived doubled and, in some cases, even tripled from the usual levels. Reason was simple; after the plague, there were significantly fewer workers than the number of jobs available, so the social contract changed in favor of the working class.

There are many ways to create a new social contract. There is no need to wait or create another Bubonic Plague, in order to get better wages. The only thing we need is to tweak the current system.

Although the idea of Universal Basic Income has been around for a few centuries, even now, for many countries, it is just a theoretical idea in a very early stage. For many others, in undeveloped countries, which do not have a GDP large enough to sustain Basic Income for the entire population, this is just a wild dream.

Basic Tax Control aims to fix this by creating a system and organizations that are built around solving sustainability issues related to the country's resources, gradually overcoming the existing system by allowing everyone to work around a common goal. By building the necessary infrastructure, they could create enough wealth to sustain the population indefinitely with Basic Income and without causing major, negative, disruptive effects.

Nowadays, as the ruling elite has a stake in the majority of resources, they can manage the social contract in whatever way they want. With an appropriate social contract, it would be difficult for the ruling elite to acquire wealth at the same level they have today.

Because a majority does not have any involvement in a share of investments, and those who are managing investments at stock exchanges – banks were allowed to earn huge amounts of money by managing other people's money without any legal or financial responsibility in case of a loss.

Basic Tax Control is a form of obligatory crowd investment, where all people, just as they are required to pay taxes, are educated to invest in different companies. In the same way as every person is obliged to pay taxes, every person should, in an obligatory way, receive investment money and should be obliged to make small investments and learn how to invest better. As everyone is working toward the common goal of Universal Basic Income, any failure would be handled without stress or pressure.

Additionally, by changing the social contract, the Basic Tax Control would create a more democratic society. By transferring more responsibility to people by directly involved them in matters that concern them (without waiting for politicians or government to fix all the issues) would shift the focus from "them" to "us", and give people more freedom in shaping their own future.

Part II
Problems

Political systems

All political systems we ever had and we have now are an illusion and they do not exist. A bold claim isn't it?

Meaning — neither of those systems really ever existed except as theoretical ideologies written on paper. We are just using different words so we can name and describe something that is not. Probable reason to do this is to feel a bit better about ourselves and to escape reality. As we all know, reality can be painful sometimes.

Name it: democracy, socialism, communism ... never existed, and the most genuine system we ever had in history is something we never had officially.

Let's start with **democracy**.

What does democracy mean? The term originates from the Greek δημοκρατία (dēmokratía) "rule of the people," which was coined from δῆμος (dêmos) "people" and κράτος (krátos) "power" or "rule", in the 5th century BCE.

We have never had "rule of the people," at least not for all of them! We have something called the election system, a process in which a ruling party is elected, and some people from that ruling party are chosen to lead the country with some type of ruler (chairman, president, premier ...) on top.

What about socialism and communism?

From the standpoint of rulership, they have been envisioned as systems ruled by the working class. The working class tends to be the majority of the population (people = demos). In both socialism and communism, everything is owned by the government, which is really only difference in comparison to capitalistic democracy. And on top, there is again a ruling party with a president.

What about **feudalism**?

Feudalism is the system for structuring society around relationships derived from the holding of land, in exchange for service or labor. The Latin word "feudum" can be translated as "fee" (payment, tribute). In this system, lords have land and properties in their possession, which are given by the monarch, and then they rent that land to peasants for a certain fee.

Now, let's examine all these systems a bit more. Although each of these systems has many variations, from political or economic point of view, they each have one very important thing in common:

Each of these systems is just a pyramidal system ruled by the elite and owned by the elite. Elite is enjoying all the privileges and luxuries and everyone else is working for the elite!

In feudalism, which is the simplest system of above mentioned, the monarch spreads lands and properties to loyal lords, and in return he gets advice, military power, and money as support in the form of taxes. Everyone else works for the lazy king and lords for their pleasure and benefit. So, on top of the pyramid is the monarch, then the lords and, I must not forget, the religious clerks. Religion is very important because when you do not have bread to eat, at least you can dine on hope. Although Christ never had this type of misuse in mind, much like Nobel, Tesla, or Einstein with their inventions in recent times, it still happened.

In communism and socialism, the problem with ruling was that rulership of the working class was just a romantic dream in which everyone works as much as they can, which is often almost nothing, but they all live in a world of plenty. The sad reality is that only the people on top (usually very cunning and skillful, with the rhetorical ability to promise things but not accomplish them – in other words lying) enjoy the wealth. Small exception to this rule, are the people who live around the elite. Everyone else lives poorly. Usually, what is government property in theory, in reality is the property of the corrupt officials on top and it is available at their disposal. Similar to feudalism, another thing is at their disposal the military and police. Therefore, even if anyone discloses this level of corruption, he or she will be gently removed from existence. Replacing "La Presidente" is similar to the process in the monarchy: **when one dies, another "silver-tongued" star rises.**

The democracy, the most promising system of them all, like the previous systems, is yet another romantic illusion. Amazingly, in the beginning, when democracy was formed, only a handful of people had the right to vote. Women, poor people, people of certain ages and slaves did not have the right to vote. That was amended later, but, over the course of time in the UK, Australia, USA, and some others,*[31] something else has happened: the multi-party system has been replaced with two highly-influential parties (USA has democrats/republicans, UK has conservative/labour...), while others have been completely marginalized, creating a good case for a two-party system without significant freedom of choice.

In each election, those parties have their own prodigies, similar to the communist silver-tongued stars, promising "hope, changes, and winning wars." The entire voting system in "democracy" is just a façade as it can be manipulated very easily (fake ballots, electronic voting machine fraud, non-exiting voters, conflict of interests, etc.). Sometimes it does not even need to be manipulated because both parties are the same - pretending to have differences and opposing ideas. Behind the curtains are the puppeteers: mighty businesses and people pulling the ropes of politicians. It is easy to recognize these individuals as they are not governed by the same laws as the little people are.

Everyone else in those system lives in the "rat race" wage slavery conditions.

All the systems we have invented have a **pyramidal** structure and some kind of elite on the top. Therefore, the best word to describe all these systems is — **aristocracy**. Perhaps no one is calling it by that name, but that is the only system we have and we ever had.

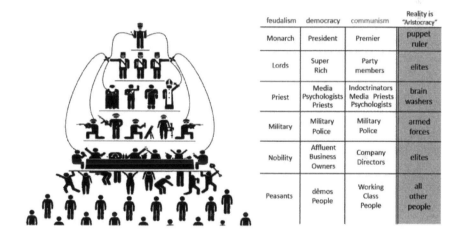

feudalism	democracy	communism	Reality is "Aristocracy"
Monarch	President	Premier	puppet ruler
Lords	Super Rich	Party members	elites
Priest	Media Psychologists Priests	Indoctrinators Media Priests Psychologists	brain washers
Military	Military Police	Military Police	armed forces
Nobility	Affluent Business Owners	Company Directors	elites
Peasants	dêmos People	Working Class People	all other people

The scenario goes like this:

Those on the top are telling tales of hope to wax the ears of the dreaming masses. They tell lies and carefully constructed empty promises of "a better, rich life" so people will start believing in those false dreams. Blinded by these lies people will continue feeding the same old idea, the same old system, thinking that any other system any alternative is absolutely impossible.

In this system, brainwashers have a significant role: they are there to calm things down, to tell people not to rock the boat. They are there to convince you that life is hard and that there is no other way – that you need to bow your head and continue working for your leader. Religious leaders will talk about the afterlife reward for your service to the elite, the media will pump stories about elite successes and how you can achieve the same, and psychologists will try to find the cause of your pain in your youth, offering you a wonderland pill [iv] that will bust your performance. All that so that, one day, you won't ask that crucial question: for whom and for what cause I am doing all this; for whom and what I am wasting my only life?

It seems we are in a game of monopoly, and the game is still on. As you know, there is just one rule to win this game: "Win all the money and push other players to bankruptcy." And please remember: don't hate the players - they are just playing by the rules of the game!

We cannot say that everything that happened was bad, although it sounds contradicting it is not. Everything in the history of politic systems had its own purpose and it could not have been "played" significantly differently with the state of the knowledge, technology and the state of mind of the majority of "players."

To begin with, it was impossible in ancient times to have "rulership of many" because majority of people were completely illiterate. The little knowledge they had was extremely difficult to transfer, and they have done it usually directly from one person to another. Written word was rare and life condition combined with a short life span had a huge negative impact on ideas and concepts that were frequently lost with most prominent members of society. Many did not know simple things, and they were far from having knowledge about matters of state. Everything that happened until this point in time in the development of political systems had "evolutionary" properties in their nature. You may say that some of these processes happened because of "revolutions," despite the fact that this is true in physical appearance, as already explained, nothing really important has truly changed.

From the psychology of civilization stand point of view – most likely, people will live in the system that corresponds to their level of knowledge and consciousness.

"But why would I care? Who cares who rules anyway?"

You do and we all do. We might not already know it, but we should care because someday we could find ourselves in the same line as someone else - on our way to the killing pit, as many people experienced during the Second World War.

There is one big issue with this "dance" of the elite: while they play their game of monopoly, they will do everything necessary to win. Sometimes, that means they will go to other countries to "educate" the people in those countries about democracy. During this "education" process military is usually involved,

---

[iv]   Reference to blue pill from The Matrix movie (1999) and green-white Prozac antidepressant pill

just to make sure no one will skip the lessons. In the process of this "knowledge transfer" – people will die.

Now, you have to ask yourself: who is guilty for these deaths? Do you think that among the millions of people who die in the process, there will be an innocent child? Who is responsible for death of that innocent child? Think about it: even if it's just one child, who is responsible for the death of that one innocent child?

You are! We are!

If you are paying taxes, you are responsible! Your taxes support military actions, and perhaps your dollar was the dollar that bought the bullet that killed a child.

How does that resonate with your religion or ethical upbringing? Are you Christian, Muslim, Sikh, or maybe Buddhist? What is the biggest commandment? Do we really think we can repent for the death of an innocent child in God's eyes?

Currently, in terms of the political system, it is in a state where it looks like neither evolution nor revolution will change anything. Does that mean we are doomed? Not quite.

What is evolution?

Evolution is a slow change through trial and error; it works by removing elements that are weaker than others. Evolution also involves gaining knowledge, by the process of building on top of existing knowledge. The main problem with evolution is our expectation that every change will lead us in the correct direction. But what usually happens along the way, is that we are removing all attempts that are not suited for the game of "Monopoly", making the game more complex and even more difficult to understand. And, by the rules of the game, only the strongest and fittest "survive." The problem there is that the strongest and fittest are just a small fraction of the entire population on the planet. If we accept that "only strongest and fittest should survive" as absolute truth, what will happen to everyone else?

What is Revolution?

By definition, revolution is a forcible overthrow of a government or social order in favor of a new system, which should be an action that creates a change – which is yet another lie. Sad truth is that every change that has happened in history just led to a transfer of goods from one "elite" group to another "elite" group.

Unfortunately, mentioned "action that creates a change" does not create significant change in reality. Look all the countries that recently went from socialism to democracy or any other "change." In most of the cases, the situation is the same and sometime worse. The same thing happened when masses of people overthrew monarchs in favor of a republic or communism, and the same is applicable for near or distant history.

Remember, when everyone starts shouting for revolution, there is a good chance that the majority of the people won't get anything out of it.

If you examine any historical revolution – take, for example, the "Great October Socialist Revolution" – the only thing that happens is that they just replace one state figurehead with another. The "socialist" party leaders replaced the royalist aristocracy, and, for the rest of the people (great majority) noting really changed. They continued working hard and struggling to survive – working the same job but for another boss.

When you are the horse that pulls a cart, the question of coachman concerns you just in the extent of how hard he whips you, how much weight he puts in your cart, and how far he forces you to pull it, but, never the less, if you stay attached to the cart, your job of pulling will not change.

Then what? We are kind of running out of options here.

The solution is – **design**!

We already have all the knowledge. We are at the point of development at which we have gained enough knowledge through history that we can make a much better system. By combining the knowledge we have with inventive design, we can create a new system that will be more suitable for the majority of the people. As most of us consider our species to be conscious and intelligent, maybe it is time to start acting that way.

Anarchy

The word "**anarchy**" ('anəki/)

Definition: A state of disorder due to absence or non-recognition of authority or other controlling systems. Absence of government and absolute freedom of the individual, regarded as a political ideal.

Origin: From the ancient Greek ἀναρχία (anarchia), which combines ἀ (a), "without" and ἀρχή (arkhi), "ruler, leader" — "without rulers" or "without leaders."

Anarchism is a political philosophy that advocates self-governed societies based on voluntary institutions — described as stateless societies or institutions based on non-hierarchical, free associations.

Theoretically, there are no issues with anarchistic society when everyone is nice, loving, and peaceful; things get very ugly when everyone takes power and justice into his/her own hands. This usually leads to chaos and destruction.

In deeply corrupted societies, governments tend to exercise its power in an oppressive, burdensome, cruel, or unjust manner. In order to restore balance, people tend to self-organize, in order to overthrow such structures and escape oppression.

As a consequence of several equally-corrupted governments, and in the fear of repeating the same mistakes, people choose to live without government or structure. Instead of putting their trust and hopes in new false leaders again, they choose a society without leaders. Often, this change does not happen peacefully, as leaders of corrupted governments do not want to lose the power and benefits they already have.

Anarchy is an antidote for oppressive government, but there is a fundamental flaw: by using violence, they are not becoming better than those oppressive governments.

Although anarchy looks like something that is meant as a good alternative for destroying oppressive government, anarchy is also destroying the society. By failing to give adequate means/institutions that will protect citizens and carry out law and justice, necessary to civilized society, anarchy creates a fertile ground for chaos, allowing everyone to take the law into his/her own hands.

Metaphorically speaking, anarchy is chemotherapy for a government affected by cancer; it destroys the cancer cells but also destroys the good cells. In most cases, it is not a cure, because a weakened body is more susceptible to the recurrence of cancer cells. This relapse, with an already weak body, can lead to a quick death. Ideally, what we want is to strengthen our immune system, so it can recognize and fight cancer cells and make the body stronger.

Therefore, we know that anarchy is not a solution, but we also know that totalitarian-democracy *[32] isn't solution either, as it is just an aristocracy in disguise.

What we need is active, direct democracy — a mix between the two ends, a golden mean, a middle way.

We need to be transparent enough that we can have positive feedback but not to such an extent to push us into a mass-surveillance police state. We need cohesion in society, but we do not want a cult. We need guidance and things to strive for, but we do not want to end up in a control-freak world where we become slaves to our own goals.

We need a solution similar to the Buddhist story of "The Middle Way": "One day, Siddhartha heard an old musician on a passing boat, speaking to his pupil: If you tighten the string too much, it will snap, and if you leave it too slack, it won't play." *[33]

Freedom

"Rare are those who understand the limits of freedom.
Even rarer are those who understand the freedom of the limits.
Eskimos say: "Do not build a door that is bigger than the house".
It means the same as to build the windows smaller than the eyes."

– excerpt from the poem "Eyes" *[34]

It is interesting how most of us take freedom for granted. And, we behave as same for many other things that do not have a price tag. We think about them only when we lose them; family, love, health, freedom ... we start thinking about them only when they are not in our presence anymore.

To be free is a great gift, but with great gifts always comes a great responsibility. You have to be always vigilant, you have to protect those gifts, you have to keep them in your sight, and you have to fight for them — with all your will and all your heart.

Past generations fought wars, they rallied against oppression and discrimination, and they spoke for those who did not have a voice or for those whose voices were suppressed.

And what is it exactly that we do?

Nowadays, it seems we do not care about our freedom at all. We are willing to accept everything under the pretext of consumeristic need/desire or false patriotism; we will accept anyone's intrusion on our privacy and our life. How quickly we forget that the very thing we are giving up so easily was, in the not so distant past, paid with blood.

During Nixon's era, the Watergate scandal *[35] was a huge issue and it caused a great disturbance. Today, we are experiencing an unprecedented level of spying. It is hundreds of times larger than Watergate, and it is not just NSA that I am talking about; small or big tech companies, governments, individuals ... it seems everyone is spying on everyone, and everyone is collecting data about everyone. It is so huge that it is almost unimaginable, but yet again, it seems that just a few people care about it. It seems that spying has become a new normal.

This very much resembles the experiment with the frog that gets boiled alive without noticing the slowly rising water temperature, and once the water starts boiling, it is way too late for the poor creature.

Unlike frogs, you have a bigger brain, so ask yourself, "What is it that they trying to heat today without me noticing? And who is trying to boil the water in which I stand?" and ask those frequently.

The novelist George Santayana once famously said, "Those who cannot remember the past are condemned to repeat it." And, no one said it as good as Ronald Reagan "Freedom is never more than one generation away from extinction. We didn't pass it to our children in the bloodstream. It must be fought for, protected, and handed on for them to do the same, OR one day we will spend our sunset years telling our children and our children's children what it was once like in the world [v] where men were free."

Heart attacks rarely manifest as sudden and unexpected blows, instead they are usually preceded by many warnings; however, many completely ignore those warnings...

Evil never sleeps. When we forget to be wary and forget that it exists, as it goes, it is very likely that we are at the verge of the same evil we have experienced many times before in our history.

---

[v]   Ronald Reagan's quote modification - Word from original quote "United States" has been changed to "world" as it is more suitable for this day and age.

Concentration camp metaphor

Long ago, a black-and-white movie was broadcast from time to time, but I cannot find it anymore; it has been lost somewhere in the winds of the past. The story is set in a Nazi concentration camp.

In this camp, there was a pavilion where all the prisoners were settled. As in every concentration camp, they lived in dreadful conditions: weak, and most of the time hungry. The man in charge of order and discipline, the so-called "capo" was not a German solder but one of their own flesh and blood, a man who was one of them not so long before. He was a huge fellow with a nasty look in his eyes — someone who would torture people with a smile on his face as if he enjoyed every minute of it. Once he was a boxer, a champion, and although they knew his name they simply called him "Champ." He was someone they had admired and cheered for but there, in that sad and dark place, he was their tormenter, their demon.

Being punched when you are well is one thing, but being punched by that huge "block of stone" when you are weak and starved, completely another. There wasn't a day that passed that they hadn't thought it would have been a lesser evil if they could have been tortured by the German soldiers; at least they would not have that internal guilt of being tortured by their own kind.

At night, while they licked their wounds, they counted those who were not among them anymore and cursed their luck; they were praying as well, praying for some kind of salvation.

On the other hand, "Champ" was drinking with the Germans every night, and as good masters do with their dogs, they would have fetch him drinks and food, and sometimes he would even get a kiss or two from some very free lady of the night, lost and clueless about the place where she actually was.

One day, a new shipment of fresh "meat" arrived. With this shipment, someone else arrived, an unexpected gift, and prisoners immediately spotted someone they had known for a very long time. Although he had lost a few pounds and he looked properly beaten, he was still a big guy, almost the same size as "Champ." As a matter of fact, he once fought "Champ" for the title but he lost by just a few points. Still, he was a very good boxer.

Slowly but surely, an idea emerged: "What if...?" But they shook off the idea as something silly — how could they even think about that kind of thing!?

But some ideas are more persistent than others, and this one kept coming back. During the days of constant torment, the idea was returning like a boomerang, and eventually one day one of the poor souls said what was already on everyone's mind: "Can he beat the Champ? If he could beat him, at least the beatings will... stop."

Someone else said, "Yes, but he is weak, and every day he is becoming weaker."

Another shrugged, "Yes, that is true."

But then someone else suggested, "What if we give him our food?"

They started thinking and after a while unanimously they decided "Yes, we will do it!"

So, every day after a meal, they gave him half of the very thin piece of bread they were getting and half of the watery pigwash they were being fed. They thought, that they were almost dead anyway and there was not much to lose.

They saw the will in his eyes, and they recognized his determination and wish for revenge.

So they spoke with him and revealed what was on their minds, waiting for a reply with trepidation. To their relief, he immediately accepted, thankful for the opportunity. He started practicing every single day. When the lights were out and no one was looking or listening, he was doing sit-ups, push-ups, and many different kinds of exercises. And, during the noisy Nazi parties, he was practicing punches on the bed mattress.

Gradually, he became stronger and stronger. In everyone's mind the day of the "match" was closing by.

On a Sunday, after the previous night's wild party, "Champ" was still dizzy as alcohol was still crawling through his veins, although being dizzy did not stop him from being mean. It seemed that the hangover just amplified his bad mood. As soon as he lumbered in through the door, he started harassing and beating people. When he got to his rival, he raised his fist to punch him. At that moment, as in a very good match, the rival struck back. In a split second the match began, but it did not last long.

At the time, when Nazi soldiers came in with hounds baring teeth and growling, all they could find was "Champ" lying down, unconscious, with bruises and blood all over his face.

. . .

What happened next?

There was no significant fuss about it within Nazi lines. For them, it was just a minor disturbance. They just replaced "Champ" with the rival, and now the rival was the man in charge.

And for the prisoners, well, something else unforeseen followed. As soon as the rival got his new position, and as soon as he stepped into the role of jailer, he, very much like his predecessor, became as brutal and oppressive.

In the final scene of this twisted reality, the prisoners looked at each other and looked at "Champ" sitting in the corner battered and bruised, and then... again, with bowed heads, they started giving up their portion of the food in the hope that this time it would be...

And somewhere, in some perpetual parallel universe, this story is still repeating.

When I saw this movie for the first time, I could not get it out from my mind, and I could not stop thinking about three questions:

Did the prisoners have any other choice?

Could they have done something else?

Is there any other solution for this?

What about you - can you imagine another ending?

The blood cell metaphor

For the human body to function normally, each of its parts has to get enough oxygen and nutrients, otherwise organs will start failing, and eventually the body could completely shut down and die.

Temporarily it is possible to stop blood flow to certain limbs or organs, but if circulation is cut off for too long and the cells do not get required oxygen and nutrients carried via blood cells, without needed protection they will start breaking down and dying. Failing parts can quickly spread an "infection of sorts," where the decaying process can easily spread to other sections of the body. If blocked circulation is not treated, this can spread to the rest of the body and can eventually become fatal.

Too much blood in one place for an extended period of time can cause coagulation and thrombosis. If left untreated, thrombosis can cause a stroke or organ failure, which can lead to death. On the other hand, ruptured blood vessels (regardless of a reason being an internal or external force) can cause escaping of blood, which can again lead to death.

Another blood disorder, anemia, can be caused by malnutrition. Anemia will cause fatigue, weakness, and a variety of other symptoms. In contrast, too much nutrients combined with lack of physical activities can cause clogging of arteries, which can obstruct normal blood flow, and again lead to thrombosis.

We can argue that certain body parts (organs/limbs) need more blood while performing different activities. Some organs need more blood than others. For instance, when we digest food, exercise, or engage in an active thinking process, various part of our body may need more blood flow. However, this will happen only for short periods of time, and afterwards the blood flow will return to its most optimal state, where there is a more or less uniform distribution of blood cells.

In our economic system, money has the same function as blood cells, *[36] and everything else goes the same... flow in an optimal way is necessary; otherwise the system will die, taking down all of its components with it.

Fighting cancer metaphor

When confronted with a "terminal" illness, the first thing people have to understand is that most of that illness is in their minds.

Do not get me wrong. I am not saying it does not exist. The illness is there. Do not be confused about that for a second. It is real, but what is more important is that you are real as well. You are real...and, if you can think and read the following lines - that also means you are alive.

Furthermore, do not confuse the things I am talking about with some hocus-pocus-mumbo-jumbo thing that some people tell you just in order to take your money. This is for free. But also, do not think that if something is free it also means it does not have a price. A price is always there: time, effort, persistence, patience... all these are prices we have to pay.

I am not saying that I have a cure for cancer. This is just something that may help you fight cancer.

Your body has a vast neural network. It is so large that, as I am writing this, the number of neural "nodes" in your body is about seven times larger than entire Internet.

Your body has "cameras," "sensors," and "secret service agents" in every corner, creating a huge amount of information in every moment of time.

Even more amazing, your body has three minds, not just one mind like we thought before.*[37] One mind is in your brain, the all-day-information-processing, thinking, voice-chattering mind that controls all at the conscious and unconscious levels. Then there is autonomous mind that controls the heart, lungs, and kidneys, never forgetting to beat, filter blood, or take a breath. And finally there is one brain in your guts. Your guts are like another dimension, a whole universe in miniature. In your guts there are between 500 and 1,000 species of bacteria. The total estimated number of bacteria is ten times (10x) larger than the number of all cells in the human body (as they are much smaller than human cells).

Those bacteria are working in symbiosis with you. Also they communicate with each other by chemical means and, as interesting as it sounds, they communicate through taste buds in your mouth and guts (isn't that amazing, you have taste buds in your guts) *[38] and other receptors, forming an extensive neural network going from your guts to the central nerve system.

Your mood can affect those bacteria. Also the "wrong ingredients" can affect your mood.

The food you are eating will affect your emotions, and your emotions will affect your thoughts. This is a very interdependent relation.

When you are sad, worried, depressed, or angry, you will probably skip a meal, eat some junk food, or try to cheer yourself up with some sweets. Also, you will not chew your food well enough. Skipping the meal, eating junk food, or not chewing well enough will cause future imbalances in your guts. Your guts will react and the bacteria inside will further negatively affect your emotions, and your emotions will cause an entire barrage of negative thoughts.

This is a vicious cycle. Even when you are healthy, this is something that can make you sick.

News about terminal illness is a difficult thing to process. Thoughts are overwhelmingly bad and you find that you are unable to stop or control them. An endless loop of a self-repeating voice that says one single thing: "I am going to die."

That single thought is the worst thing that can happen to an ill person. Stopping it will perhaps not cure you but not stopping it will most certainly kill you faster. Negative emotions and negative visualization will weaken your organism much faster than illness.

Repeating that one sentence constantly is a self-fulfilling prophecy. *[39] By thinking negatively, we become what we have set as a negative outcome because all that fear and negative emotion will create fertile ground for negative habits, and negative habits will feed illness. When a body is under constant emotional stress, it cannot work properly and it cannot turn on the appropriate immune response.

In contrast, when we are happy and in a loving environment, if we laugh a lot, our organism will be relaxed and more oxygen will flow through our veins. Consequently, our body will trigger natural immune systems in order to fight illness.

Now, how to stop that one thought repeating like a broken record?

This seems an almost impossible task to do, similar to when they ask you to stop thinking when practicing meditation. If you try stopping your thoughts by thinking about "not thinking," the only thing you will end up with is one more thought about "not thinking."

The same is true with the "I am going to die" thought. If you try stopping it by sheer will, the only thing you will end up with are thoughts about how to stop thinking about the thing you do not want to think about, and you will be caught in a paradox, you will still think about it. This will drain your energy very rapidly.

What is the solution then?

Focus on something else, something that will give you positive feedback regardless of how small. Something to cheer you up, and something to make you smile. This is something that should give you energy by the pure power of thought.

The trick is to replace that self-perpetuating sentence with something else, something positive, a sentence that will lift you up instead putting you down.

This is not the same as occupying yourself with lots of things to do in order to escape reality, like playing video games, watching movies, chasing hedonistic pleasures, or working to exhaustion all day long. Do not get me wrong. I am not against playing video games. But you have to understand that sitting in one place for several hours while producing a significant adrenalin response will create a suitable environment for the illness and its development. Also, it will not stop your negative thinking loop; that loop will be gently pushed into the background but it will be there.

Movies that can make you smile can be helpful, as can working on something you love. But probably the best option from the lot is reading books, if the book is interesting enough, this will push out all other thoughts as you read.

Remember, the general rule of thumb is to avoid things that will nail you to one place for a very long time while creating additional stress. This applies to video games, work, hobbies, movies, and books as well.

The goal is to train yourself so that whenever you get a negative thought you have to replace that thought with positive ones, the ones that will make you happy and will give you positive feedback.

This is very important. When you decide to choose your replacement sentence, it must be true at all times.

For instance, imagine that both sentences you are choosing are knights. One sentence is an evil knight. (You can choose any color for his suit you like. The only thing you have to remember is that the knight is evil and he is trying to kill your body.) The other one is a good knight. He has the task of protecting your body from the evil knight. If the good knight is not strong enough, he will fail in his task and the evil knight will continue his reign.

For instance, choosing to replace the sentence "I am going to die" with "I am better every day" can be a good thing as it can lift you up. But at the times when you get even the simplest cold, that sentence can seem to be a lie and can bring back the evil twin very quickly.

The trick is to choose your good sentence in such way that it will be positive and true most of the time, or even to have different sentences that will correspond to different situations. This is very much like having an army of good knights that are fighting on your side. Maybe your favorite one won't always be in shape, but there will always be one good enough to replace him.

The evil side also has an army, and the "I am going to die" knight is not the only one. There are a huge number of them who are there to poison you mind with negativity, and you have to fight back, you have to fight back if you want to get better. You have to fight because and you must remember that in this world, there is always someone who would miss you very much if you were gone and that you are an important piece of the larger puzzle.

Replacing these bad thoughts with good ones is important, as good thoughts will create good emotions, and good emotions will lead to good habits, and good habits will help fight illness.

And lastly, do not give up! It will take time and patience to heal. There is a saying that one needs the same amount of time to heal as the time spent in developing the illness.

"You have to stay focused when fighting cancer!"

Concentration camp part II: alternative

Have you found an alternative ending for the "Concentration camp" story? If you were there in their shoes, what would you have done differently?

I like to believe there is a solution for every problem we have, and in order to find it, we just have to step out of our usual box and think outside of it.

There is an old saying that a double-edged sword has one side pointing at the enemy and the other pointing at the wielder. Another one says, "He who lives by the sword dies by the sword," lastly one of Newton's laws says, "Every action has its opposite reaction." In "Concentration camp" story the prisoners used force to cancel the force, and all they got in return was – force. They returned to the same point from which they began.

If we leave all these quotes aside for a moment, we can see that the prisoners' biggest and most unfortunate mistake was actually defining problem in the wrong way. They thought their biggest problem was the warden, and they completely overlooked the real issue, which was there from the beginning.

Their problem was not the warden but the deprivation of their freedom.

Regardless of how banal and funny it sounds, the only problem they had was that they were being held captive at the concentration camp in the first place.

A peaceful path would have said the only thing they needed to do was to find a way to get out of there. The other mistake in their plan was a grave misjudgment of character.

When planning or looking for solutions that crucially depend on people, we do not usually look for the strongest people. What we need instead are the most intelligent and trustworthy individuals. And, in life and death situations, we would most likely look for the people of such **integrity** and **honesty** which couldn't be disrupted even at the price of their own lives. Without issues of **trust,** by having people with perfect, incorruptible integrity on your side, the only thing left is to focus on the technical realization of the plan.

Instead of having a fistfight, what about digging a tunnel? What about investing in people who have the same problem like they have? Instead of force, aggression, and revenge, they could have "invested" in knowledge and integrity.

Haven't we, for all these years, invested in similar bullies?

In our case, bullies have nice suits and ties, loads of money, and silver tongues. Instead of abusing us physically, they molest our minds, morals, and needs.

Isn't it time for a change?

How about finding an engineer, instead of a politician, to resolve the problems we have?

The odd games we play

Throughout history, games have played an important role in our society and have been used as a means of education, fun and even manipulation.

If we go back in time to Ancient Rome, we can find an interesting Latin proverb "panem et circenses", *[40] which can be literally translated as "Bread and Games", which is a metaphor politically used to describe the creation of public approval, not through exemplary or good public service or public policy, but through means of providing a diversion to satisfy the immediate, shallow requirements of the people.

Having that in mind, let me address one particular type of game that had and still has a huge positive, but, at the same time, detrimental toll on our world as it is today: **competitive games**.

It seems that everything we create nowadays and everything that is already out there, is all about competition. So, we have all sorts of crazy competitions: beauty competitions, science competitions, spelling competitions, art competitions, even poetry and food competitions.

The Guinness Book of World Records is a prime example showing how many things we have turned into some form of competition. Almost everything we do can be perceived as a competition ... isn't that silly?

Please, stop for a moment and try to think about that... ask yourself, why, why, why? Why the blip do we do any of these things?

Let's take food competitions for instance. If something has not gone terribly wrong in the process of cooking, how will you decide who is the winner? You may say that the judge will decide. But what does the judge know about me, my taste buds and what I like?

Maybe I don't like the food that the judge has chosen as the winning one and I would have preferred it done differently, maybe cooked a bit longer or maybe spicier, while maybe someone else would have picked a completely different meal.

It's the same with music, poetry or art ... the things I like someone else might not like, and vice versa.

What is the point of saying that something is the best meal, when the entire winning part is susceptible to subjective taste?

"De gustibus non est disputandum" is old Latin saying and can be translated to "In matters of taste, there can be no disputes".

So how did we get to the point of having art or music competitions?!

In fact, why do we even need the entire concept of winning and losing?

Thousands of years ago, when human behavior was more animal-like, competition was useful. It established dominance within a community and created social structure and order. This was essential for the survival of the species. Now, when we consider ourselves intelligent and empathetic beings, we have to abandon the way of animals. If we regard ourselves as superior to the animals, then we have to act accordingly.

Naturally you would ask yourself, if competition is the problem what is the opposite of competition?

And most people, if not all, will answer cooperation.

But there is another issue - we have created cooperative games that are still competitive.

Football, basketball or many other team games per se are cooperative games but they are still competitive in their nature.

Hence, again we have created winning and losing sides and again there are more losers than winners because now the number of losers is multiplied by the number of members in the team.

In most team games, only one team can win. That means one winner but lots of losers!

Ok then, what is the real opposite of competition?

It is a plain and simple playfulness.

Like dancing, when you are listening to music and you are relaxed enough, your body will follow the rhythm naturally, and if you lose yourself in the rhythm, regardless of how skilful you are, you will enjoy it. But then, somewhere around 1900 someone invented competitive dancing. *[41]

But what is wrong with competition; after all doesn't competition encourage people to perfect their skills?

Yes, it does!

Fear also does the same thing. When human beings are under stress or in danger, they learn crucial skills a lot faster than usual, but that does not mean we should torture or deliberately create fearful circumstances, just so people could learn a few new things.

Why not love? Love perfects skills more than any competition, and, when you love and enjoy doing something, you will perfect these skills anyway, and you will even enjoy the process of getting there.

We take competition games so seriously that we got to the point where a football player is paid more than a surgeon!

One of the issues with competition is that stops large numbers of people from even trying. Talking about culinary wizardries does not make your stomach full, preparing food and eating it – does. So, if you like something, don't just watch or sit there and talk about it, and don't just enjoy it in a passive way, instead go and do it, everything else is just a waste of time.

Yes, competition can be a good thing, it can mean progress and it gives us drive to explore more about ourselves, our bodies and our limits. Issue is not just a competition per se, but more how competitive activities have soaked through all the layers of our society, talking, cheering, liking, hating, planning, showing others that we are better than they are...

Following the same thread, we have to ask: what is the next thing we are going to invent?

Maybe a breathing competition!?

And, that already exists in the form of free diving or competitive apnea!

For a moment, imagine this setting:

Two friends, after they have enjoyed very good and long lives, are lying next to each other in the hospital on their deathbeds and are talking: "I had a good life you know", says the first. The other replies, "Yes, but mine was better, I have done more than you!"

I can already see the big Circus title: "The Ultimate challenge! Life as a competition! Do not miss your chance to see this event!"

Hooray for that, but let's get real for a moment.

Life is a personal experience - why compare it with anything?

And - that is the best thing ever. Everything you have felt, dreamt, laughed at or cried about, is just yours. Yours — and no one can take it away from you.

Yes, we like to romanticize about these things in that way, but what about dementia or memory erasing brain surgery - well let's not worry about these things now, we are probably safe for a few more years.

Let's say that you do not experience any memory altering event during the course of your life, on your deathbed, if I had chance I would ask you following:

Have you enjoyed your learning time or was it painful?

If you have had a choice, would you repeat your "life" (experience) all over again?

There are more than seven billion people on this planet, and, probably, there is something to learn from each person. Each person, regardless of being good or bad, rich or poor, has his or her own stories — every single one like a pearl — each unique in its own way.

Yet again, in our minds, we live the lives of some other people. Movie stars, sport stars, politicians, TV people, Internet stars...we watch them, we talk about them, we follow them, we invest our emotions in them, we admire them, and we use them as role models.

How many people are in the media spotlight in all countries? 1,000? 10,000?

The media will keep them in focus all the time — the same people, over and over again.

For how long — how many years? 10, 20, 30 years? Some of them, for their entire lives.

Every person who reads or watches the news is subject to the same brainwashing machine, with an unprecedented level of mass hypnotic influence. Regardless of being in peace or war, the elite, ruling party, the media, and religious leaders will push out their political, commercial, religious, or patriotic propaganda. As a result, people will continue rolling the same rat wheel, and, in times of war, countless lives will be lost for a bag of empty promises and false ideals. We are being served the same pictures and the same patterns, making our lives one big 'Groundhog Day' *42 – a constant repetition of the same boring day.

The same ruling elites stay on the top, squandering resources created through the sweat and tears of those on the bottom. They do not care about fixing the real issues we have on this planet; the only things they care about are how to gain more power, money, and control over strategic resources – the same resources that may, sooner than we think, end us all, along with all other life on this planet.

Maybe it is time to snap out of it, to wake up, and start living our own lives. Maybe it is time to explore, experience, and play our own game – the game in which we would play the main role, instead of being the silent audience.

The most dangerous game - Monopoly

The simplest way to explain how the current "game" works is by talking about the board game Monopoly.

Interestingly enough, the history of Monopoly $*^{43}$ can be traced back to 1903, when an American woman named Elizabeth J. Magie Phillips created the game as an educational tool to explain Single Tax theory of Henry George. She hoped the game would help explain the negative aspects of concentrating land into private monopolies, which will lead to change. Since then, instead of becoming an educational tool and serving its main purpose, Monopoly caught on as a highly competitive, addictive game, selling over 250 million copies worldwide and educating kids and grownups, although not in the way that was originally intended.

What is the goal of the game Monopoly?

"Players move around the board buying or trading properties, developing their properties with houses and hotels, and collecting rent from their opponents, the ultimate goal being to drive them into bankruptcy."

Personally, I never liked the game, but not because I was losing more often than winning. Quite the opposite: I didn't like it because of the realization I had when I won for the first time.

When I was losing, I was thinking about the game and other strategies to win, and sometimes I would envy the winner. Eventually, instead of being happy when I won I was sad because I realized something rather obvious: If there is one winner, everyone else ware losers, meaning that the number of people who were happy would always be multiple times smaller than the people who were unhappy.

Now consider this: one way we learn is by repeating actions, so every time we "win," our brains reward us with emotions such as thrill, excitement and pleasure, and our brain remembers entire sequences of events because we want that pleasure again. But do not forget that the loser's brain also learns.

Stop for a moment and try to compare reality and the game.

Are we transferring patterns we have learned in a game to real life?

What if reflection of this game has become our reality?

It would not be fair to blame Monopoly for all the issues we have in this world; the game we play has been here for thousands of years, long before Monopoly came into the light.

In the game of Monopoly, the number of players can range between 2 and 12. At the end of each play, there is one winner and a maximum of 11 losers. In the game of life, the number of "players" is much larger-hundreds, thousands, millions-and it follows the same principle, there will be a couple of winners and billions of losers.

Many wealthy people have the same simple business philosophy as Kevin O'Leary, something along the lines: "Every morning, when I wake up, I want to think I am richer than the night before." *[44] What this person is saying can be summed up with the following: "I want **MORE** money". Most of these people do **not** have a goal or a definite number to reach-if they have one million, they would like two million; if they have hundred million, they want two hundred million; and even if they have one billion, they want two billion...and so on. They have more money than they could spend in their entire lifetime, and yet all they think is, "How do I get more?" So why is that? If you talk to a politician, you hear something similar: more money, more power, more influence, more votes...

It seems we could use just one word to define the current state of our political and economic systems in - "more".

One huge issue with "more" there is a certain point where "more" becomes "no more."

Like Monopoly, our world has its own limitations. Like a game, our world is limited by its size, the number of players and the amount of money in the game.

And there is one more thing. In Monopoly, we are playing our rounds and getting richer or poorer, and as the game progresses, sometimes slower or sometimes faster, one person will emerge on top. Sometimes, the winner will use his money to help, by giving loans and chances to others, and if the other players are lucky enough, the game will be extended and they will get a couple more turns with the dice.

But eventually, if everyone is playing by the rules, the game will end after some time, and a single, solitary person will win!

Similarly to Monopoly, in our world there is a playing time, although we do not call them games-we call them "cycles". As with Monopoly, in our real world "game" we have a few winners and a rather ridiculous number of losers. Although in Monopoly there is no name for the end of the game, in our world, we call such an event an economic crisis. You already know the pattern: the rich become so rich that they push all others into bankruptcy. They do, and they will do in future, after all, isn't that what they have learnt to do in life in the first place!?

There are other side effects in our world at the end of a cycle, such as riots, financial depressions or wars. You have to ask yourself-why is all this necessary?

You have heard already "History repeats itself". Of course it does, there is nothing strange about that, we have been playing the same stupid game all along.

But, be honest - you like playing the game, don't you? You like the thrill, and you like idea that maybe you will be a winner this time. For most of us, it does not matter how poor people around the world are. We are ok, we think we have a good job, we are secure, we are not losers and losing our small amount of wealth can't happen to us. So, we decide not to think about the big picture around the world. The truth is painful. Although the solution is easy, we do not want to listen about solution.

The simple solution is to stop playing Monopoly! Stop playing the game! Just stop this nonsense! Stop it, all of it - the entire concept of playing competitive games with each other, cheering the winner, belonging to these games and endorsing the system of winning and losing. Just stop!

There is a much better way to enjoy the game of life.

But that is not as easy a task as it seems. Forcing yourself to stop a bad habit is often an almost impossible task because of our nature. In terms of our habits, we are very much like a bottle filled with gas - if we force the gas out, what is left is a vacuum. In a gassy environment, the bottle will quickly "suck" back the surrounding gas in, or, to be precise, because gasses always fill all the surrounding space, they will push their way back into the bottle. Therefore, in order to replace bad gas with desirable gas, you have to fill the bottle with that gas while keeping the same pressure. The other option is to change the environment, so that, when we push the old gas out, whatever is outside will fill the bottle.

Can we build a new kind of "game," where everyone will win?

Fairness

Have you ever thought about following, "Why do I think that the world/society 'needs to' / 'should be' fair?" and "Why do I think that fairness should be our end goal?"

There are certain things that many of us take for granted in such level that we expect everyone should think and feel the same way we do, without any questions, but, most of the time, that is not the case. The first time I was asked the same question; I was left speechless, struggling to find a meaningful explanation. Although the question about fairness looks like something one would likely dismiss with the wave of our hands, accompanied with a "What a silly question" type of comment, it got me thinking for a while.

To begin with, a question of fairness is not the question of a goal, but more of an ability. It's like asking, "Do we need lungs?" Maybe we do not, but, if we don't, is there a better option that can provide oxygen for our body, and, in that case, would we need oxygen at all?

So, why do we need fairness?

Studies have shown, that fairness is not something that is exclusive to humans, but it is a property that is hard-coded in many other animals. Prof. Bekoff, who presents his case in a new book "Wild Justice," said, "The belief that humans have morality and animals don't is a long-standing assumption, but there is a growing amount of evidence that is showing us that this simply cannot be the case." *[45]

Fairness is baked into the brains of all mammals and provides the "social glue" that allows often aggressive and competitive animals to live together in groups, giving them a better chance of survival.

We can think about fairness as a trait that decreases the unpredictability of a system. The more unpredictable members of the society we interact with are, the lower our chance of survival.

Unfairness is in some sense directly correlated with unpredictability. We communicate, make agreements, shake hands, and have unwritten rules of trust, in order to make our lives easier and to allow us to live longer. In order to fulfill its purpose, society has to increase predictability by controlling communication channels and improving the accuracy of exchanged information.

The simplest way would be to imagine two robots: one is white and one is black. To keep moving, they need to find new batteries, but the batteries for the black robot are hidden under white pieces, and vice versa. Each robot is programmed to only touch objects of its own color; the only way to get new batteries is to ask the other robot for information on where they are and for help in retrieving them. However, whenever the black robot asks the question, the white robot gives the wrong answer. After a while, the black robot will shut down, running out of charge. Even if the black robot has been providing correct information to help the white robot, the shutdown of the black robot will make the white robot lose the ability to find new batteries. The only option for both robots to survive is to transfer information truthfully in both directions.

Our society is very similar to this example; we need one another in order to survive.

Unpredictability in the above context does not mean knowing exactly how will one person behave, but it means knowing enough to determine that the other person's behaviors or actions won't be dangerous for our survival. It is predictability of the nature of a behavior (god/bad) rather than predictability of the behavior on its own.

At the same time, this is the reason why we are hesitant to make new friendships with people about whom we do not know much. If we do not have some kind of track record, we do not have much to begin with, and that can be intimidating. We can rely on gut feelings, trust, and facial expressions from the other person, but, if we really get in trouble with a true predator, none of those things will help, as a true predator always has methods to trick his prey. That is the reason why we chat, gossip, live in a communal society, and, in some weird way, doing all those things helps others. Whatever happens to one person ripples through society, with a number of messages to give warnings to others.

Imagine what the world would look like if someone would pull out a gun every time we smile and extend our hand in greeting. It would be chaotic, drastically unpredictable, and would have been understood as predatory behavior, endangering lives.

By the rule of group survival, we try to eliminate any such member of society, in order to decrease danger and the possibility of harming one or more member of our society.

In the movie "The Ghost and the Darkness," a fictionalized account of the true story about the two lions that attacked and killed workers in Tsavo, Kenya during the building of the Uganda-Mombasa Railway in East Africa in 1898. Portrayed lions represent a typical example of the force of nature that is:

unpredictable and cannot be controlled. This force presents a real danger for the members of society, and society decides to eliminate the threat by killing the lions.

It is the same reason why we lock up murderers and other criminals. Their unpredictability and violent nature presents a danger for the other members of society, the majority of whom have a shared social contact of living peacefully by contributing to the betterment of society. In order to decrease suffering, this majority can exclude or banish such members from what is otherwise a cohesive group.

Theoretically, it is possible for some members to gain enough power that they will become stronger than the group, giving them the ability to operate beyond the rules of the group. In that case, fairness would not be applicable, and the group would be fully subjected to the temperament of that one entity, regardless of how crazy that entity may be.

Wealthy people, dictators, and politicians usually have a similar advantage, but there are always ways that even the weakest link can restore balance or destroy the entire system.

At the end of the day, we are faced with the question on whether we prefer chaos or order, uncertainty or trust, fairness or deception. Whatever we choose, we will have to deal with the consequences.

Economic inequality

The most common argument for inequality is that we are not equal and that we should not be equal. Furthermore, the argument says that inequality is an actual driver for innovation and economic prosperity, leading to the conclusion that we, in fact, do not want to reduce inequality and that implementing some of the more progressive economic ideas would inevitably lead to socialistic society and stagnation.

Although the introductory premise of the above argument is correct, everything else is wrong.

Yes, we are not equal — not biologically, not with our abilities, or by our mental capacities — and I agree that we as a society should not aspire to create a nation of clones. Our differences and uniqueness are what make our lives more interesting. Although this is true, in an economic sense, it is pretty misleading.

Imagine a hundred meter race in which everyone would not start at the beginning, but, instead, someone would start way behind the starting line and someone else next to the finishing line.

Would you watch that kind race?

Why would you bother watching the kind of race where all the outcomes are known at the beginning and where you could immediately tell who the winner would be before it starts? Even WWE Wrestling is less predictive: it has different variables and some kind of scenario, but, usually, no one will tell you what the outcome will be.

We all know that we are different, and that is not an issue; some people are taller, stronger, smarter, or more creative. The most significant issue of economic inequality is the **unfair advantage**. We are not starting the race from the same starting line. Those further from the finish line have less chances of succeeding. Therein lies the paradox of economic inequality we are facing now: often, that unnatural advantage has not been earned by merit or effort, but it is given by birth, by inheritance, not reflecting the true value of individuals.

This means that, regardless of how smart or talented one individual is, if she/he has a bad starting position, rough environment, poor food, and bad health conditions, that person is destined to fail.

Imagine: even if ten thousand people succeed in lifting themselves out from the bottom, that is only 0.00014% of the entire population. If we measured this in terms of IQ, you would need to have a coefficient of 174 *[46], which just a very small number people have. In comparison, the average IQ is considered to be between 90 and 110, and a genius IQ is generally considered to begin around 140 to 145. This means that not even all geniuses will succeed, and, if all of them will not succeed, the real question is what will happen with the remaining 99.9998% of the population.

What is it that that we want as society?

Do we want to glorify behaviors which will benefit our society or the ones that will have a damaging impact on it? Or maybe idea is to glorify eugenics sliding back to Nazi times?

Who would you rather give significant access to funds: people who will waste it on drugs, sport cars, and wild parties, or people who can actually benefit society with science, art, and culture? If we do not praise members who are really talented, what are we praising exactly?

Ideally, what many people want is that every person has the same, equal rights at the beginning: a loving environment, healthy and nutritious food, decent housing, enough care, good education, and a life without fear that one day she/he may experience unemployment and struggle to survive.

Many before us struggled to create a society where we do not need to fear hunger and starvation. Although, now we have all the means to create a world of plenty, it seems that we want to create some kind of survivalist, dystopian horror game out of this planet, by polarizing the world into some simplified version of a Darwinistic "survival of the fittest" race. There is absolutely no need for that. Countless generations worked hard in order to crate future where we don't need to. There is no need to create an artificial scarcity, in order to sustain someone's sadistic idea of power and control.

Doing it would be an evident sign of lack of intelligence and imagination while solving problems we have now and we are going to face in future. Just like having a hammer in your hand does not mean that smashing is the solution for everything.

What is fair economy?

After the big economic crash in 2008, many have realized that our economy is a quite fragile and easily breakable thing, especially for those in middle and the bottom of our society.

Additionally, people around world, with the exception of Iceland, did "remarkable" things — they bailed out the banks that were, as they said, too big to fail. And, just the following year, they saw the same banks paying large bonuses for their managers.

Banks have the right to take your home, if you do not pay just one installment, and they have all legal instruments at their disposal to do that. At the other end, for the money (tax money) they were given from the people to save them from failing, they are allowed to never pay it back. Clearly, reciprocity does not exist, and those law-abiding citizens are at an obvious disadvantage. It seems what financial trends constantly show is that, for ordinary people, voodoo magic has a better success rate than the current economy.

Where does the issue lie? Is it just wrong policies, is it people, or is it something else?

The issue is more fundamental. The basic concepts on which we've based our economy are just plain wrong. Why I am saying this? And how can I be confident that what I am saying is true, even though I am not using any advanced mathematics and complex vocabulary?

Behind almost every man-made concept, there is very simple logic.

The current economy is based on the concept of infinite growth. In an economic sense, that means that one country must continuously increase its gross domestic product. That would be fine if we could have access to all the infinite resources of the universe, but we do not — we live on a finite planet.

Even if we had access to the entire Milky Way galaxy, as Federico Pistono explains in his book "Robots Will Steal Your Job," *[47] with exponential growth in energy demand we would, energy-wise, exhaust the entire galaxy of 100 billion stars in just 2500 years.

Now, how did economists overcome this paradox?

They introduced the magic concept called — inflation. This means that the price of one product will rise over time, and as purchasing power is tied to the work or services provided, the purchasing power of the money you have already earned will decrease with time.

Let's put all that aside, and let me ask you a question:

Imagine that we had an agreement, in which we decided we would build two houses, one for me and one for you. First you will work on my house until my house is done, and while you are working on my house, I will give you vouchers; every voucher means that for every day of your work, I will guarantee a day of my work. And, after a year of hard work, my house is eventually completed. Now it is time for me to work on your house. But because of inflation, the price of the work has increased, so now the vouchers I gave you do not have the same value anymore. Halfway through the second year you have already used all the vouchers I gave you, and you have ended up with your house only halfway done.

Would you accept that deal? Would you work for me under these conditions?

Most people would say no, but yet we all agree to work under those same or worse conditions in our daily life.

How is that fair?

Some may say that "life is not fair, deal with it," but, for me, that looks like a defeatist type of statement. We are the ones who live on this planet and it is ours to create rules, the rules that will govern our lives, not just for a small number of privileged people but for everyone.

Have you ever heard anyone getting PhD for inventing perpetual motion machine [vi]?

Over the years, the economy, despite having a paradox at its foundation, has become a science with huge number of branches. And people, same as for perpetual motion machine, have perfected many different solutions, some simple but other very complex. They have earned PhD titles and many high honors and still their science, which runs the world, does not work, at least not for those who are not at the top.

If a thief learns his skills to perfection, would you give him a PhD or maybe a Nobel Prize for his achievements, or would you maybe take another approach and send him into the jail?

All the thieves locked up in all jails in the world in the last century have not stolen the amount of money that vanished in last market collapse.*[48] In some form or another that money ended up in the pockets of a few wealthy people and still not one of them went to jail. How is that possible?

Pension funds, house mortgages, savings... for which people worked very long hours, for years, all diminished. People ended up on the street, and instead of blaming those who rigged the game, we blamed the people who became homeless.

If I asked you to lend me $1000 or just $100, and if I honestly told you I will never give you that money back, you would probably refuse my request. But again, people are willing to give much larger sums to "trust" funds with the same end result.

Money is just a construct, an idea, nothing more.

---

vi   A perpetual motion machine (also called Perpetuum Mobile) is a hypothetical machine that can do work indefinitely without an energy source.

Although many think that our civilization would completely collapse and that it cannot run without money that is not true. We cannot breath, drink, or eat money; why the worry then whether it exists or not?

What is important for you is clean air, water, food and shelter - not money.

No, I am not an anarchist, and I am not preaching about destroying money, but I am saying that it **has to** and **it will** disappear eventually. Soon enough we will realize that it is an outdated concept; it is just a matter of time. With all the recent technological advances we will eventually realize that there is a better way, or all the resources will just end up in the hands of a few and everyone else will starve to death.

We humans have only one real currency and that is time. Time is our only asset; everything else is just an illusion. Even that asset is very limited for each of us. Even if we could live for ten thousand years, that is nothing in comparison with the age of universe, and yet again we live for a much shorter time, and during that short life we are troubled by many things.

Our economy is an economy of time. When we trade, we do not trade with money, we trade with our time, and we vouch with our promises. Every closed transaction is a promise fulfilled and every reduced transition is a promise betrayed. Everything relies on trust. When trust is broken, things, sooner or later, start falling apart.

In a fair economy, with all the advances in automation in technology we have nowadays, one should expect to always get more value for money earned, not less.

In the IT industry there is interesting economic phenomenon going on from the beginning. If you have $1000 and you want to buy a PC or mobile phone, in two years, for the same amount of money you will get double the computing power.

Now ask yourself what is so special about food, housing, and many other fields where prices are surging when demand is going up?

We have built houses for thousands of years, and by now we should know how to do it very cheaply. Why are housing prices skyrocketing then?

Nothing is different, really — nothing. It is just artificially created in order to sustain the silly game we play. All that exist in order to keep us in the loop in which the structure of the pyramid will be preserved, while our heads are buried in the work we do not need to do, so that we can buy the things we do not need and we won't think about things that really matter.

A fair economy should be something that gets a better side for every single one of us — a system that will help us realize that our lives are not just about what can we do for our personal pleasure but also what we can do for other people and all other living creatures on this planet.

Whatever we decide, it is on us, as there will be no one else to help us. Not God, messiah or aliens ... and if you believe in these, then you have to consider that maybe they do not want to help us, as they are just testing us: are we responsible enough to continue as species or not.

In "their" eyes maybe, if we cannot overcome our own problems we do not deserve to be alive...

Inheritance

While debating about the rights and ownership of the things around us, regardless of your country of origin, we tend to forget that most of the things we have are not due to our personal effort. Claiming that certain people deserve more than others is something we need to question.

Most of the things we have — as individuals and as a collective — we have because we inherited them from our ancestors. Our entire present world, for better or worse, is inherited from past generations; everything we have, including our lives, is because of them. For many generations, they mated, worked, explored, learned, and did many other things, in order to make possible the kind of life we have now.

Think about it: the first species of the genus Homo appeared about 2.5 million years ago, and the first Homo sapiens (Latin: "wise person") appeared about 200,000 years ago. During the last 2,000 years, and before the advent of birth control, the average length of a generation remained close to 30 years each. Using 30 years per generation, Homo appeared 83,000 generations ago, and Homo sapiens appeared 6,700 generations ago. All those generations — and who knows how many other generations of bacteria, insects, fishes, amphibians, mammals, and other transformations before that — allowed you to live.

Now you are alive. What are you going to do with that life? Are you going to go into war against other people, believing that your God is better than their God? Are you going to die, so that someone else can make money on foreign oil, comfortably sitting in his chair and drinking whisky, while you roll in and eat the dusty of some desert world?

We know that we equally inherited our lives and troubles, but access to knowledge, wealth, and power is not equally distributed. That is a serious problem. Concentrating control in one single point of failure can lead to the collapse of the system.

Discussions about redistributing wealth usually lead to the most common claim against ideas like Unconditional Basic Income: "It is wrong to give something for nothing." Now, **if we genuinely believe that nobody should receive something for nothing**, as the British professor Guy Standing said, "Then **you should be against all forms of inheritance**." in order to avoid hypocrisy, we should be consistent.

The point is that the reason for our income and current state of welfare is more due to the effort of past generations than any effort of our own. If our ancestors had not contributed with their efforts, knowledge, ideas, infrastructure, roads, buildings, etc., you and I would probably still be bashing one rock against another.

Therefore, distributing wealth, especially wealth made by fully-automated machines, would be similar to giving a social dividend on the investments of our ancestors, and as we do not know whose particular ancestors did the most, it would be fair to distribute equally to meet the basic needs of everyone. You do not have to believe my words, as this is more or less what Thomas Paine – an English-American political activist, philosopher, and political theorist – said more than 200 years ago. The same Thomas Paine who was the author of "Common Sense" a pamphlet that inspired people in the Thirteen Colonies to declare and fight for independence from Great Britain in the summer of 1776.*[49]

The problem of an unfair advantage in economic inequality in present society is mainly created by unfair subsidies of wealth inheritance in the first place. Lets' be honest: land and property inheritance, along with birthrights, are ancient royalty concepts, reinstated to give preference to one group of people over another and give them advantages from birth. Those who were born with more money have a much bigger advantage than those who started with zero. In ancient times, this was the way to save bloodlines and secure power, the royal throne, and survival of the selfish-gene.

But, that idea is created under a false pretense: if their genes were good, and if those newborns were equally capable to their parents, they would find their own way to succeed, and they would have survived or maintained power on their own.

Think about this: the federal estate tax exemption in the US (that's the amount an individual can leave to heirs without having to pay a federal estate tax) was $5.43 million in 2015. On top of this, shares in a private company are subject to an Inheritance Tax, but there is a very valuable relief, known as the business property relief. When the business property relief rule is applied, the shares can be transferred upon death or during a person's lifetime free of Inheritance Tax. *[50]

Imagine what kind of head start you would have, if you had that kind of money at the beginning, and no taxes were taken out of it.

Just from the education point of view, that is a lot, and it would buy you a top education. If you had even basic understanding about investments, you would probably not run the rat race — chasing ways to earn money and pay your monthly mortgage installments all your life.

Unfortunately, even for wealthy families, there are exceptions and cases where fortunes did not do them any good.*[51]

There are many ideas on how to deal with wealth inheritance and wealth distribution, none of which are mine. Some of them are more radical than others, and many of them were conceived a long time ago.

For each of those ideas, it seems that the largest fears the intelligentsia has are that civilization will become dormant – most of those fears are wrong.

People are not driven only by the fear of survival. As the famous American psychologist Abraham Maslow once explained, with the so-called "Maslow's hierarchy of needs," there are many other things that drive humans to work, once the basic needs of survival are satisfied.*[52]

War

All wars that ever broke out have been fought because of two reasons: territory and resources.

Territory in ancient times meant access to more resources: gold, silver, lumber, food, and often free labor, in the form of slaves. Now, territory also means a strategic advantage, in a military or economic sense — the way to control enemies and distribute more products to allies.

Different types of resources, over the centuries, were attractive for one reason or another, but, over the last 100 years, almost all wars have been fought in order to gain access to and control over fossil fuels. Even now, when we are under the threat of extinction from climate change, as result of overconsumption of fossil fuels, countries still militarily intervene and go into wars over the dominance of fossil fuels.

In the 21st century, while surrounded with all this technology, and being connected like never before, trying to resolve things with wars is like trying to send a message to someone by setting the keyboard on fire and then making an effort to communicate by sending smoke signals.

Excuses for military intervene are many, especially after an attack on a civilian population; the media will blame radical religious groups, drugs, or different extreme ideologies. Accordingly, the military will be sent into a war on drugs, war on terrorism, war to spread democracy, or even a war to bring peace.

Attributes like skin color, religion, and ethnicity are not main reasons for hatred and wars. People are people, and they can hate each other for all kinds of silly reasons; religion and race do not have to be, and usually are not, the only reasons. In that picture, educated, freedom-loving, knowledge-seeking people are not good for war; in contrast, uneducated people fuelled by hatred are! Plus, it is very easy to control them. When someone wants to hate, he/she will easily find an excuse. Maybe the best example of this is the Rwandan genocide. During the colonial period, German and Belgian colonial powers split Rwandan people into two groups, Tutsi and Hutu, just because of their different facial characteristics — in this case, the size and shape of their noses. Fast forward to 1994, after more than 100 years, the same characteristic was used as an excuse to fuel hatred that killed around one million people in something that can only be described as autogenocide.*[53]

Imagine a country — a nonexistent one — and label that country as a source of terrorism. Then, imagine the people in that country without any specific attributes. Let's name our imaginary source of terrorism as the country "Yellow."

Currently, there is a civil war in Yellow that has been going on for several years, and most infrastructure has been destroyed by now; economically speaking, they barely produce anything. Yellow does not have its own weapons factories, as those were the first things that were destroyed at the beginning of the civil war.

Yellow is surrounded by four neighboring countries — Blue, Red, Orange, and Green — and all the surrounding countries have strong economies and, more significantly, they have their own weapons factories.

If Yellow does not have its own weapon factories, the question arises: where do they get guns, ammo, explosives, and all other types of weaponry? We could argue that they had stocks from before, but, if the war has lasted for years, these stocks should be long gone by now.

The simple answer would be that all the neighbor countries supplying Yellow with arms and thus prolonging the conflict. For each of the neighbor countries, war is a good source of income, and, by the logic of maximizing profit, a long-lasting war is a good opportunity to increase the country's wealth. The longer the war lasts, the better, as more arms will be sold.

If you've ever played any strategy PC game like War Craft, Age of Empire, or Civilization, you know that the easiest way to win the war against your enemy is to cut off supplies and resources, so the enemy won't be able to build a future army or make any kind of meaningful progress.

War is similar to fire: the best way to extinguish a fire is to suffocate it by depriving it of oxygen, fuel, or heat. When the fire is already started, the easiest way is to deprive it of oxygen; at that point, you cannot lower the heat, and fuel is usually everywhere, so the best chance is to cut its access to oxygen.

In war, the heat is hatred, the fuel is people, and the oxygen is arms.

So, if you take the guns out of the picture, the job of stopping war will be much simpler and easier. The only tasks left will be to deal with any ignited fuel, then lower the heat, since it would be desirable to prevent new fires in the long term. But, current wars look more like deliberately pumping oxygen into an existing fire while adding new fuel.

The Blue and Red countries were already involved, in one way or another, in military actions against militant groups of the Yellow country. Militants from Yellow, seeking revenge, make occasional attacks within neighbor countries but mainly attack the civilian population, causing panic and unrest. The media in all the neighboring countries disturb the masses, using a panic effect to call for military actions. This propaganda loop is suitable for the weapons industry, because now everyone needs more ammo and more guns, as all countries are involved in war. Even countries that were not involved previously are afraid of terrorism and willingly agree to join in action against the threat.

During wartime, the war industry will gladly supply allies with arms. But, they will do the same for militant groups from the Yellow country, in order to extend the war as long as possible and therefore increase profit as much as possible.

At this point, one could ask: Why does the leading country just not stop supplying militants?

The reason is simple: if any neighbor country stops supplying terrorists, the other countries will fill the market gap. The logic behind this is very simple: "If you do not do it, someone else will — for the sake of profit."

In this day and age, finding out who is trading and supplying terrorist organizations shouldn't be overly difficult. The only thing necessary is to follow the money. If the algorithms behind Amazon can figure out, with just a few items you have purchased, whether you are expecting a baby or whether you are potentially dealing drugs, how difficult would it be to track large amounts of arms? The only thing necessary is to track money transactions for the necessary components or the final "products." After that, cutting the supply of guns would be an easy thing to do.

Unfortunately, we should not discard the possibility that everyone already knows, and everyone is responsible, but they're just playing the same old game of pretending. So, the next time you hear a politician or public figure saying how we should buy more guns, in order to secure peace, ask, "How many shares does he/she have in the weapons industry?"

The nature of the current economic system is shaping our minds and directing our moves; it is a type of human behavior control imposed by design. Although we would reluctantly admit it, it's very easy to pull our strings; it's easy to convince masses of people that religion is to blame, race is to blame, a different regime is to blame, or any other thing is to blame. The Milgram social psychology experiments showed how powerful influence of authority figures can be and how obedient ordinary people can become — completely turning off their sense of morality in directed actions.*[54] In the same sense, we rarely question the morality of the system in which we live, and, when we do, it is even rarer that we do something about it — just as people with limited choice continue working in drug cartel factories, in order to feed their children.

With enough resources and influence, you can create conflict in any country, regardless of how polite or civilized people of that country think they are. If there is no sense of unity, and without education, it is possible to create polarity about something without significant effort. All they need is to follow the rules of spreading fire: bring the heat, add the fuel, and pump the oxygen.

That been said, looking at the world from the game of "more," strange as it seems, it is reasonable for super powers to militarily intervene or install puppet governments, in order to secure their own economies. Also, as the weapons industry provides a very big chunk of the world's economy, it is reasonable that the economically most powerful countries will spend crazy amounts of money, just to stay on the cutting edge. But, the more they spend, their opponents, by the rule of positive feedback, will spend even more, creating some kind of magic loop, which is impossible to escape.

Somehow, when you hold a hammer in your hand, the only thing you can think of is that everything looks like a nail.

Technologically, we have advanced a lot in the last 200 years; our knowledge, understanding of nature, and tools we make have improved exponentially, but we still have the same hunter-gatherer mindset like 50,000 years ago.*[55] Similar to the metaphor from the Abrahamic religions about Cain (working in agriculture), who killed his brother Abel (working with livestock), society switched from a gatherer society to agricultural society, but the hunter stayed.

Why is the discrepancy between mindset and technology such a big issue?

Imagine we live in a world where, among humans, there is a living, walking being so powerful that it can create and destroy the world at will. The question is: would you rather live in a world where that "god" is neurotic, moody, and often angry, killing subjects for every petty mistake, or you would rather live in the company of a "god" that is patient, loving, and forgiving figure? Or to bring things down to the ground, would you rather live in Norway or North Korea?

With the advance of our technology and increase of powers, we are increasingly capable of destroying our civilization just by mistake,*[56] and surely having neurotic or psychotic politicians or generals does not help, either. Russia, for instance, has a system called "Dead man hand," which is basically an automated system that will detect atomic explosions by different types of sensors; in case of an emergency, it will first try to contact the Russian government, and, if it fails, it will launch the entire nuclear arsenal to predetermined targets. The question arises: what if there is a glitch, and no one succeeds at responding to the false alarm?

Many countries have already stockpiled nuclear weapons to let each other know that the retribution for an attack would be fatal and catastrophic. This concept was called Mutually Assured Destruction, or MAD, for short.

Over the last few years, now and then, it is possible to hear analysts suggesting that the only way to overcome the current economic crises would be similar to the beginning of the 20th century: to go into a world war. The others suggest that what we are seeing now are signs that we are already in World War 3. On the other end of the rope, there are conspiracy theorists who say that elite circles want to prevent the collapse of the Earth's biosphere by creating an event of human depopulation, directly influencing the mortality rate.*[57]

The war-fearing and mongering way of thinking is a sign of a fundamental lack of understanding how much we have advanced and how today's world works. Let's consider what would happen, if there was another world war.

First, it may start as a local brawl about some economic or territorial dispute. From that point on, as everyone is already under tense emotions, someone can make a miscalculation and shoot down a plane or boat, like Turkey did with a Russian jet fighter in Syria.*[58] From that point, things can quickly spiral out of control. Unlike during the First and Second World Wars, weapons now are capable of reaching any corner of the world in just a few hours. This means, instead of days and months, armies could advance and fights could develop significantly faster.

At the point when war is fully fledged, nuclear weapons can quickly replace conventional weapons.

Now, if nuclear war begins, even a local one, there is a great likelihood that the human race will go extinct.

At present, we do not have a backup planet; we do not have a space colony, where people could live or migrate for a long time during periods of war. **If nuclear war happens, we are all gone.** Forget about underground bunkers; forget about long-time food storage; no one will survive, and this is why:

In nuclear war, there are four major effects:

- First, there is a direct impact, in the case of usage of fission hydrogen bombs: temperatures will exceed 100,000,000 degrees at the centre, instantly evaporating everything within hundreds and thousands of meters from the impact. At the same time, EMP (Electro Magnetic Pulse) will instantly fry any electronic equipment miles away from epicentre. Shockwave will follow and destroy all in its way, miles from the explosion. During this first effect, it is probable that 1/3 of the whole population would vanish, and all major towns and cities would be destroyed. This exchange, between countries could last for several days, but, at some point after all missiles were fired, it would stop.

- After the first impact, those outside of shelters who got burned by gamma radiation, and those who were in the vicinity of radiation clouds – somehow surviving the blast – will start dying a very painful death. As electronics are fried, including all our vehicles – as all of them are heavily dependent on electronics – and as major infrastructure is destroyed, those in need of medical help will not be able to get it. Acid rains and radiation in the air will continue poisoning air, water, and land. Some will die from radiation poisoning and others from lack of food and drinking water. This will last months. During this period, only those in underground bunkers in far away mountains will survive.

- The third effect is nuclear winter; after a few weeks or months, the amount of dust particles thrown into the stratosphere could cause global cooling, and the resulting ice age would last hundreds of years. During that time, crops will not grow, and the rest of the population that comes out of their bunkers will die, as result of cold or food starvation. Some say that the current nuclear arsenal is not enough to cause global cooling, as the nuclear potential was significantly reduced during the era after the Cold War; although the stockpile was significantly reduced from 68,000 (in 1985), those remaining **16,300** *[59] nuclear warheads beg to differ this point-of-view. Furthermore, the development of future nuclear weapons, like R-36M and RS-28 Sarmat — with yield measured in megatons — is a reminder that nuclear winter is not something we can easily rule out from this scenario.

- Lastly, easily forgotten while thinking about these scenarios, is that there are **440 operational nuclear power plants** *[60] in the world, mostly located in the Northern hemisphere. Just the two nuclear disasters we had in the last two decades poisoned huge amounts of the earth and sea. We partially managed to contain those disasters, but, even now, people are still struggling to find any meaningful way to clean those sites and prevent future disasters by building structures like a sarcophagus. The Chernobyl explosion put 400 times more radioactive material into the Earth's atmosphere than the atomic bomb dropped on Hiroshima.*[61] Some experts say that the land around Chernobyl will stay polluted and inhabitable for humans for at least the next 10,000 years. In addition to all nuclear power plants, there are 55 countries that operate 245 research reactors, and 180 nuclear reactors that power some 140 ships and submarines.*[62] Now, imagine a combined nuclear disaster of all of them, without the ability to contain or prevent the future spread of radioactive fallout. Nuclear bombs, both fusion and fission, are quite efficient at burning fuel; strange as it seems, in the case of war, nuclear power plants are more dangerous than nuclear weapons.

At the end, we have to consider 60 years of nuclear waste that is stored in waste management locations. Each year, nuclear power generation facilities worldwide produce about 200,000 m3 of low and intermediate-level radioactive waste, and about 10,000 m3 of high-level waste, including used fuel designated as waste.*[63]

If we multiply 16,300 warheads, with an average yield of 375 Kilotons of TNT per warhead, we can calculate that the total arsenal power is around 6000 Megatons of TNT. Then, if we add to that number around 600 Chernobyl-like nuclear reactors, with a yield of 6 Megatons of TNT (400 * 15Kt TNT Hiroshima), we get a total yield of around 9600 Megatons of TNT.*[64]

A nuclear capability of 9600 Megatons of TNT is enough to **completely level all habitable areas on the planet.** Definitely, this amount is not enough to destroy the plant, but, surely, it could destroy the entire human race.

Some may say that hiding in some deep underground bunker for a few months, until the ashes settle down, will save at least someone, but that is true only for the time being. The already scarce resources of drinking water would be poisoned and completely undrinkable, and the land would be poisoned with radiation, preventing cultivation and crops. If nuclear winter does not kick in, it is quite possible that, by burning all woods and plants, global warming will just become even faster, triggering the release of methane hydrate.

Even if people stay in those underground bunkers more than 100 years (although it is unlikely they could survive more than a few years), after coming out, the land and sea would be still uninhabitable for any type of mammals; the only thing that would maybe recover are viruses, bacteria, plants, and some insects.

The population would revert to the Stone Age. Gadgets we once used with pride, in those circumstances, would be worth less than rocks. There wouldn't be any Internet, computers, cars, machines, fridges, dishwashers, electricity, or any other modern means of communication. Survivors would not have a critical mass to transfer and maintain knowledge of the 21st century, and, even if there were no residential radiation, we would need at least the next 1,000 years to recover to the same technological level. In the process, we would need to reinvent almost everything all over again.

Radioactive pollution, exposure to elements, and diseases, all without access to modern health care and medicine, with an already weakened DNA, would kill us quickly, and newborns would come to earth with different disabilities and deformations having very short life spans. The human population of the Earth would, only in a few years, gradually decline to zero.

From the perspective of climate change, that may be a good thing. It would maybe cool off the planet and give the biosphere a chance to recover. But, from the perspective of human survival, all that would mean was the end of the game. History has already showed us that the planet has nurtured people capable of doing atrocities to members of their own kind — people like Hitler, Stalin, and Pol Pot.

Not so long ago, the Daily Mail regarded Genghis Khan, a man responsible for the death of 1/3 of Earth's population, as the greenest leader in the history, with the title "Genghis Khan the GREEN: Invader killed so many people that carbon levels plummeted." *[65] It almost looks like a challenging invitation for future psychopaths.

I hope, by now, I have succeeded in convincing you that war is a bad idea, especially nuclear war. Regardless, being a bad idea or not, the top countries of the world continue spending crazy amounts of money on military advancement, in order to gain a strategic advantage. This year, the combined military expenditure of only the top 16 military powers exceeded $1.68 trillion US.

Paranoia is fuelling fears, and fears are pushing military technological advancements with the simple goal to stay in front and obtain a tactical advantage. But that is only an illusion: a "tactical advantage race" only creates a more likely extinction.

In nuclear war, tactical advantage is a very murky concept. One side will try to obtain a closer territorial position; the other will use submarines to get closer to the shores. One side will use lasers and missile defense; the other, EMPs, rail guns, and supersonic and hypersonic rockets. In that race, one day, the superpowers of the world will come to the conclusion that human reaction time is not good enough, so they will hand over controls of their command war tables to AI (Artificial Intelligence) and computer algorithms. When that happens, they world may end just as a consequence of some glitch in Artificial reasoning; there will be no Stanislav Petrov *[66] to cool down the situation and save the day. In those circumstances, for us, the world as we know it could end in just a matter of minutes. It would not be enough time even to take shelter.

The question is, is it possible to change this; can we stop the arms race?

Almost every culture has some kind of nonsensical mythology/prophecy about a future big Armageddon, but none of them says when that may happen, so, there is frequent confusion on whether those events have already happened or whether they are just about to happen. That entire charade about prophecies is one terrible thing, and this is why:

What we believe, that we become.

If you drive a car, do not sit behind the wheel if you think, fear, and constantly worry that, one day, you will crash. If you think you will crash all the time, the likelihood of crashing is significantly higher — not because your belief made that happen, but because spending time thinking and worrying about it made you concentrate less on what you should actually do and be focused on and that is driving.

All ancient prophecies had a single purpose — to scare people, so they would behave better — but all of them have one glitch. People were attracted like a moth to a flame; instead of using those stories as "what may happen," mostly, they have been using them as "what will happen," creating self-fulfilling prophecies.

If someone knew what the future would be like, and we in the future cannot change it, why would he say anything?! We would live much happier lives without worrying and fearing what may happen in the future, so it is a logical choice of that prophet not to say or write anything at all.

Prophecies are easy to change; we just need to replace them with good dreams. By replacing dark prophecies with the idea that, one day, we will all live in a beautiful world of love and understanding, our future will change accordingly.

Our current political and economic systems are very similar to those prophecies. Many of us think – and most of us are even convinced that – our current system is inevitable and impossible to change – a blind alley from which there is no escape – but the thing is they have never even tried. They never tried to think about how to make a change. The system (political/economic) is just the mind's creation; it can be changed, like everything else.

Currently, the rules of the game are urging players to fight and compete with each other, but, if we could change the way the game works, by fixing it, so that the system would start encouraging people to work together, instead of turning us against one another, then everything is possible.

There lies the beauty of it all: we are the masters of the game. We can change the rules.

When we achieve that, maybe, instead of spending stupidly huge amounts of money on the means of our own destruction, we will use that money for education, health, science, green energy, and other things that would actually promote peace, instead of war.

Climate change

News popping out all over the Internet is that the UN *[67], NASA, and many others have announced that the year 2016 is the world's hottest year on record.*[68]

Instead of thousands of words, only two images from NASA *[69] are enough to sum up what is going on:

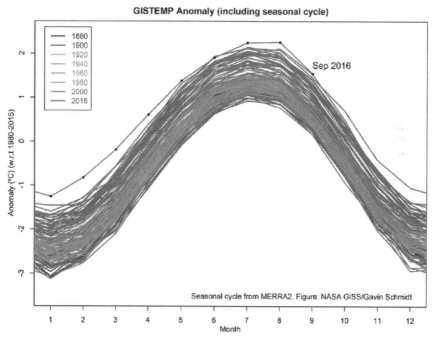

If there was any doubt before — about global warming — after seeing these graphs, there is no possible reasonable argument one can give to deny it, and that is not the end of the bad news; it is just the beginning.

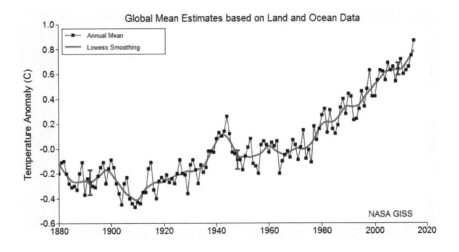

Scientists believe the North Pole is soon about to disappear,*[70] triggering even more rapid global warming, as, after the ice is melted, water will start expanding, causing a rising of sea levels and, as a consequence, creating massive coastal floods.*[71] When ice melts, it can absorb large amounts of energy, as much energy as it would take to heat an equivalent mass of water by 80 °C. During the melting process, the temperature remains constant at 0 °C.*[72] As oceans reflect around 10% of light that touches their surface, the planet's ice caps represent huge regulators of the planet's temperature by absorbing energy and also by reflecting sunlight from the planet's poles.

Ice located in high mountains, like the Alps and Himalayas, is also melting, adding to the total water levels.

If all the Earth's ice melts, water levels worldwide will rise by 70 meters; although this is something that could happen in 25-50 years' time, even a one meter rise worldwide will have dramatic consequences for our civilization.*[73] Global sea levels rose about 6.7 inches (17 cm) in the last century. The rate in the last decade, however, is nearly double that.*[74] The more ice we lose, the warmer the oceans will get. Swelling as water molecules will move further apart from one another.*[75]

To add to the issue, if the Himalaya mountain range loses its ice, this would trigger long-lasting droughts for a country that needs to supply water to a population of 1.5 billion people. That could easily trigger massive migrations of people and war between neighboring countries like India and Pakistan — both with a nuclear weapons capability.

The increase of the planet's temperature is already causing more extreme weather: on one side, long-lasting droughts, and, on the other, severe floods, sudden, deadly heat waves, wildfires, tornados, and hurricanes will be more frequent and more destructive, and people will start seeing them in places that were not typically known as areas known for those kinds of weather patterns.

Although warmer oceans can look like a good thing for tourism, just a slight rise of temperature can have devastating consequences for marine life. Increased levels of CO_2 already have had a negative impact on the oceans. Surface acidity has increased by 30%, having a direct impact on species like clams, oysters, shrimps, and corals are also at risk, putting the entire ocean food web at risk. In Australia, an aerial survey has revealed that 93% of reefs are hit by coral bleaching — the devastation caused by abnormally-warm ocean temperatures.*[76] All this will directly impact 1 billion people who rely on the ocean as a primary source of meat.

The second very big news that shook the planet is that Antarctic CO_2 has hit 400ppm (parts per million) for the first time in 4 million years.*[77] Although this looks like a symbolic mark, the last time there was this much carbon dioxide (CO_2) in the Earth's atmosphere, modern humans didn't exist.*[78]

Dr. Michael Gunson from NASA said, "The world is quickening the rate of accumulation of CO_2 and has shown no signs of slowing this down. It should be a psychological tripwire for everyone." *[79]

Some say that, by passing 400ppm mark, we do not have a chance anymore and that we have passed the point of no return, where the positive feedback loop *[80] will kick in, and global warming will drive itself, creating a world similar to the planet Venus. Others still believe there are things we can do on both global and personal levels, like recycle and reuse, use public transportation, turn off idle electronics, eat less meat, eat locally-grown foods, or spreading the word, which, all combined, may help to deter the threat.

The safe level of carbon dioxide in the atmosphere is 350 parts per million. The only way to get there is to immediately transition the global economy, personal habits, and way of living in a radically different way.

James Butler, director of NOAA's global monitoring division, said, "Elimination of about 80% of fossil fuel emissions would essentially stop the rise in carbon dioxide in the atmosphere, but concentrations of carbon dioxide would not start decreasing until even further reductions are made, and then it would only do so slowly." *[81]

Carbon dioxide is not the only problem we have, in regards to global warming. Methane (CH_4), another greenhouse gas, is 25 to 85 times (depends on over how many years) more damaging than carbon dioxide. The total current amount of methane in our atmosphere is around 5 Gigatons — around 1.8ppm and 200 times less than CO_2 — but, if we multiply the methane amount with the potency, we get number that is equivalent to an additional 30-70ppm of CO_2, which adds up to a dangerously high amount of 400ppm of CO_2.

The issue does not stop there: methane exists in one more naturally-occurring form called methane clathrate, *[82] or methane hydrate. It is a solid form, in which large amounts of methane are trapped within a crystal structure of ice. Clathrates are stable at -20°C and are generally found at depth in sediment, in the sea bed, and in land permafrost.

It is estimated that, under a thin sheet of Siberian permafrost (soil, rock, or sediment that is frozen for more than two consecutive years), there is approximately 100 to 1,000 of Gigatons of methane hydrate ice.*[83] Increasing planet temperatures (oceans and land), due to climate change, could cause the sudden release of large amounts of natural gas from methane clathrate deposits. Only 1% of that deposit is required to double the atmospheric burden of methane, causing runaway climate change that cannot be halted. That would mean extinction of all life on planet.

Giant holes bursting open in Siberia with explosions that can be heard from tens of miles away,*[84] as well as satellite images that show increased emissions of methane over the Northern part of oceans,*[85] are signaling that the process has already started, and that we do not have a lot of time before it gets entirely unmanageable.

What does global warming mean for humans?

While an increase of a few degrees is barely noticeable for humans, each degree will have huge consequences for the life on the planet.*[86]

A temperature increase between 0.5°C and 1°C, as we are already experiencing, is already bad; we have a shift in weather patterns, floods along the coastlines on one end and long-lasting droughts affecting agriculture on the other. More frequent tornadoes, hurricanes and wildfires occur.

Just in the UK, the average damage from weather disasters has reached an average annual cost of $10.8 billion *[87], with thousands facing financial ruin.

A temperature increase between 1°C and 2°C would mean extreme summers taking human lives in numbers reaching hundreds of thousands. Crops will bake in the fields, and forests will die off and burn. People will start migrating from the Mediterranean further to the North. Central London would be flooded. Bangkok, Bombay, and Shanghai would lose most of their area, and, most likely, most of humanity would have to move to higher ground. As mountains lose their glaciers, so people will lose their water supplies.

A temperature increase between 2°C and 3°C would cause catastrophes of Biblical proportions. At this point, carbon-cycle feedbacks could tip the planet into runaway global warming by the middle of this century. All soil will be affected by the rising heat, but the Amazon would be the worst affected: it would become a desert. Drought and heat will cripple it; fire will finish it off. Currently, the Amazon's 7 million square kilometers of rain forest produce 10% of the world's entire photosynthetic output from plants.

A temperature increase between 3°C and 4°C would trigger one of the most dangerous of all feedbacks: the runaway thaw of permafrost. Scientists believe at least 500 billion tons of carbon is waiting to be released from Arctic ice. With the Amazon's collapse and the carbon-cycle feedback reaching three degrees, therefore, that leads inexorably to four degrees, and then five. Cities would fortify, struggling to survive on what is now an almost alien world, with temperatures reaching a casual 45°C in most of the world's places.

A temperature increase between 4°C and 5°C is like looking at an entirely different planet. Ice sheets have vanished from both poles; rainforests have burnt up and turned to desert; massive migrations of people and fights for food and water are common. Wild life would disappear, as supporting a hunter-gatherer lifestyle takes 10 to 100 times the land per person that a settled, agricultural community needs. Any armed conflict, particularly involving nuclear weapons, would decrease surface area habitable for humans. Whenever the stockpiles of food were discovered, the householder and his family may be tortured and killed. It is very likely that cannibalism would be quite common.

A temperature increase between 5°C and 6°C would look like the time between 144m and 65m years ago — an era that ended with the extinction of the dinosaurs. The sea would frequently release huge pockets of methane, causing explosions equivalent to the explosion of multiple Tsar Hydrogen bombs *[88] at the same time. At the end, stagnant oceans would start releasing poisonous hydrogen sulfides, silently killing all remaining life. No more complex life would exist on the planet after this.

What is causing global warming?

By crossing out the Earth's wobble, the tilting of Earth's axis (40,000 years cycle), 11 years Sun spot cycles, and other naturally-occurring causes, scientist have concluded that human activity and the emission of carbon dioxide, methane, and a few more other greenhouse gases is the root cause of global warming.

The bottom left graph, taken from the EPA (US Environmental Protection Agency), shows the ration of greenhouse gases that are the main cause of global warming.*[89]

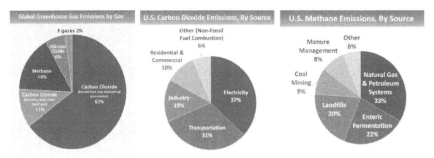

In the middle, we can see the US Carbon Dioxide emission per industry type.*[90] The main human activity that emits CO_2 is the combustion of fossil fuels (coal, natural gas, and oil) for energy and transportation, although certain industrial processes and land-use changes also emit CO_2. The main sources of CO_2 emissions in the United States are described below.

On the right, we can see US methane emission by source.*[91] Globally, over 60% of total CH_4 emissions come from human activities. Methane is emitted from industry, agriculture, and waste management activities, like landfill and manure management.

The primary sources of greenhouse gas emissions in the United States are:

- **Electricity production** – electricity is the largest single source of CO_2 emissions in the U.S., accounting for about **37% of total U.S. CO_2 emissions** and 30% of total U.S. greenhouse gas emissions in 2014. Approximately 67% of our electricity comes from burning fossil fuels, mostly coal and natural gas.

- **Transportation** – accounts for about **31% of total U.S. CO_2 emissions** and 25% of total U.S. greenhouse gas emissions in 2014. It primarily comes from burning fossil fuels for our cars, trucks, ships, trains, and planes. Over 90% of the fuel used for transportation is petroleum-based, which includes gasoline and diesel.

- **Industry** – accounted for about **15% of total U.S. CO_2 emissions** and 12% of total U.S. greenhouse gas emissions in 2014. Primarily from burning fossil fuels and the emissions from certain chemical reactions necessary to produce goods from raw materials, in order to produce cement, or for the production of metals, such as iron and steel.

- **Commercial and Residential** – electricity is the largest single source of CO_2 emissions in the U.S., accounting for about 10% of total U.S. CO_2 emissions and 12% of total U.S. greenhouse gas emissions in 2014. Primarily from fossil fuels burned for heat, the use of certain products that contain greenhouse gases, and the handling of waste.

- **Agriculture** – accounted for **9% of US greenhouse gas emissions** in 2014. Primarily from agriculture and livestock, such as cows, agricultural soils, and rice production.

- **Land Use and Forestry** – accounted for 11% of 2014 greenhouse gas emissions in the US. Land areas can act as a sink (absorbing CO_2 from the atmosphere) but also decaying biomass and deforestation, combined with frequent wildfires, are all sources of greenhouse gas emissions.

On a global level, total CO_2 emissions for the year 2013 *[92] looked like this:

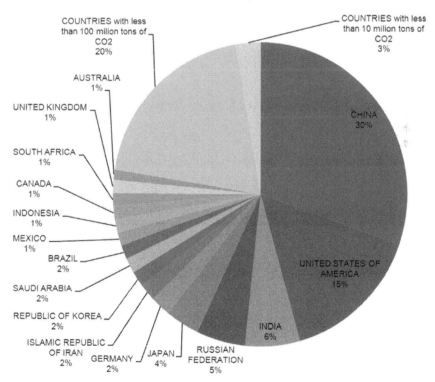

The top 16 developed countries, led by China, USA, India, and Russia, account for 77.6% of total CO_2 emission. The next 55 developed countries, with emissions below 100 million tons of CO_2, are responsible for 19.7% of CO_2 emission, and the rest of worlds 148 mainly smaller or undeveloped countries are responsible for only 2.7% of total CO_2 emissions.

China has double the CO_2 emissions of the USA, but it has a 4 times larger population. If Chinese would consume like Americans, they would have double of the emissions they have now. The reason for the "lower" emissions rate is that China, along with India, just recently emerged as developed countries. This means that CO_2 emissions of those two countries will probably continue to grow. China and India have populations with more than a billion people each, making up more than 35% of the total world population. Although the economical boom they are experiencing is very positive thing, from the perspective of global warming and the planet's ecosystem, if everything continues in the same way, there are very low chances that this will pan out in any positive way for all of us.

All the issues we are experiencing can be summed up in the following terms: overpopulation, overconsumption, excessive waste, and usage of fossil fuels. It is important to understand that it is not possible to pinpoint a single problem as the biggest, as they all have a combined effect on the planet and planet's biosphere.

Overpopulation

To this point, we have not found any intelligent way to control our numbers that would actually work. Wars, diseases, food shortages, natural disasters — like tsunamis, earthquakes, floods, and volcanoes — have all failed at reducing total human population numbers significantly. Unlike all other species, humans do not have a natural predator. By evolving our brains, we put ourselves on the top of the food chain, but we forgot to use that same brain to restrain our own reproduction rate, which can turn out to be a means of our own demise.
Almost every global issue we are experiencing now would be less significant, if the world's population was smaller — especially in the case of those top 16 countries that emit the most CO_2.

Again, saying that population is the only problem is not true; if we would use 100% renewable energy, we would not have issues with global warming. Maybe, we would experience some other issues, like food shortage or excessive pollution, but we would not have issues with CO_2 emissions. But, it is worth mentioning that things get very gloomy, when we combine a large population with overconsumption and usage of fossil fuels.

Future increases of population will create additional burden on resources and the planet's ability to provide for all citizens. We may invent new technologies, in order to increase the planet's carrying capacity, but, eventually, there is a finite number we can sustain. Today, if the entire population of the Earth would live the USA's style of living, there is an estimate that we would need 4.1 additional planets like Earth.*[93]

Some suggest that, in the future, we will need even more rigorous child policies than the Chinese one child policy. Who knows — maybe, one day, we will have some kind of permit to conceive and raise children, without the ability to choose the preferred sex of the child. Others, more futuristically-inclined, say that it is even possible that we will design and grow children in artificial wombs — altogether moving away from natural way of childbirth and conception. Although I would not go that far, it is obvious that we will need to do something, and, the sooner we do it on global level, the better.

Hans Rosling has shown many times that a good way to control the population of one country is to increase its standard of living. Statistics show that, in wealthier societies, the number of children averages 1 child per couple. But, as mentioned before, with the rise of living standards, the usage of fossil fuels becomes an increasing issue.

Many countries fear about their economic future, because of a fast-aging population and issues connected with providing for them in the future, but that fear is not justified.

The growth of jobs in the USA, for instance, is not enough to satisfy population growth, and we have not even started talking about the future effects of automation and technological unemployment. As recent trends are showing, most of the jobs in the future will be carried out by machines and robots, not humans, so the fear that the economy will fail under burden of an aging population does not have a basis in reality.

With a smaller population, at least until we find other planets suitable for colonization, everything would be easier, and, also, we would give a chance to other species – important for maintaining diversity and the stability of the ecosystem.

Overconsumption

Overconsumption is the usage of resources in a way that exceeds the sustainable capacity of the ecosystem.

In the year 2016, we used up the planet's resources in less than eight months, and, each year, this number is decreasing.*[94]

The current capitalistic system is driving overconsumption, as the main — and often the only — goal is to maximize profit, a reasonable strategy is to convince customers to buy as much as possible of things they actually do not need.

Proof of this is the fact that the inhabitants of the developed nations are consuming resources at a rate almost 32 times greater than those of the developing world, which makes up the majority of the human population.

Although capitalism could be pointed to as the driver of population growth, as more people means more customers, it seems, as Rosling has shown, that does not happen, and the primary reason is that people of developed countries are more preoccupied with things they posses than by families. Better education and the ability to choose gave women the ability to pursue careers and also the right to choose smaller families, so they could take care of them better, and those things are good both for the people and the planet.

Fossil fuels like coal and petrol, and the need to power always-hungry consumers has created the situation where we are now. For global warming, pollution of land and oceans, deforestation, land erosion, loss of biodiversity, and depletion of minerals can be blamed on overconsumption, a throw away ideology, and low rates of reuse and recycling.

All those things we've made, all household items, means of transport and communication, clothing, food, and many others, that created the comfortable life we are enjoying in our current Western world — just like narcotics, in one way — created pleasure and a false sense of security, concealing the true effects that will kick in later, maybe too late to do anything about it.

Waste

Hand-in-hand with overconsumption, we waste, and we waste a lot. Each year, new electronic gadgets will arrive, with barely noticeable improvements, and, as soon as it becomes available, we will throw away the "old" gadget and spend crazy amounts of money just to get the "new" one.

There are many examples of the throw-away economy: clothing, household items, and electronic — rarely do those items live to see the end of their lifetimes, and, even worse, companies deliberately build in planned obsolescence, an artificially-limited useful life, and, by this, companies urge customers to buy more and buy more frequently.*[95]

Global quantitative food losses and waste per year are roughly 30% cereals, 40-50% root crops and fruits and vegetables, 20% oil seeds, 20% of meat, 20% dairy, and 35% of fish and seafood.*[96]

Fact is that roughly **one-third of the food produced in the world** for human consumption every year — approximately 1.3 billion tons — is lost or wasted is absolutely mind-boggling. Those food losses and waste per year account for roughly US$ 680 billion in industrialized countries and US$ 310 billion in developing countries.*[97]

On top of this, on one end, there are 2.1 billion people — nearly 30% of the world's population — who are either obese or overweight, according to a trend data analysis from 188 countries,*[98] and, on the other end, around 795 million people (roughly 11%) in the world do not have enough food to lead a healthy, active life.*[99]

Apart from not providing food for entire populations, there are several other issues with food waste. During the production phase, food requires land, water, and huge amounts of energy; also, energy is required for transport, which means that CO_2 emissions could be significantly smaller, if we would stop wasting food.

Food waste usually ends up in landfills, causing even more issues, where, while rotting, it produces CH_4 (methane), a more aggressive and damaging greenhouse gas, in large quantities. Cattle produce large quantities of methane while they digest food, and, later on, their manure will continue releasing methane. The waste of 20% meat and milk means that 20% of total methane emitted yearly by animals and manure was needlessly released.

However, definitely the largest waste we produce is in the energy sector.

Out of the total energy produced in the USA in 2015, **59.1% was rejected.***[100] This is enough to power the UK for 7 years. This trend is similar for other countries around the globe, which is quite odd, considering all of the issues we are facing would be significantly less harmful, if we could use the energy we generate more efficiently.

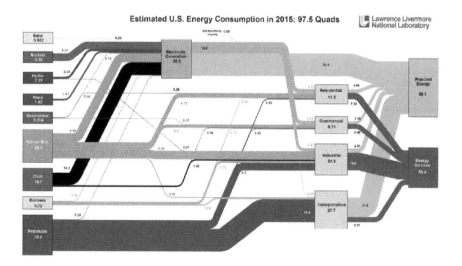

Estimated U.S. Energy Consumption in 2015: 97.5 Quads — Lawrence Livermore National Laboratory

Most of the energy waste comes from electricity generation, as most power plants are relatively inefficient, and there are significant losses during energy transmission, because of the old electric grid. Transport sector waste is due to vehicles' internal-combustion engines being infamously inefficient, wasting between 60-90% of what they burn.

Fossil fuel usage

Our dependence on fossil fuels has changed the climate of the planet. Excessive use of coal, petrol, and natural gas altogether, with cement production, use of chlorofluorocarbons (CFCs) greenhouse gases chemical industries, and methane emission from the animal stock worldwide has caused a sharp rise in greenhouse gases, since the beginning of industrial revolution.

The only way to make a change is to shift our economy completely from fossil fuel dependence, if we wish to detour from the path of global life extinction; the sooner we do it, the more chance we will have to fight climate change and future damage.

But, it seems we have not stopped with global emissions; actually, trends are showing that we have increased emissions from fossil fuel and cement production from 8.363 Gigatons of CO_2 in 2006 to 9.795 Gigatons of CO_2 in 2014.*[101] In August 2016, total carbon in the atmosphere was approximately 3130 Gigatons of CO_2, which is equivalent to 400ppm.

It seems that neither big oil companies nor the governments have any intention of changing this course, and why would they? If the only goal of the game is to maximize profit, the game will be played until the house burns to the ground.

But, there are a few ways we can change that.

How to fix those issues?

There is no silver bullet for climate change and pollution; just as there are multiple factors credited with creating those issues, there are multiple solutions that all need to work together, in order to fix this. The principle is simple: with one note, it is possible to make a rhythm, but, in order to make a melody, you will need a few more.

There are some general strategies we can follow:

- Abandoning fossil fuels
- Consuming less beef and dairy products
- Managing methane
- Reduce

- Reuse
- Recycle
- Recover
- Innovate
- Changing the system

Abandoning fossil fuels

New planetary temperature data have shown that we urgently need to stop using fossil fuels — not in 20, not in 10 years, but yesterday.

Regarding our transport vehicles, the best option would be to switch to electric cars as soon as possible. The only obstacle is batteries: the range is not good enough, compared to gasoline, but it is still good for city transport. Additionally, batteries are improving, and, with each passing day, there are new discoveries, and prices are dropping dramatically. Currently, there are 1.2 billion vehicles on the world's roads. Tesla can, at best, produce around 500,000 a year; if Tesla would increase production to 1,000,000 cars a year, we would need at least 50 more companies like Tesla to replace all cars in a meaningful time (24 years). At the same time, that would mean plenty of new jobs and lots of opportunity for economic growth and development.

Self-driving cars could reduce expenses of buying a new car and also reduce the number of cars on the road, as network communication between cars would increase safety, efficiency on the road, and the utilization of cars.

A side effect is that we could use those electric cars to power homes and therefore make our electricity grid more resilient.

When we are talking about power plants, the same rule is applicable: we have to move away from any type of fossil fuel or biomass that produces CO_2. Solar, tidal, and wind are becoming cheaper every day, and, with the drop of prices for home battery pack solutions, renewable green energy is becoming a viable, long-term solution.

Going green in the energy sector would also mean lots of new jobs in solar, wind, tidal, hydro, and many other similar sectors. Smart electricity grids that are required, if built with battery packs for houses, streets, and city blocks would have a significant positive effect on overall consumption, and they would reduce waste electricity, especially during peak times.

Nuclear is still an option, but only if we talk about fusion and molten salt thorium reactors; currently, the wide-spread old type fusion reactors are probably not something we want to continue for very long, as they are too expensive to build and too dangerous to operate, and, at the end, radioactive waste that is currently piling up is still unmanageable, which makes them an unprofitable investment.

Consuming less beef and dairy products

Cattle bred for meat and dairy products require lots of land and huge amounts of water and energy. In addition, out of the total methane emissions, 22% comes from enteric fermentation, 8% from manure management, and a portion of the 20% of landfill methane emission can be credited to wasted meat and stock feed. Cattle methane emission is huge: some even say that cow burps are causing more global warming than all the cars on the roads.

It is obvious that we have a slim chance that the entire planet will become vegetarians overnight, but, at least, we can reduce consumption of meat. World obesity statistics are showing that we have plenty enough room for improving health and reducing the amount of food we eat.
Governments can help by putting caps on the amount of meat that can be produced, which will decrease over time. This would increase prices, because of supply and demand rules, and that is not bad, as farmers will not lose their earnings, and people will eat less meat.

In the meantime, labs around the world are working on finding burger and beef alternatives that will solve two problems: meat-craving dietary habits and the moral question of killing animals.

One of the ideas is to create a plant-based burger that tastes the same as a meat burger.*[102] The other is to grow meat from animal stem cells in labs; *[103] this is basically very much like a forerunner of the Star Trek food replicator, where we could take living cell from any part of animal and grow it in a lab, while the animal will stay alive and safe, running somewhere in a field.

In this way, the entire chain of methane emission and CO_2 emission would be reduced by tens and hundreds of times.

What else can we do?

Managing methane

When we talk about cattle and meat production, unavoidably, there is the issue of methane from enteric fermentation, landfills, and manure.

Currently, there are 1.2 billion vehicles on the world's roads, and there is a similar number — ranging between 1.3 and 1.5 billion — of cows.

Beef cows produce between 150 and 250 liters of methane each day, and dairy cows will emit around 500 liters of methane.*[104] *[105]

The average mileage for four-wheeled vehicles was 7,900 miles (12,700km) in 2013 in the UK, meaning that we would need 2 cows to fuel one vehicle. If we would scale this method significantly, we could power around 700 million cars in this way, and, by switching to methane, reduce total gasoline or diesel usage, respectively.

As methane CH_4 is fuel, by capturing it and then burning it, we would convert it into less dangerous CO_2, and, in the process, we would have energy. When enough electric cars kick in, we could burn methane in power plants, without the need to use gas, petrol, or coal deposits.

One day, maybe we will even decide to burn methane hydrate (clathrate), in order to convert it into carbon, as part of a long-term, future planet safety policy.

Reduce

To reduce was once advertised as a slow solution; now, that is not enough, as, instead of reducing, we have increased production and consumption. We are running out of time, and it is necessary to make dramatic cuts of fossil fuel consumption and the amount of things we consume on a daily basis as soon as possible.

In fields where we cannot find immediate replacements, we need to reduce usage. In others, like the airline industry, there are already some viable bio replacements — jet fuel can be a good example.*[106]

It is necessary to reduce the amount of goods and food we throw away. If we would just cut food waste, a significant amount of energy, water, and land would be saved. Furthermore, methane emissions created by the mountains of food in landfills would be considerably reduced.

There is a huge need to change our consumerist habits. Planned obsolescence should be banned, and recycling strategies should become part of the product life cycle.

In a highly-automated society, where the goal of technology is to work for all — not just a privileged few — it is much smarter and more efficient to build things that last longer, so that they can be used and reused multiple times, sometimes even combined,*[107] ideally repairing and cleaning themselves on their own.

In the future of clothing, one day, instead of having ten or twenty shirts, we could have only one, a shape- and color-shifting second skin that could change according weather conditions, our needs, mood, or the necessity of events we are attending, and that will be a tremendous saving of natural resources.

Reuse

There are multiple websites that are part of a sharing economy that will help you find unwanted furniture, clothes, toys, electronic equipment, home appliances, and, in some cases, even cars. Instead throwing things away in dumpsters (ending in landfills), more and more people is deciding to participate in an economy where they can give away or exchange things they do not need for little or no money. Charity organizations already have locations where they collect unwanted stuff and freecycling websites use the Internet to connect people.

On the manufacturing side, we should think about reusing and recycling before manufacturing new things, in such a way that allows for multi-functional usage, easy disassembling, and then recycling or repurposing of the parts.

Instead of manufacturing and buying non-rechargeable batteries, for instance, we could buy rechargeable ones that can be used many times over, without the need to throw them away, and, when we are finished with them, they should be easily recyclable or decomposable, so their parts will not pollute or poison nature.

Items, like car tires, which are dumped by the billions and can pose serious environmental, health, and fire risks, can be used as building materials for sustainable architecture *[108] but also can be fully recycled, converted to road base, or back to diesel fuel and energy.

Recycle

We are consuming too much, and, in the process, we throw away a lot, creating huge piles of garbage. In the past 20 years, the recycling industry has advanced significantly, but there is still room for improvement. At the beginning, recycling was regarded as the thing of green-nature-loving-hippies that are too concerned with nature; nowadays, recycling is considered a source of lucrative income and companies compete in order to gain possession of other people's garbage.

There are five major groups we can recycle: glass, paper, plastic, metal, and organic waste; all of them can be used multiple times. Some of them, like glass, can be recycled infinitely, without losing any of its original properties.

Food and other organic waste, including our poop and pee, can be turned into methane in biodigester facilities, and later on produced methane can be used as fuel and the remaining biomass as good fertilizer for our crop fields.

Recover

This can be done in many ways for the purpose of lowering greenhouse gas emissions and increasing energy efficiency.

It is possible to recover organic waste from landfills and reprocess it in bio digesters, producing biogas (methane) in a controlled environment, so it can be used as fuel later on. The same process can be applied to manure and sewage water processing, lowering the usual cost of management or creating additional streams of revenue.

It is possible to recover precious metals from electronics or to use some complex, chemical mixtures, in order to revert them back to raw commodities again. Plastic bottles polluting rivers and seas could be recovered and convert back to oil.*[109]

Waste steams or heat recovery from industry can also save lots of energy; generally, in any type of industry that operates at low efficiency, it is possible to find ways to recover waste energy or some of the materials used in the process.

Innovate

Innovations — regardless of talking about finding ways to plant and grow more trees or some technical solutions for batteries, the way to desalinate water, the way to clean plastic trash from oceans, or a method to more efficiently remove CO2 from the atmosphere — all solutions are equally welcomed and, combined with a system that backs them by providing investments, which can create a profit for business owners, can actually save us from our ill fate.

Changing the system

In a system where maximizing profit is the sole goal, it is easy to turn a blind eye to any issue. Climate change, pollution, products that cause cancer or diabetes, and similar issues can be put aside by using corporate money to wax a few politicians or scientific peer reviews, which will eventually lead our species to destruction.

Recent data about CO_2 emissions increasing, instead of decreasing, urging us (us all as an ordinary people) to take matters in our own hands. The way to do that is to find ways to redistribute wealth and then use that same wealth (work + human time) to fix those very issues that threaten our way of life, our families, and our own existence on this planet.

Therefore, the first and foremost task is to change the system in such a way that, by its design, will incentivize and reward cooperation and solutions that work for everyone, in the process preventing the influence of corporate money on politics. With time, if done properly, this strategy will starve cancerous behavior, as each member of society could act as a monitoring party.

By working together, we can increase velocity enough to solve the challenges that are threatening our survival, and, in the process of fixing them, we could economically prosper and create a healthier society of abundance that works for all of us, not just for the privileged few. This change would have great potential for creation of small businesses that would align forces around unified goals. Self-organization would replace waiting for slow giants to show mercy by violating their main rule of making profit, in order to solve our existential problems for us.

This means shifting toward distribution and control of the planet's resources in a way that will be suitable for the long survival and thriving of our species — as well as the other species with which we share this planet, allowing them to evolve in their own, natural way.

Basic Tax Control and **Universal Basic Income** are complementary systems that, by nature of their designs, can serve as the foundation necessary to solve the issues of crony capitalism we currently have, creating a better market economy for everyone.

Technological unemployment

One of the largest problems we will face, even sooner than climate change, and yet we rarely talk about it, is the issue of technological unemployment. The term "technological unemployment" means fewer jobs for humans, as a consequence of a technological change typically involving the introduction of machines or more efficient processes. But, technological unemployment is far from being a new thing; this process has been going on for quite some time.

The earliest evidence of water-driven mills,*[110] used in processes such as milling (grinding), rolling, or hammering, in order to produce many material goods, including flour, lumber, and paper, can be traced to the Perachora wheel in the 3rd century BC, in Greece. Even earlier, the screwpump *[111] used to pump water (invented by Assyrian king Sennacherib [704 - 681BC] and later reinvented by the Greek polymath Archimedes of Syracuse in the 3rd century BC), can be described as one of the earliest examples of **automation**.

Only with the first arrival of what can be considered modern weaving machines *[112] and windmills in the early 18th century we can see a historic turning point: the beginning of the Industrial Revolution, in which it started being noticeable that machines were displacing human labor.

We can roughly define automation as the usage of technology to multiply or replace human output. In that sense, if human output is multiplied enough to meet maximum demand, decreasing the necessary human force to tend to machines, it is possible to get to the point where machines will not need any human force whatsoever; at that point, the cost of labor is neutralized, and the future efficiency of the system can be improved, with future savings made only by improving the machine itself.

In a society where everything is shared, this does not pose the problem as removing the drudgery of work means more free time; unfortunately, we do not live in that kind of society.

With the first industrial revolution, soon came those who were against machines — unsatisfied because they were losing jobs. In the 1810s, the "Luddite" movement emerged in response to machines·taking jobs; people tried sabotaging machine frames, but the effort did not last long, and the machines prevailed.

Now, we have similar issues, but, this time, the extent of machines replacing human labor is much greater than anyone could have anticipated, and it seems that predictions are being realized much faster than expected, not leaving necessary time for the market to adjust to a new change.

Arguments that scaring people with these types of stories is comparable to the "Luddites" just does not hold any ground anymore, as, this time, replacement is so rapid, and the scale of automation is so large, that it will ripple to all pores of our society, potently creating massive unrest.

Let's go through some of those new advances that will rapidly replace the human working force.

Autonomous vehicle

Self-driving cars could soon replace professional drivers. Just in the USA, there are around 3.5 million professional drivers.*[113] Within the next 5 to 10 years, all those jobs could disappear.

We can find evidence for this in the present effort of companies like Mercedes-Benz, General Motors, Continental Automotive Systems, Bosch, Nissan, Renault, Toyota, Audi, Hyundai Motor Company, Volvo, Tesla Motors, Peugeot, and many others, who are rapidly working on self-driving, autonomous car solutions.

Elon Musk, owner of Tesla Motors, announced in August 2016 *[114] that a Tesla update that will arrive soon will lead to 4th level (out of 5 levels *[115]) of autonomy. While this book was still in its final stages of editing, in October 2016, Tesla showcased self-driving Level 5 autonomy. Elon Musk has pledged that, by the end of 2017, he'll produce a Tesla that can drive itself from Los Angeles to New York City without human assistance.

Uber, the multinational, online transportation company, which allows consumers with smartphones to submit a trip request, which the software then automatically sends to a driver, is aggressively pushing to replace their voluntary drivers with self-driving algorithms.*[116] Uber is not stopping there; recently, they announced that soon they will release their own version of a self-driving truck.*[117]

In Helsinki, Finland, *[118] Trikala, Greece, *[119] and Perth, Australia, *[120] **self-driving buses** have already hit the roads, and this trend will soon spread to other towns and cities, as well.

Self-driving trucking start-up Otto has made a definite goal to put its software in the hands of long-haul truckers by the end of this year (2016) for testing. *[121] At the end of October 2016, Otto's self-driving truck packed with Budweiser beer made its first delivery in Colorado, making it the world's first such commercial delivery. *[122]

In agriculture, on crop fields, **self-driving tractors** are already working at full speed, doing everything that once was a human job. *[123]

At Amazon, for few years now, 30,000 **robots** are working at warehouses, taking care of the busy movement of orders and managing storage and retrieval systems, almost entirely without a human working force. *[124]

On rivers, seas, and oceans, soon, **robot sailing boats**, ships, and tankers will transfer goods and passengers with very little or no human crew. *[125] Floating **drones** will roam freely on the seas, monitoring the waters and collecting data, replacing old-fashioned coast guard and explorer ships. *[126]

Self-driving vehicles are getting better with every driven meter or sailed mile. Soon, they will be more reliable than humans; they will be able to map and remember roads, they will talk to each other, informing waste networks about road blockades and traffic jams. They will never experience lack of sleep, hunger, or thirst; they will never get tired, drunk or be under the influence of narcotics, and they do not get distracted by loud noises, phone calls, or SMS messages. They will not need a salary, and, in every aspect, they will be better than humans. And, if they have not reached that point now, they will be there very shortly.

Banks, shops, and restaurants

Automated teller machines (ATMs) have already reduced the need for bank visits to obtain cash and carry out transactions, eliminating the need for a significant number of branch offices and, eventually, a significant number of staff who would work there.

In shops, self-checkout machines have significantly reduced the need for human cashiers. To deal with thieves who think they can get away easily when shops are automated, the company DeepSee has taken care to create an automated theft detection system with deep learning. *[127]

McDonald's spokesman Paul Horner has recently told reporters that, because of the demand for a $15/hr minimum wage, the company has been playing with the idea of a restaurant run entirely by robots for years and believes their "McRobots" are the answer. *[128]

On the other end of the world, in Japan, they made a fully-automated restaurant, removing the need for waiters. *[129]

Manufacturing

Robots are already used for many types of manufacturing jobs, and every industry can benefit from them: car assembly lines, electronic companies, home appliances, furniture production, the food industry...

In May 2016, Foxconn — a company known for manufacturing iPhones, iPods, and iPads, as well as many other products for Sony, Microsoft, Amazon, Dell, Google, and Nintendo — laid off 60,000 employees, replacing them with AI driven Robots. *[130]

New industrial robots are not like those expensive industrial robots we know; they are smarter, and they are capable of learning and improving their functions through their own mistakes.

On the other side, 3D printing is becoming a huge game changer, promising that, in the near future, we will have the ability to "produce" very cheaply almost anything in our homes, in a very similar way to replicators from the "Star Trek" TV series.

This is not limited to home utensils alone. 3D printing is slowly finding its way into every field: the car industry (engine blocks), aero industry (airplane parts), space industry (parts of rocket engines, building habitats on the Moon and Mars), medicine (yaws, bones, kidneys, blood vessels), housing (building homes autonomously), food industry (printing food, mixing ingredients)... and it is quickly picking the pace.

Construction industry

The above-mentioned 3d printers already have their giant versions, capable of printing entire homes, just in a matter of days. Except for being able to build large objects in a short period of time, without significant human involvement, those structures can be incredibly resilient and complex shapes, obtained by printing what would not be possible to make with standard construction techniques.

The example of small, printable houses, castles that can be assembled from printable parts, and support columns that can be printed in unusual ways, giving them additional, static properties *[131] are just small examples of what can be done with this amazing technology.

Unfortunately (saying unfortunately only because of the system we are currently living in), at the same time, this will mean that humans would not be needed any longer for similar types of jobs.

High education jobs

The automation process is not limited only to low-paying jobs and skills; Artificial Intelligence is constantly showing that jobs that require higher education are also endangered.

Robots Radiologists are already really, really good at recognizing X-Ray photos (30 times faster and 20% more accurate than humans) *[132]; by using artificial intelligence and deep learning algorithms, at first, they won't replace humans. Instead, they will work alongside them. But, in the long run, this will reduce the need for trained radiologists, who need years and years of training and experience, in order to become good at what they do. *[133]

The Emma AI is starting a fund that hopes to outsmart the humans and computers that make a living trading stocks, aiming to replace hedge funds at financial markets.*[134]

Linklaters and Pinsent Masons have become the latest law firms to invest in artificial intelligence, as the legal profession tries to automate the mundane tasks that have traditionally been the preserve of junior lawyers. *[135]

In journalism, at this very moment, automated, artificial journalists are tirelessly writing sport reports, and, probably, most of us can hardly tell the difference between a human and a robot writer.*[136]

Artificial Intelligence

Moore's law *[137] is the observation that the number of transistors in a dense integrated circuit doubles approximately every two years. That means that computers double their power every 2 years for the same space occupied, and this law is quite persistent; it has proven to be correct since 1965.

In 1996, in its first match, IBM's "Deep blue" lost to Garry Kasparov, world chess champion. One year later, "Deep blue" accomplished the feat of defeating the top human player in chess.

In the year 2011, another IBM's child, "Watson," won at "Jeopardy!" — TV show that features a quiz competition in which contestants are presented with general knowledge clues in the form of answers. This type of task quiz was generally accepted as a human specialty and something very difficult for a machine to do. Unlike beating a human player in chess using a brutal force search algorithm, here, they use deep learning and AI networks to search and decide between 200 million pages of data.

In March 2016, Google's DeepMind computer AlphaGo beat Lee Sedol 4:1 in the ancient game of Go. Really, special about it is that the game's numerical estimates show that the number of possible moves in a game of Go far exceeds the number of atoms in the observable universe (on a table 21x21, the number of possible moves is 2.5×10^{976} [*138]). Even more amazing is that AlphaGo AI taught itself how to play the game.

With recent progress in quantum computing (D-wave Google),*139 creating a quantum leap in comparison to the current progress of Moore's law, reaching a point where a machine will be able to think on its own may happen even sooner than we think.

What other jobs are at risk?

The "This is Money" web portal made a list of 100 occupations that are judged most and least at risk of automation.*140 Looking at the list, it seems there will be no secure jobs anymore; sooner or later, all jobs will be under the "threat" of automation — even for those that are identified as the least at risk, it is possible to envision that, in 10 years, that will all change.

Companies aim to replace even what some may refer to "The World's Oldest Profession." In the not-so-distant future, sex robots could replace sex workers; with advanced technology, they could give options that would fulfill any type of sexual fantasies and desires, so much that experts warn that robots could be dangerously good (more patient, obedient, good listeners), causing addiction, as it will be available for sex at any time, which could, in the long run, cause the inability to form relationships with real people.*141

The nature of work is changing, and, as all trends showing, there is no coming back; we will probably get there even faster than we expect. The only thing left is to find what will be our purpose in a society that does not require us to work and how we are going to provide for each person.

A very good read on this subject is Federico Pistono's book, "Robots will steal your job but that is ok," *47 in which he tries to present many issues that we are going to face with increased automation, additionally providing his thoughts on how to solve those things.

In the beginning, Federico writes, "According to Voltaire, 'Work spares us from three evils: boredom, vice, and need,' and having a job has undoubtedly been the driving force to combat them up until now. Later on in chapter 9 he says "We do not need 100 times the amount of food, water, and housing that we did 50 years ago. We could have easily reduced the work week. Instead, we work more than ever before, on average. This is pure madness: the purpose of technology was to free our time so that we could dedicate it to higher purposes. Instead, our jobs have become the purpose."

To add to this, I would like to say that we have indeed freed up our time, but what is freed is not for everyone. Thanks to the current system, we have freed up time for the elite at the top, who currently waste what can be defined as social dividends. Expensive homes, parties, private jets and yachts, destabilizing trading markets and other governments... Now, how high those purposes are is something we can argue about.

This issue is very similar to Orwell's "Animal Farm," where "we" does not always mean "WE," as "some of 'we' are more equal than others."

Federico, like me, does not agree with Voltaire's assumption that work (the old-fashioned way) is the only way to spare us from evils, and, in the following chapters, he gives a way in which everyone could live richer lives without the need to spend our time working repetitive and boring jobs, liberating us from the drudgery and toil.

Martin Ford, in his book "The Rise of the Robots," does not provide many solutions but thoroughly explains the economic consequences we are facing now and will face in the future, describing the effects of automation and the potential for structural unemployment and dramatically-increasing inequality.

Recently-deceased author Alvin Toffler, in his books "The Third Wave" and its predecessor "Future Shock," describes three types of societies, based on the concept of "waves"—where each wave pushes the older societies and cultures aside.*[142]

- **The First Wave** is the society after the agrarian revolution; it replaced the first hunter-gatherer cultures.

- **The Second Wave** is society during the Industrial Revolution (ca. late 17th century through the mid-20th century). The main concepts are industrial and based on mass production, mass distribution, mass consumption, mass education, mass media, mass recreation, mass entertainment, and weapons of mass destruction, combined with standardization, centralization, concentration, and synchronization; these inevitably lead to bureaucracy.

- **The Third Wave** is the post-industrial society. This type of society is frequently referred as super-industrial society, Information Age, Space Age, Electronic Era, Global Village, technetronic age, or scientific-technological revolution. It is characterized by demystification, diversity, knowledge-based production, and the acceleration of change.

Building upon his books, other authors argue that growing trends signal the emergence of a Fourth Wave. The fourth wave will take hold through the social fabric. Seven important trends underlie the emergence of a new worldview:
- a shift in consciousness,
- disenchantment with scientism,
- new inner sources of authority and power,
- a re-spiritualization of society,
- a decline in materialism,
- the spreading of political and economic democratization,
- and a movement beyond nationality.

As Herman Bryant Maynard and Susan E. Mehrtens explain in their book, "The Fourth Wave: Business in the 21st Century," in the Fourth Wave, people will tap into the full range of human cognitive and perceptual abilities, including some not yet known. The shift to a leadership role for business in this Fourth Wave can be made through "thinking globally while acting locally." The key is a global perspective that extends beyond the traditional and includes a sense of responsibility for the whole planet.

Although I agree with many of Toffler's wave insights, I would argue that all waves exist, and they will exist simultaneously, but, during certain times in history, some of those waves will be more prominent and influential than others. Automation is only a problem in the context of the existing political and economic system. Our belief system and what we think is right or wrong, in terms of economy and politics, just needs an update — it just needs a patch that will allow us to move on and live happily in the universe. Yes, we will still have issues, but at least we will know how to work on them, uniting our forces.

However, many believe that it is very hard, or even impossible to change the governing context. In this book, I am trying to challenge that assumption by giving solutions that represent steps how to replace this context and also how to move further from the system that should serve only as a temporary replacement.

Psychology and technology

Most of our problems are not a question of philosophy but rather question of our psychology.

- Why do we do things in the way we do?
- Why do we get annoyed, when we see idle people?
- Why do we force people to receive education?
- Why do we go to wars, why do we have slavery, why do we admire "success," why do we work…?

There are many similar questions.

The way things work now, economically and politically, is deeply rooted in our psychology and has been carried across many generations, in the form of male dominance and the desire to control. The Alpha male, testosterone competition that has as a goal to propagate, has a message saying "my penis is bigger than yours," or "I am better than you are," and "therefore you must do what I want."

The famous actor and comedian Robin Williams said, "The problem is: God gave man a brain and a penis and only enough blood to run one at a time."

In ancient Greece, people celebrated small penises. To them, only grotesque, foolish men who were ruled by lust and sexual urges had large penises. Except for the obvious advantage while running or being in a fight, Greeks associated small and non-erect penises with moderation. Statues of the era emphasized balance and idealism; the ideal Greek man was rational, intellectual, and authoritative, which was one of the key virtues that formed their view of ideal masculinity. Art history blogger Ellen Oredsson writes, "He may still have had a lot of sex, but this was unrelated to his penis size, and his small penis allowed him to remain coolly logical." *[143]

Competition is the metaphorical expression of dominance — the desire to show that some members of society are better than others, and, therefore, they are many-fold rewarded for their success. When a rich person buys a house, private jet, a luxury yacht, or marries a beautiful model, it is just to show off — regardless of gender, the only thing he/she is trying to express is dominance and power.

Our corporations are largely organized around slavery — to be specific, wage slavery — concepts, with the central argument that it is necessary to force someone, in order to achieve progress or make things happen.

But, you have to ask: what are we trying to achieve, and why?

What is the purpose of the progress we are trying to achieve?

What is the goal we are chasing so eagerly, stressing about it all the way?

Therein lies the paradox: we say that we try to reduce suffering, but we use other people's suffering, in order to reduce it. Isn't that already a too familiar concept? Haven't we heard that one somewhere else?

We have heard different governments saying something along the following lines: "We need to kill criminals, in order to reduce the murder rate," or "We need to go to war to stop war," or "We kill people who killed people to show people that killing people is wrong."

We still think and teach people that, in order to gain the means to survive, people need to work hard, and people need to suffer. So, it is not a wonder that our system is failing; the real problem is that we have a medieval mindset, but we are surrounded with 21st-century technology.

Our perception has to shift, and our psychology has to change, or we will willfully create machines that will enslave us, because that is what we do. We know how to invent things, and we are really good at it, but we do not know how to un-invent them.

Artificial Intelligence and machines do not have penises, and they do not have a need to show off, but, yet again, they will be capable of doing any job humans do now, significantly better than any man or woman on this planet ever could. News about Google's "Alpha Go" AI recently beating the best human player is just the beginning of what can be expected in the future.

The real problem we have now is in our minds. If we realize that we can play the game in a different way, maybe by helping others, understanding will follow, and we will enjoy life more, being surrounded by happy people — dreamers who like learning and exploring uncharted territories of our existence.

To understand the nature of work, for a moment, forget about capitalism, socialism, aristocracy, economy, or any similar socially-constraining construct, and also forget money. Instead, try to think about everything only in terms of time and effort.

Back in the 90s, I had a computer PC 286. Back then, if you wanted to use a computer for different things, you needed to configure you computer each time for a different purpose. Under DOS (Disk Operating System), when the computer starts, the computer first reads the information included in the BIOS (configurable from the 80286 by setup).

So, each day, when I pressed the power button, I would wait for computer to boot and then, after the command line appeared, I would manually write commands, depending what I wanted to do. Whether I wanted to do some office things or play games, I was writing different lines. If a game froze from some reason, or there was a power shortage, or I simply turned the computer off because I was going out, it was necessary to repeat the entire process again after the next boot. Each time, as I did not know touch typing at that time, I was losing around 3-5 minutes of my time, the process was painfully slow, repetitive, and boring but still I needed to do it, if I wanted, for instance, to play games.

I knew there must be another way. On PCs back then, there were two files, AUTOEXEC.BAT and CONFIG.SYS, and all I needed to do was to modify those files and save them. The next time, I would have simple menu options. Easy!

CONFIG.SYS	AUTOEXEC.BAT
Device = c:\DOS\himem.sys Device = c:\DOS\ Emm386.exe Noems DOS = high, UMB DEVICEHIGH = c:\mouse\mouse.sys BUFFERS = 20 FILES = 40	Path = c:\dos rem check programs in DOS Keyb US Prompt p g set temp = c:\temp LH c:\dos\doskey/insert

But, at that time, somehow, my brain calculated that it would take around 15-20 minutes to do that, and I said, "Nah, it is too long," and I continued in the same way, until, one day, after experiencing several power shortages and PC restarts in a short period of time, I got fed up with manually writing and rewriting all those DOS commands, and I said, "That is it! I am writing the bloody file."

```
CONFIG.SYS

[MENU]
MENUITEM = normal
MENUITEM = games
[common]
Device= c:\DOS\himem.sys
[normal]
Device = c:\DOS\ Emm386.exe Noems
Files = 20
buffers = 10
[games]
Device = c:\DOS\ Emm386.exe RAM 2048
files = 40
buffers = 40
[common]
DOS = high,UMB
DEVICEHIGH= c:\mouse\mouse.sys
```

Those consequent power shortages made me realize that what matters is cumulative time, and that, basically, by not doing a more difficult and longer alternative, I am losing more time in the long run.

It took about 25 minutes to read the manual and modify the files. Afterwards, I never lost any significant time rewriting the same commands again. Even better, my friend had similar problems during that time, and I simply copied my file to a disk and gave it to him; he also stopped wasting time with boring and repetitive sets of actions.

Now, try imagining you are a member of some tribe on some island, far away from any modern civilization. You live in the cave that protects you from the elements. That cave is one mile away from the mountain spring — the only source of clean drinking water. As you have seen that other members got sick after drinking water from puddles, you refuse to make the same mistake.

So, every time you get thirsty, you will walk to the mountain spring to drink water. Soon, during those hot summer days, you see that walking every little while is not very effective. In order to solve the walking issue you make a bowl out of wood bark and clay. With it, you can bring more water, and there is no need to walk so frequently. Again, that water will last only for one day.

Then one day you get struck by a eureka moment: what if I make a larger bowl? So, you build a bowl big enough to carry water for 3 days, but, as it is larger and heavy, it is difficult to carry down the hill. Therefore, you realize that this is not effective.

Next, you get the idea to use a canal, diverting the stream your way, but soon you realize that water gets stuck often and that animals can urinate and crap in it. Soon after, an idea pops into your mind to connect bamboo sticks and transfer water through them; so slowly, stick by stick, the first water pipes are created.

At that moment, you have clean water all the time; you have automated the process. And, as water flows all the time, there is plenty enough for everyone else. It is there, free and available for everyone to use. It is a huge time saver for everyone in the community.

In some different scenario, imagine that the village chief instructed you to do the same thing, but now water is not free; although you have done all the hard work of creating the bamboo pipes and laying them all the way to the stream, the chief is forcing you to pay for water, as long as you live.

Is this a scam or slavery?

Why do we allow some people to hoard and control our planet's resources?

Now, think about some task you do all the time, some kind of job that is boring and repetitive, and yet you need to do it almost every day. For instance, imagine you are a bricklayer; your everyday job is to make walls. In your job, there is specific set of actions you need to do, in order to build a wall and finally build a house.

Let's say you are building your own house, and you know that, to do that job, you will need around 60 days; also, you have some mechanical skills, and you know that, to build a robot that will do the same job, you would need 180 days to build the robot, and 15 days for that robot to build the house on its own. (By the way, while I write this, the bricklaying robot that can build a house in 2 days has already been invented.*[144])

If you build just one house and one house only, it is reasonable to build the house manually, but what if you need to build 5, 10 or 100 houses? By giving away the bricklaying robot, houses will be built at zero-cost of labor and just a small price for fuel, and, if you manage to get energy from wind or solar, that means that building houses costs almost zero money.

But, initially you have lost your time and resources, in order to build the robot; therefore, community owes you something. Things that the community owes you are time, materials, and effort (intellectual, physical) spent while building that robot; if they repay you in, for instance, food and other services, there is no reason why you should not give away that machine for the community's benefit.

In a fully-automated world, any physical and even intellectual work can be similar: food production, transport, telecommunication, water and waste management, and many others. So, question is: if there is no human effort, where are all goods and services coming from?

They are coming from the intellectual and physical effort (thinking and work) of a past generation. In fact, everything now, and everything that will be built in the future, will be built on top of that same foundation, using the joined efforts of our earlier physical and intellectual work, combined with machine work and intellect.

Recently, news voices have been drumming disturbingly bad ideas: supposedly, the only way to get out of the economic crisis is to create a new World War, after which production will be boosted.

Furthermore, to propose anything along those lines requires being psychologically classified as a suicidal maniac type of personality or to be ignorant enough to completely dismiss how powerful and deadly technology is in the present moment. More importantly, everyone needs to understand that, if we allow World War 3 to happen, the population will be zero — no ifs, no buts, there will be no human beings to boost any production.

On the other hand, it is not strange that world super powers use wars and military actions as tools of securing their own economic stability. Regardless of how expensive war may look, economic collapse would have much larger consequences; therefore, countries with strong military capabilities will always first try to influence smaller countries of economical significant importance in different ways. Sometimes, this is just by installing puppet states and, in some other times, by military interventions. By this, they are basically imposing their own rules, just as kids would occasionally rig a game by arbitrarily changing the rules, so they could win all the time.

Although the reasons for military interventions and justifications of them are somewhat understandable, in the modern world that we live in, imperialistic way of thinking is a really, really bad idea.

The same absurdity happened during the Great Depression of the 1930s, when the stock market crashed, and, although people were surrounded with immense material wealth – like never before in history – influential economists of that time theorized that the way to overcome the issue of money was to create war.

Professor Harry Cleaver, *[145] in his course, "Introduction to Macroeconomics," in the section "The Great Depression and the Keynesian Solution," *[146] explains: "War was definitely good for business, in that it created a whole new set of markets and a great deal of government subsidization of new investment. There were vast operations built during the war by business, but run by government, which were subsequently turned over to private business. One example was the nitrogen plants built to produce TNT. After the war, they were turned over to private business to stimulate a boom in the production of inorganic fertilizer."

Unlike a hundred years ago, with the current state of technology, the issues we are experiencing are comparable to being healthy and being surrounded by an abundance of food, yet starving to death, thinking that there won't be enough.

Imagine there is Fruit Inc., and they produce only fruits; the only type of food they eat is those fruits. Everyone has some fruit trees in the backyard, but still, to get enough to survive, all ten villagers work at Fruit Inc. The rich owner has 99 times more than they have. The Boss of the company hoards all the fruits he harvests and uses that fruit to make the other 9 villagers work for him in different types of jobs. Over time, The Boss has hoarded so much fruit that he realizes he does not need so much working force anymore. As he cuts the working force, workers start begging to keep their jobs, even at lower salaries. In order to keep them all, he reduces all salaries. In that way, he hoards even more wealth. At some point, he decides to create machines to replace people, as they do not complain, do not have breaks or sick leave, and he does not need to pay them. People are eventually laid off. Fruit Inc. loses customers and, with customers, its purpose, as it does not have a market to which it would sell its product anymore.

At one point, The Boss will have so many fruits, and others will have so little, that the entire Fruit Inc. will stop working. At that point, he will have full storage of fruits, and people will be on the brink of starvation.

To solve this problem, they have following options:

- They can burn the storage house and everything he has. In the process, a few people will die, but that will restart production from zero, and the game will start from the beginning. (This is the War option)

- The workers can decide to revolt, break into the storage, and then take over and divide what they find there. In the process of protecting "his ownership," The Boss may die, and then someone else will declare himself the new boss, and game will again start from the beginning. (This is revolution)

- The Boss can decide to take a certain small percent (let's say 10%) for himself, and then distribute the remaining 90% equally to other people, because they were responsible for creating that wealth, the company, and machines. (This would be the philanthropic approach)

- There is a forth option. If The Boss does not want to distribute his wealth, and workers do not want to create riots, and no one wants to go to war, workers can simply decide to organize themselves to participate in a sharing economy, excluding Fruit Inc. from the loop. With time, all the things they make will go into the community, and, slowly, they will phase out Fruit Inc., and its monopoly will cease to exist. At the end, no one will need to work anything physically, as machines will replace all work, and then everyone (even the scrooge boss) will enjoy the fruits of technological progress. (This is Basic Tax Control with Basic Income approach).

Purpose of a machine is to make repetitive, hard, and boring work obsolete. That is what the goal was from the beginning. That is what we have worked for all this time. Now, when we are almost there, and we have achieved the goal, we somehow do not know how to live without the work.

So, we invent boring, unnecessary, administrative, bureaucratic jobs we really do not need, just to keep people busy. We create them, because we think that human beings need to work, as if that is the only way to live.

Money is not real; it is just a quasi construct we have created, in order to measure our time and physical/mental effort — nothing else and nothing more.

Never in history have we had a wealthier society with more goods, food, or services than we have now. In no other period in history, despite what you can see on the news, have we lived more secure, stable, and prosperous than we do now. It would be a real shame to throw away all that — everything generations of people have worked for — and create some stupid, senseless war, in which we would all die, just because we could not understand that the mental construct we have created does not serve the same purpose it did before.

C(oope/orpo)ration

The concentration camp story is a parable about our elective process in the political arena and the system that never changes. It is a tale about every person that has already gone through the "democratic" elective process, with hopes that, this time, the government they choose will be the one — the one that will bring change. A better world for everyone. Not long after an election, realization follows that there is no any significant difference.

While in power, politicians usually spend their time focusing on how to stay in power, instead of doing the things they were elected for and actually need to do. Four or five years after, people are in the same situation all over again, lining up to elect the same bunch, like they did before — maybe some other faces with different clothes and a slightly adjusted tone, but, again, everything stays the same.

When a waltz is playing, those who know how to dance do so with predefined steps, with the skills according to their knowledge, and those who do not know how to, usually step aside quickly. It is the same in politics and economy: nothing ever changes, because the music is playing the same tune, and no one is brave enough to improvise new steps or ask the orchestra to play something else. It is an endless loop, which can be solved only if we redesign the system from inside out and start dancing to a new tune with completely different, never-before-seen steps.

We all seek freedom, but being in the same cage for so long, we have forgotten what freedom means and what the world beyond the cage looks like. Most of us take the game (system) for granted, trying to adjust to the inner workings, unwilling to participate in the process of change, unwilling to fight for something else.

Soon, the world as we know it, will transform. With advancement of Artificial Intelligence, computer technologies, sensors, and robotics — there won't be secure jobs, and, willing or not, in order to survive, you will be forced to think about the future society and your own role in it.

The main question in the society where the top 1% controls 99% of the wealth and requires you to work, in order to survive, is this: what will you do if "work" does not exist? Some say we would need to upgrade our skills and learn continually, but what if there are not enough jobs for higher education? Even now, there are examples of people with college degrees working in fast food chains for minimum wage. Additionally, a high supply of highly-educated work force will just drive their salaries to a minimal level, undermining the years and money invested in education, pushing the highly-educated middle class below the poverty line. Is society supposed to invent useless jobs, just in order to artificially sustain an archaic system that was once invented to get us here but now is unfit for technology and the current stage of progress?

By the rules of the game "Monopoly," we are destined for periodic economic crises, as they serve to leverage bad investments and neutralize effects of overproduction of useless things. If we continue with the same system, and the same economic rules we have now, the gap between rich and poor will continue to grow, making it impossible for a majority to reach financial safety during their lives. Even worse, the pension funds and insurance mechanisms will fail to deliver their main purpose.

Finally, the destruction of the middle class will lead to suicide of market capitalism. Without people to buy things and services, suddenly, we will end up in a world with factories that have high production capacities but without customers who are able to buy those product or services — therefore imploding under their own rules and weight.

Nowadays, money means speech, corporations are people, and lobbying (giving huge amounts of money to politicians, in order to influence their opinions) is not corruption. We have allowed corporate money (controlled by billionaires) to influence politics, shaping policies in their favor and rigging the process of democratic elections. On the other hand, if the same would happen in some other non-democratic country, we would call it a human rights violation and accuse those governments of corruption.

In democracies (including the widely-adopted representative model of democracy), all people, regardless of their gender, race, or income, should be able to participate in the political process, and could run, if they wanted, for office, without asking for money from the wealthy and the powerful.

In order to create a better society, we have to cut the influence of money from politics, especially from corporations and wealthy individuals.

There are many ways to do this:

The first necessary step is to remove policies that treat companies as people. Companies are not people, and they cannot be part of the political process.

Next is to stop subsidizing giant corporations and giving them taxpayers' money. Instead, we should force them to pay the fair share of taxes they owe or are usually trying to evade. This would require a change of international laws to prohibit the existence of tax heavens, which now mainly exist for the purpose of money laundering and tax evasion. Some time ago, the BBC had a show "The Town That Took on the Taxman." *[147] In one scene, they showed the real scale of the tax evasion scheme with mind-boggling numbers. Just in Amsterdam (Holland, Netherlands), for the year 2013, there was a total of 14,668 companies that were registered there for the sole purpose of evading taxes; the total amount of money flown at the end of that year was $7.861.000.000.000 (~ $8 trillion US dollars). That was more than 10% of the world's GDP *[148] that same year.

Any company, regardless of how powerful and highly valued, can be terminated, if it loses all its buyers or its entire working force.

Consider Apple – one of richest companies in the world *[149] – and consider that they have not yet switched to a fully-automated, AI-driven mode. If all the employees would leave the company and, for some reason, no one else wanted to take their place, the company would cease to exist. Also, if, for some reason, customers stopped buying Apple products, fed up by the company's policies or repeatedly non-innovative new releases, Apple would implode, diminishing the wealth of shareholders in the process. A similar scenario already happen to BlackBerry Limited, in November 1999; the value of its shares was around $7 and then, at the peak of their fame, in July 2007, the value of their stocks was high as $230 per share, but, soon after, not being able to follow new market trends, the share price plummeted, hitting a $7 share price in 2012 and never recovering since.

If you ask any human being what should be the goal of society, he or she would probably answer something like: a safer, healthier, friendlier, and fairer society. Unless there is something terribly wrong with a person's mind, you will not hear that someone wants to live in society where he or she would live in a fear all the time, struggle for water and food, starving to death, or have the experience of bombs exploding all around.

So then, what is our goal; what is the ideal we are fighting for?

What does it mean to win as a society?

Goals are what drive people and companies to succeed, and societies are not much different. Up to this point, we had a very simple goal that was driving our system, and that goal was more stuff, more things, more bridges, more money, "more, more, more," and we created a name for that growth: GDP (Gross Domestic Product). The larger the GDP, the better it is; more GDP meant that we are winning. In the process of this artificially-created competition, we polluted nature, exhausted our natural resources and we brought ourselves to the brink of the Third World War. Obviously, we are doing something wrong. Maybe the issue is that we concentrate our energy in the wrong direction.

Instead of "more," we need a "better," "smarter," "healthier," and "happier" society.

Annie Leonard, author of "The Story of Stuff" *[150] project, in one of her short movies, "The Story of Solutions," *[151] uses the GOAL acronym to explains what is necessary to do, in order to make game-changing solutions happen.

- G stands for **G**ive people power – take back the power from corporations and give it to people, which is necessary to build fair democracy.

- O stands for **O**pen people's eyes to truth – that happiness does not come from buying and having more stuff, but from community, nature, health, and a sense of purpose.

- A stands for **A**ccounts for all cost – it includes the toll it takes on people and the planet. In other words, it internalizes costs, instead of externalizing them, as most businesses do today.

- L stands for **L**essens the wealth gap – between those who cannot meet basic needs and those who consume way more than their fair share.

Annie continues: "We all know we need to get businesses out of our democracy. But, cooperatives go even further and bring democracy into the businesses. Sustainable, democratic, equitable."

The role of Universal Basic Income and Basic Tax Control is to enhance and speed this process up. Metaphorically speaking, if we would imagine sustainable businesses (as Annie has mentioned) as electric cars, then Universal Basic Income and Basic Tax Control would be the road and the factory that creates not only those cars but also all the traffic lights and communications necessary to organize people faster around mutual GOAL.

The question that arises is how to define sustainable business, and can we end up in a situation where we just have lots of small polluters?

A good metaphor is sealed terrarium: a glass container that has enough ground, water, and nutrients so that plants inside of it can create a mini ecosystem capable of sustaining itself indefinitely, only by getting a bit of heat and light from the external environment. David Latimer from Cranleigh, Surrey, created one such system that was watered just once since 1960; completely sealed, plants are still thriving inside of it.*[152] Those plants have managed to find a balance between life and death, managing available resources in a perfect way.

A sustainable company is the company that is able to control its financial, social, and environmental risks, obligations, and opportunities in a friendly manner. A sustainable company's impacts are sometimes listed as profits, people, and planet. They are expected to be democratic, allowing people to participate in the process of growth, as well as share in the wealth. They are fair and treat all rivals equally, fulfilling all responsibilities to society (paying taxes, respecting human rights, taking care of the planet), showing that companies and their employees will be accountable for their actions.

The majority of current businesses are far from this goal; they are off the balance so much that they are pushing the entire system and life on the planet out of balance.

Wealth wise, we live in a society where all the butter is pushed to one corner of the toast. One side is dry and almost impossible to swallow; the other has so much butter that it leaves disgusting taste in the mouth. To change things, we need a table knife and just a bit of skill to spread it equally.

By cutting subsidies to larger businesses, and concentrating investments in small, democratic, sustainable businesses, we could shift the focus from giants to ants. This can be a gradual process similar to boiling a frog: by deploying a Basic Tax Control platform, people will have time to adapt to a new change. As a result, the positive change will pass unnoticed, and the risk of unrest and destruction would be largely reduced.

One positive thing that can be drawn out of the Concentration Camp story is that at the end it is still possible for large group of people to find consensus and self organize about one single goal and be persistent enough to follow it till the end.

In order to achieve this mind shift, we need to find way for people to understand that cooperation is a positive thing for everyone and that it can work equally for both the society and for personal goals. This would require willingness to cooperate with someone, having in mind that we deliberately want to create circumstances that will work in favor of other people and ourselves.

Why would we do that — isn't it our personal goal just to pursue our own happiness?

In the movie "A Beautiful Mind," mathematician John Nash is portrayed correcting Adam Smith's idea that, "In competition... individual ambition serves the common good" — or, in other words, that, the "best result comes from everyone in the group doing what's best for himself" — by saying that Adam Smith's idea was incomplete. He builds up upon the sentence by saying, "**The best result will come... from everyone in the group doing what's best for himself... and the group.**"

In the famous scene, [153] John Nash is at the bar with couple of his friends. A pretty blonde girl enters the bar with a couple of her friends and immediately captures the attentions of all his friends. So, Nash explains that, if they all go for the prettiest (the blonde) girl, they will all lose, as the blonde will not be able to pick one out of many, and her pretty (but not that pretty) girlfriends would not like to feel like second choice. Instead, he explains that the best choice would be to use a bargaining strategy, in which they will ignore the pretty blonde completely and go after her friends; in that way nobody would lose, and they would all score. [vii]

Current capitalism is in the stage where, along the line, someone figured out that that blonde is free, and, as everyone is busy with her friends, he should approach. He married the blonde, but the advert that she is available is still in the newspaper. Other people read the advert and still try to fight for her attention, not realizing that she left long ago, to live in some other city.

For us, what is most important is to understand that the best outcome will come when we **work for ourselves and others at the same time**. The notion that, along with our personal needs, we have societal needs and requirements leads to the conclusion that the best — and maybe only — way to create a positive outcome for our future is to work together and to **cooperate**.

[vii] I feel compelled to defend Adam Smith: in the movie, they used a depiction of John Nash picking on Adam Smith to emphasize John Nash's genius, and, somehow, they felt that the best way to emphasize his genius was by correcting another genius. However, Adam Smith basically recommended the same thing through the ancient "propensity to 'truck, barter, and exchange,' or bargaining: 'give that which I want, and you shall have this which you want.'" Actually, one of Smith's most famous quotes is, "Man is an animal that makes bargains: no other animal does this–no dog exchanges bones with another." When Adam Smith talked about "the best result will come... from everyone in the group doing what's best for himself," he was talking about competition, but bargaining is not competition; it is actually a cooperation strategy.

Part III
You/We Can Change the System

What does "change the world" mean?

In recent years attitudes about changing the world, or at least about talking about changing the world, have shifted in a positive direction. Just a decade ago if you publicly spoke about how you would like to change the world you would quickly get strange looks, and in some more severe cases you were at risk of being locked in the loony house, dressed in the shirt with comfortable long sleeves buttoning at the back. And if you went a bit further back in time, you would find that not so long ago, humans were very eager to place other fellow humans on a burning pile of woods just for mentioning any similarly sounding ideas.

That was happening because "Changing the World" has two not so very different but very unpopular synonyms: "Saving the World" and "Saving Humanity."

The first one, **"Saving the World,"** is an obvious impossibility, as we are basically adding emotion to unemotional objects. Although, metaphorically, it means the same as the other two, a literal interpretation can quickly lead to an argument.

Usually, arguments range in the following ways:

- "Our planet has existed for billions of years, and we humans are technologically capable of some very small impact just in the last fifty years."

- "If nature wanted, it would have gotten rid of us a long time ago."

- "We are very ignorant, if we think we could have any impact on our world."

- "Save the planet!? What a stupid idea; you cannot save the planet."

All of these arguments are true, to some extent. Although we are still fragile, and we cannot master nature's forces, we are constantly increasing our knowledge and powers, and it is just a question of time when we will be capable of controlling them. Furthermore, nature does not have a mind to decide whether it will let us live or die; it is not revengeful, angry, or justice-seeking. It is just nature — nothing else and nothing more.

Maybe we look insignificant, but, if we would unite around a mutual goal to blow up the planet (for some strange reason), I believe that, with the constant improvements of nuclear weapons and through increased manufacturing capabilities, we could "convert" our planet into dust 10 to 100 years from now.

I am mentioning this just to show that it is still possible to have a significant impact at the planetary level.

And, it is true: if we would succeed with our "Dr. Evil-Destroy-Earth-plan," the rest of the universe, given its size, wouldn't be significantly disturbed by the event — just as an ocean does not have a reason to be bothered about losing one grain of sand or drop of its water.

In our history, the "saving the world" task was usually entrusted to gods, demigods, or especially God-gifted people, which some people call prophets. So, by saying you want to do something similar means that somehow you want to take their jobs, and other people would get really upset about this, so you would again risk being locked in that special loony house ...

"Saving Humanity" is the subset of "Saving the World." It is a people-centered task, task that puts humans in the middle of its affairs, like they really matter. And saving humanity is a reasonable subject of self-preservation, and probably any species would do the same.

But in the case of us humans, for some reason this subject usually creates many points for very long debates, generating questions like: Why do people need saving? Is there any point to saving humanity? Do humans deserve to be saved? What do we need to be saved from? Who will save us? And the list goes on, and on, and on.... In fact, that long list of arguments is more disturbing than any actual problem we have to face or any solution we may think of. In order to outline the simple problem and propose a solution, one needs to pass through the nine levels of hell of a deep philosophically-emotional scientifically-religious discussion.

This approach, like his bigger brother, suffers from the same illness, a belief that saving humanity has to be done by someone with super-special-god-like powers. So, if there is some individual or group of people who can really do this correctly, it has to be the God, the son of God, the official person from the God service — usually known as a prophet, angels, aliens, or something else unknown, everything except humans, especially not the live ones. This attitude basically means that a huge percentage of the population thinks that humans are capable of creating huge piles of issues but not very capable of cleaning up after themselves. In their minds this can be summarized with the following distribution:

Humans = Troublemakers 100%, Responsibility 0%.

"Changing the world" is the most politically correct term to use, as its literal meaning is the same as its metaphorical one, so there's no confusion. Just by being on Earth, at any given moment, and doing something or even nothing we are already changing the world. Furthermore the construct "Changing the World" is not even a statement of intention, but a scientific and obvious fact, similar to breathing — something we do all the time. And, beauty of it is that no one can blame you for something that everyone does all the time. That being said, you are now safe to go about your business, safe from the obnoxious people willing to endlessly argue about your plans and disturbing your dreams.

"Changing the world" is also very good because it does not place any expectation on you — you do not have to save, help, or rescue anyone, because change simply means change. For instance, if you start working on your plan and then at some point you hugely f*ck up, you can still say that this is exactly what you wanted in the first place. If your plan blows up in your face you have still won, as any change — positive or negative, small or big — is still a change. So you are safe from every possible side and angle.

Now, the only thing left is for you to decide what kind of impact you want to make — do you want to make a positive or negative change in this world.

How big that change will be sometimes will depend on you and sometimes on society. Unexpectedly, things can become an instant-overnight hit and change the lives of many, or they can go completely awry.

But don't sweat it!

If you have dreams, and you think you can change the world for the better — just do it. Never allow your insecurities to get in the way of your dreams. Never allow other people to tell you what is possible or not; you are the one who needs to discover these things for yourself. Maybe you will fail miserably and maybe they will be right on some points, but the knowledge you will gain on that journey will outweigh the possible failures you will face and will help you to achieve some amazing things.

How to change the world?

By this, I strictly mean: how to improve our lives, how to live more sustainably on this planet and what are the common strategies to make this happen? The way we currently live has been shown to be unsustainable; we lack the resources to provide the same quality of life for the all world's inhabitants, we are losing the battle with the planet's weather and, on top of everything, our behavior could wipe us off of the surface of the planet.

As I do not want to spend more than this sentence explaining morality and the justification for saving humans as well as other existing species, I will continue writing with attitude that every living or dead but resurrectable species *[154] is immensely precious and that variety/diversity of life is the most important thing in the universe.

Having said that, let us explore some possible ways to change the world/system:

Imagine that you have a system or an organization (we will call it "Oxygen Inc."), where there is a number of people. You are the person in charge of those people — the manager. Every person has his own moody behavior, which does not accord with the corporate rules. To complete one task, using simple math, you can estimate that the expected completion time should be around two hours. Also, you know what the desired outcome of that task should be, but, whenever you ask those people to complete a job, you always get a different outcome and delivery time. In order for the system to work normally, you have to find a way to make those people work in line with the required/desired parameters.

Elements are: **system**, required output (the **goal**) and the **people**.

In order to achieve the desired result we know that something has to be changed, because the way the system currently works will produce serious consequences.

So, let's start with **goal**:

When we see that we cannot accomplish a task in the given time, we can simply change the time in which we need to deliver something. Therefore, we can still accomplish the goal and have success. This option involves tweaking rules; the issue with it is that most of the time it does not work. Maybe tweaking the rules is a good strategy in the short run, if, for instance, we fight personal procrastination, but in many other real world systems this is not economically viable. Simply put: if you produce oxygen in an enclosed space slower than you use it by breathing, you will suffocate very quickly.

Although there is a tolerance time, there is always a maximum time after which the product will not be cost-effective anymore. When I say cost-effective, I mean more as a broad abstraction, not necessarily in the economy-market-capitalistic sense.

For the above example, let us imagine that two hours is the maximum time to deliver. That means that <u>we cannot change the goal</u>, as change, in this case increasing the time, will reflect on the life span of the system.

To make things more rigid, we will imagine that the task is oxygen production and that all the people in the system are living under the same dome (on Mars for example) and they are all the part of the same enclosed system. If the system "dies" (runs out of oxygen), then all the people in the system will die/suffocate. [viii]

Knowing that changing "goal" would not help, let us move to **people**:

As most of our organizations have a pyramidal structure of management, we will split people into two groups: a manager, in this case you and a work force.

Consequently, in order to produce a positive impact on your "Oxygen Inc.", there are also two things you can change: management or the people.

We will start with management, or **changing yourself**.

Often you can read inspirational, almost spiritualist, quotes, such as the following:

- "When you stop trying to change others and work on changing yourself, your world changes for the better."

- "Yesterday I was clever, so I wanted to change the world; today I am wise, so I am changing myself."

[viii] This simplification is necessary in order to make a few points, although in some sense it is very similar to the issue that we are experiencing on our planet with climate change.

- "If you want to change the world, first change yourself, then tell the others how you did it. Never demand that people change. Inspire them to change as an example instead."

Many of us believe that this will work, but if you apply a simple analytic approach and rely on history, you will see that this is not efficient enough. I am not saying it would not work; just that it is not applicable to an entire system.

If you decide to "vote" for this one, you will have multiple choices what to do. You can change yourself emotionally, or you can choose to upgrade your skill and therefore become smarter and more efficient.

Emotionally you have a few choices.

- First you can become a nicer person.

    You can be polite to everyone, help out whoever needs help with their own tasks and, generally speaking, do good things for others. But even becoming the nicest person in the world will still not finish the job, as you are dealing with lazy and moody people who do not want, or do not know how to do their own share. You may end up in a loop where other people are using you to do their own job. Although the idea of doing else's jobs may work in small organizations, in big ones that would not be physically feasible as you would not be capable of covering for everyone. Even when you have become a better person, your "Oxygen Inc." has not produced enough of the main product – and as a consequence you have died along with everyone else.

- What is the second option?

    You can become a tyrant, you can be terrible to people, you can start chasing them, you can try to force them to complete the job, but if the organization does not have strict rules, you will still fail. Basically, if you do not have anything to back up your rigid approach, you will quickly discover that all your threats and intimidation are just empty promises and that no one cares. During my professional life I have seen companies struggling because they have a very weak policy about dismissing people. Being a manager there is quite a challenge, as they have the very difficult task of managing people in order to meet demands.

- What is the third option?

    You can stop caring. A non-attachment or defeatist approach where you rely on the policy "whatever happens will happen" will not yield any mentionable outcome either, although it will give you peace of mind till the end. The system will end up as the sum of all individuals and in this case the date of failure will be random. This is the favorite approach of the group of people who think that we are too insignificant to make any significant change, although they frequently forget the part where we are significant enough to mess things up. This is pretty much in line with the saying that "evil prevails when good people fail to act."

Burying your head in the sand will not make scary things go away. If you want to live, and you would like for your children to live as well, this approach is not an option because it is destined to failure.

On the other hand, learning new skills may help you up to a certain point. Everything depends on how skillful you are and whether you will be able to create a miracle device to replace everyone in time before you are completely out of oxygen. On this path, people similar to you can help you by taking interest in the things you are doing. They will probably do it for the sake of fun anyway. And using this approach together with becoming a nicer person will also help.

Also consider this: generally speaking, we are not very kind to our leaders. We envy, complain and gossip about them and very often make their lives a living nightmare. Through history we even used to burn them, crucify them, assassinate them or chop their heads off. So, you have to admit at least one thing: being a spiritual leader, as history has showed us, is a tough job to do — and probably not the first or happiest choice of occupation you would sign up for.

How about changing **people**?

That is a Sisyphean task, to say the least. Trying to change people in order to resolve a problem is a most impractical thing to do. I am not saying it is not possible, but, by the time you change people in "Oxygen Inc.," everyone will be long gone — mainly because this is against human nature, and, the older people are, the more difficult they are to change. I am not denying that people have changed during the course of history, and that they are mostly domesticated, but this process is painfully slow. Generally speaking, character change requires more time than learning a new skill does. For just a small change of character we need months and years, and even then one can easily slip back into old habits.

If you ever decide to go down this route, it is worth mentioning that there are a variety of methods if you want to succeed in this, but going around preaching that people are lazy, stupid or wicked is the one — that will certainly fail.

Population-wise, there is one more case worth mentioning — an additional, unexpected new player in the game: Malthusianism *[155] is generally known as a school of ideas where a population is actively controlled, in order to avoid scarcity events. With the coming of AI (Artificial Intelligence), the ongoing discussion is that giving a general AI machine the task of solving our problems for us (in the case of our "Oxygen Inc.," the production of oxygen), while failing to clearly define the parameters of the solution, could end up really ugly. Basically, we could end up extinct, as the machine may think of us as part of the problem and, therefore, in order to resolve the problem (because the machine is not burdened by the morality of its actions), it could depopulate the system completely, thinking that, if humans do not exist, the problem of losing oxygen will not exist anymore.

Lastly, what can we achieve by **changing the system**?

There is a general notion that our system is like a moving car, and that changing the system would be equal to changing motor parts while it is running. Although this looks a scary prospect, it should not scare us at all. We just have to remember the field of medicine called surgery. Surgeons have been doing this for more than a hundred years now, on a more complex system than a car, and they are quite good at it. They can operate on limbs or internal organs, they can replace parts, they can bridge kidneys or lungs, or stop hearts and brains (medically induced comma) and they can do all this while you are still alive and your body is running without killing you or causing any permanent harm to your body. How can they do this? Well, it is all about knowledge and following the rules of the system.

Let's go back to our "Oxygen Inc.". Just like any other organization, it can be complex, but applying changes inside an organizational system is a far from changing the engine parts of a speeding car. Organizations have bodies, people, structure, laws, policies and rules. If we just tweak these a bit we can change the way in which they function significantly, and that will not stop them or break them.

So what will happen if we change the rules in our "Oxygen Inc."?

If we change the policy regarding discharge?

Or/and if we monitor people closely and make them aware that they are being monitored?

Just changing these two would change behavior and productivity [156] significantly. Objective feedback combined with punitive measures, creating an atmosphere of fairness would have an effect both on productivity and also on the people in the system, and this might be both positive and negative, all depending on what kind of changes we are making.

There is one more rather technical approach to changing "Oxygen Inc." that has built-in-control-by-its-design and will also work for everyone. Managers could stop releasing produced oxygen into the dome and, instead, start packing it up into personal tanks. The company will, for the workers who are producing oxygen, as a form of salary, refill their personal tanks with oxygen, so they could use it or share it with their families. All the excess oxygen is ending up in these huge tanks to cover for periods of volatility.

Now, this raises a few questions:

- What if all the issues with people who are not willing to contribute anymore are just because the oxygen is not evenly distributed?
- What if some people decide that it is easier to steal someone else's oxygen tank, instead of working for it?

- What if certain people in the organization receive more oxygen than they can spend and they keep it stored in special oxygen tanks, not allowing other people access to it?

- What if those same individuals are creating artificial demand, which means that the system does not need that much oxygen in the first place?

- What if people have been misled to think that there is not enough oxygen, so that they will work harder, as a result producing huge amounts of excess oxygen, while workers have not got any share out of this? Who should own that excess oxygen?

- At the end, what will happen when machines start producing all the oxygen without the need for any human workers?

The system and the people have a unique bond. The system influences the behavior of the people and the people can also have an influence on the system. The issue arises when the rules are followed blindly, overlooking the system behavior while having impossible or unsustainable parameters, which will usually cause failures of the system and everyone in it.

Change the system first, and change in people will follow. When rules change, people will change, too. Bruce K. Alexander's "Rat Park" experiment can be used as a good example of this, and it gives great hope regarding positive influence on people, when the system/environment is changed.*[157]

We have enough technology and enough resources and people to make this change. When people are immersed into a learning environment they will make positive change effortlessly. So we have to consider that maybe it is our cage that mostly makes us behave in the way we do now.

If we can consider the system as the source code of a computer program that is already running but does not need compiling, then when we change the code, the way the system behaves will change as well. It may crash, but if everything is carefully planned and tested, the chances of that happening are very low. Especially if we apply small incremental changes and we test first on a small number of people before applying a final version to the entire system.

The good thing about large systems is that you can always create an experimental/test environment to run under the new rules and assign people to live under these new rules. Monitoring people's behavior for a certain period of time can provide enough data in order to make a decision about the applicability of change to the system as a whole.

Think about Monopoly, and how players behave in it. Now imagine that our game is a computer program instead of being a board game. We can still play it on the computer by taking turns (pass-and-play) in the usual way, but we can also write a small computer program (an autopilot) that will play the game on its own indefinitely. Every player will still have all the resources necessary to do whatever he wants, but he does not need to stay in front of the screen. So while the game plays itself, you can choose to do whatever you think is more interesting thing to do or spend your time on.

Most of our civilization's advances we can attribute to our ability to change our systems, to optimize them, and make them run better and more efficiently. We do all that because our laziness is driving our constant desire to create more with less. Therefore, there is nothing wrong with being lazy; actually, we should embrace it and work toward it, so that, in the end, we will have more time to do things that require our brains more than our muscles.

Utopia semantics

500 years have passed since Thomas More first published his book Utopia,*[158] and it seems that his legacy has not stopped haunting anyone who even tries to think about any other system that should replace what we have now.

Many other fields have experienced significant changes, but, in an economical and political sense, nothing really radical and significant was changed for very long time.

The word utopia was coined from two Greek words: οὐ ("not") and τόπος ("place"), meaning "no-place".

Now, what is interesting about Utopia is that, nowadays, it is largely considered as a synonym for the perfect society that cannot exist by any possible means. But, if you put aside this stereotypical meaning of the word, when you read the book, you will find the following: Utopia is far from the perfect society, and, ironically, what our society has become at present has more in common with the Utopia then we would like to believe.

We cannot even start discussing Utopia without taking into account Thomas More and his personal context.

More was born just a few years after England ended the Hundred Years War with France and in the middle of the other very long-lasting civil war "War of the Roses," a struggle for power between two English families: Lancaster and York *[159] (basically, a real-life, historical version of the TV show "Game of Thrones").

From that long-lasting war, the Tudors came as victors, and Henry VII was crowned king. His son Henry VIII, *[160] who succeeded him, was, to say the least, a womaniser, he did not like the church bossing him around regarding who will he marry or divorce. So, Henry decided to make life easier for himself by following the Protestant Reformation view, which was more relaxed regarding his matrimonial issues. He decided to split from Catholicism and to put himself as the head of the Church of England.

Now, at the time, Thomas More (you can imagine him as Ned Stark) was the Lord High Chancellor of England, in the centre of this dispute between two powers, but on the wrong side. He was Catholic, and he considered the Protestant Reformation as heresy. Henry (you can imagine him as the King Robert Baratheon), on the other hand, really liked women and didn't like anyone standing in the way, so the poor fellow Thomas was accused of treason, and he lost his head.

Let's go back to Utopia. If you read the book, you will see that Thomas is actually trying to influence the people of his time by this story; he was not even trying to create a perfect society (as like the word Utopia will get the epithet in later centuries by forgetting the real context) but trying to say "look, people: this place I will talk about does not exist (although I will try to convince you it does), but aren't the things I am saying closer to what should be common sense, and what actually Christianity is teaching us?" The book was first printed in 1516 in Latin, 16 years before his death, and in English in 1551, 16 years after More's execution.

His attitudes about premarital sex and the fitting punishment for it shows More's puritan upbringing, but they would probably not be acceptable by any means in our society. Punishment for repeated adultery, the concepts of hierarchy, privacy, freedom of movement, and labor, as explained in Utopia, are far from anything we would consider a "dream land," and a majority of people of this century could hardly see themselves living comfortably in such a society. More's views on religion, sex, and marriage are conservatively patriarchal, and they represent messages he is trying to convey in contrast to the views of his king, and, obviously, as he lost his head, he was not diplomatic enough.

On the other hand, his explanation of a magistrate is very similar to some form of elective democracy, and the concept of "slavery" or forced labor is very similar to what we have now in our judicial system, where, for some type of offences, a person can choose between spending time in a cell or doing involuntary/ community work. On the other hand, we need to consider that slavery in the British Isles existed and was recognized from before the Roman occupation until the 12th century. But, slavery virtually disappeared after the Norman Conquest and was replaced by feudalism and serfdom. Having all that in mind, it is understandable that people during that time still considered slavery a perfectly normal concept. Also, it is important to notice that the moral meaning of the word "slavery" has changed since More's time (back then, it was a morally acceptable punishment for offence that "good" people would use to punish "evil;" now, it is how "evil" people prey upon powerless people).

Furthermore, More's description of Utopia towns is almost a replica of Plato's dialogue "The Republic," in which he describes what the ideal polis (city/town) should look like. More does not even try to hide this fact; actually, he deliberately mentions Plato several times, along with other influential philosophers and poets (Aristotle, Theophrastus, Plutarch, Lucian, Aristophanes, Homer, Euripides, Sophocles, Thucydides, Herodotus etc.); it is like he is trying to convince his readers that they should read those books.

It would be interesting to find out how Utopia earned the epithet of an ideal society, as the lives and locations in the book are far from advanced and also ever farther from a perfect society. Utopians from the book still have different kinds of issues: they can be exposed to the elements and plagues, they still have occasional wars, they use manipulation and capital punishment, and, admittedly, they can also be unhappy.

Saying that the Utopians are all happy all the time or that Utopia is the ideal society requires either to base conclusion without reading the book or having the same mindset as a person who was brought to the USA from a third-world country (just by showing him/her around all the technological advances, and all the happy people enjoying life, he or she would easily think that this is the richest and happiest place on earth — a paradise — dismissing any possibility that anyone in the USA could have any reason for war or to commit any type of crime).

So, here's where we intersect with Utopia: banishment of capital punishment, public hospitals and schools for free, easing pain and suffering, dedication to health, the way we read bedtime fairy tales (moral stories) to children, tolerance of religions, and even the concept of euthanasia. Of course, in the real world, this cannot be applied to all countries and all people, but, on average we can say that we are there — sort of.

Where we have surpassed Utopia is in knowledge and schools, and that is somewhat understandable. There was no way that More could imagine that we would have mobile phones, cars, computers, airplanes, satellites, space ships, industrial machines, robots, or the other inventions we use instead of slaves for completing hard work. If we could bring Thomas More from the past, he would probably think that we live in Eutopia. [ix])

But, the biggest thing we have not accomplished — but we will get there someday, in one way or another — is the concept of wealth and money. In Utopia, money does not exist, and, as More explains it in the book, money, where it exists, only reflects the society behind the curtain — a yet another elaborative scheme of the rich envisioned to prolong the slavery and the misery of the poor, securing their own position at the top. He ignores the possibility that having "wage slavery"/ "stick and carrot approach" was the only way we could imagine to guarantee ourselves constant progress and advancement.

With the advancement of AI and automation, it is just a question of time when we will be forced to rethink our current system. In a world where machines

---

ix   Play on words. In English, Utopia is pronounced exactly as Eutopia, but in Greek Εὐτοπία [Eutopiā], contains the prefix εὐ- [eu-], "good" and τόπος ("place") meaning "good-place".

are the only slaves, and people are not, we will need to find a new, more meaningful purpose for ourselves.

Knowing all that, we must ask why people so often use the "Utopia argument" as a derogative way to dismiss any future discussion about a new system?

If we rule out the obvious issue of cognitive limitation, which does not allow a person to understand the benefits of new things, even when evidences are clearly outlined, we can highlight following:

- **Emotional acceptance** – Being afraid of anything new, a person would rather sacrifice the chance of having something better for the sake of what is already there and known. Everything known is good, and everything new is bad.

- **Power of habit** – living too long under certain circumstances can affect both adaptability and the willingness to adapt to new situations. This is similar to people who spent too long in prison and do not like being in the outside world.

- **Obedience** – absolute submission to authority without questioning (drone effect).

- **Ignorance** – a person makes conclusions without the necessary knowledge about the subject. Often, ignorance comes as a choice or as a consequence of the lack of will to learn and understand new concepts.

- **Self-Interest** – a person is choosing deliberately to ignore what they know, in exchange for gain. Self-interest does not need to come always as monetary gain; it can also come as a personal satisfaction from wining petty debate points by undermining serious discussion.

In a discussion about Universal Basic Income, now and then, someone will pull the "Utopia card," implying that UBI is an attempt to create a perfect society. Now, as explained earlier, a perfect society does not exist, even when we reach the stage of a "Star Trek" society,[161] or Type III civilization on Kardashev scale,[162] where every possible job that can be imagined will be done by machines; being humans, we will still find ways to be miserable and unhappy. Like many rich people are unhappy, despite the fact that they have material wealth enough to sustain entire countries.

Basic Income is not a perfect solution, and it will not solve all of our problems, but it is better than what we have now, and it is step in the right direction. If we are willing to try new things, along the way, we will find something better. In an advancing society, every solution should be just a temporary solution, and it should be used until we adjust to the future society that will come through a process of research and new discoveries.

Speaking of Basic Income, the biggest question is how to implement it in realistic way without causing additional issues, and there are already many ways to do it — one of which is Basic Tax Control.

Will the future society be a Utopia (non-existing)? Well, if we do not do something terribly wrong, probably not.

Will it be a perfect society? Most definitely not!

Being human means to have issues, and the nature of interaction with other sentient beings always has its own challenges. There are always differences of contexts, ideas, and opinions.

Even when we are on our own, we tend to suffer, and, often, our emotional suffering is what builds our character. Many famous and successful people said that they are who they are because of the mortal toil they have suffered. In that sense, suffering will be here to stay with us, at least for a while.

Only when we get to the point where everyone has the same knowledge and acts in the same ways we can discuss the possibility of a society without any issues. That is also the point where individuality ceases to exist. Just as the Borg in "Star Trek" all became one, if humans start sharing consciousness on larger scale — becoming one larger, unified mind — we would also become similar to God(s), which would logically lead to the disappearance of society. So, basically, a society without issues is a non-existing society.*[163] Some may refer to this point in time and development of the species as a **singularity**.

We should stop using the word "utopia" or any word in that sense, especially in the context of something impossible to reach. The future has already surprised us multiple times and probably will continue to surprise us. When someone tells you that something is a childish dream, just wait a bit, give it a few years, and then ask him/her to tell you that again.

The fallacy of the "It never happened ..." argument

Zeitgeist nowadays is not an easy thing to keep up with. All the information flowing around about technical unemployment, automation, Artificial Intelligence, genetic engineering, the possibility of a nuclear war, singularity, curing aging, the future political system, fusion, and many, many more just do not make things any easier.

As expected, now and then, there are debates. They are usually very shallow, but, again, we cannot complain — at least there is something, and something is definitely better than nothing.

And, in almost every one of these futuristic debates, there is an argument: "It never happened in history, and that is the reason it will not happen." Even more disturbing is that this type of the argument is coming from the mouths of well-educated people: famous philosophers, thinkers, people who have a proven technology background.

Every time I hear that argument, I start constructing a scenario in my head — one in which those debaters, similarly to politicians, are not on opposite sides, but, instead, they are on the same side trying to create a "fake" debate — in order to gain popularity, fame, or just to prepare people for what is coming next — gently trying to check the pulse of the masses.

Why "It never happened (before)..." is not an argument?

Several reasons:

- **We never had cars, but we have them now.**
  Before 1768, when the first steam-powered automobile capable of human transportation was built by Nicolas-Joseph Cugnot, people thought it would be impossible to have a carriage without horses or some other animal.
- **We never had aircrafts, but we have them now.**
  Before December 17, 1903, when brothers Wilbur and Orville Wright made their first flight, people were saying that it would be impossible to

fly a machine, but it did happen, and — even more amazingly — we are now flying metal airplanes with hundreds of people in them.

- **We never had satellites, but we have them now.**
  Before October 4, 1957, when Sputnik I was lunched, people also though that it would be impossible to keep the object in space, but we have done that also.

THEY SAID

It will never work ...

- **We never had metal boats, but we have them now.**
- **We never had phones, but we have them now.**
- **We never had television sets, but we have them now.**
- **We never had computers, but we have them now.**

This list goes on and on and on ...

Probably 90% and more of the things we have now did not exist 200 years ago. If we go back in history, just few thousand years ago — which, for our universe, is just a blink of an eye — we will find out that we have not had many things to begin with.

As a general rule of thumb, if we are not talking about violations of fundamental laws of physics, and if it is more or less an engineering problem — or the matter of human behavior — do not use the "It never happened..." argument.

Creating an animal with two heads by genetic engineering or having a human being with three hands could be possible; having bacteria that will produce electricity or recycle nuclear waste by "eating" it, is also probably possible.

What about Artificial Intelligence or longevity?
For any problems that looks a bit harder to solve, we need to just remember one thing and ask one question: Is there something in nature that can think and have consciousness, or is there a creature that can live for a very long time? If the answer is yes, then it is possible.

Nature has created us, and we are living, breathing machines. If we can think, there is probably something else that can think too. That being said, we can probably create something that can think similar to the way we can.

In terms of longevity, there are many species that live longer than humans. Giant Tortoises can live up to 250 years, and a Bowhead Whale can live up to 170 years. What's even more amazing is that there are living beings like "immortal jellyfish" that can revert to its youngest age when forced with stressors — basically being able to live forever.

Regarding human behaviors, such as unemployment, wars, human extinction, and many others — are subjected to the same principle.

"It never happened..." is not a valid argument, and no one should use it as such. If people need an opposing argument, they should find a better one.

It is wrong to judge the future by asking "how" and then if we get a negative answer for the present-day, draw a conclusion that whatever we are talking about is never going to happen, as it is impossible. Predicting the future is not a question of "how" but rather of "when." With time, "when" for many questions we are asking now, will turn to "how," therefore making the impossible possible.

Currently, we all look at our world through a very long peephole, and we see only one small part of a very large picture. We all have different ideas on how things work and how they should work. Maybe, instead of trying to persuade people to follow the small part we can see trough our personal lenses, it would be better if we would share our pieces, cooperate, and create something that will eventually be better for all of us.

Solving the puzzle

For a long time I believed that logic was the only thing you needed in order to know or apply something.

But somewhere along the line, I have learned that sometimes even when we know something, even when we know every aspect of it by heart; we have nothing but a passive knowledge of it. It is there, somewhere in your brain, as a fact - resident but completely dormant. It's like a piece of a jigsaw puzzle left forgotten under the child's bed.

In order to solve the puzzle, you will need that part. You will need to find it again - and very often it will be right under your nose. To fit that piece into the puzzle, you have to look at all the pieces from different angles, you have to turn them upside down, and you have to think where they might fit - if anywhere at all.

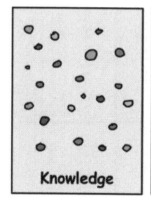 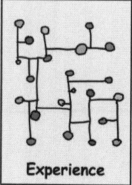 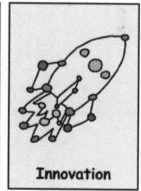

This can be hard, exhausting and tedious. Sometimes, just to get the motivation to start looking, you will need to be given a push. To become an explorer, you need to have a pinch of curiosity, a pinch of childishness, a pinch of love and the desire to solve problems - simply to keep you moving forward. At the end, once when you slot that piece into place of the puzzle, you will - depending on how large a chunk of the puzzle you have now completed - be rewarded with that "Ahhhhhhh !" feeling.

The truth is that we all share the same puzzle. And we all have elusive pieces. So in order to solve the puzzle, we need to exchange our pieces, we have to share.

There is no need to be shy; share your piece of the puzzle, even if you think it is worthless. That piece might well be someone else's most important one or the one that can create a better future for all of us.

Changing perspective

We live in the most abundant period in history and still we are constantly afraid, afraid that there won't be enough for all of us. A third of the planet's population is overweight, another third is malnourished, and all that while we waste 30% of the food we make – on top of this, we still think there is not enough food for everyone. In a world where so many people think that there is not enough, it does not come as surprise that there will be fights for resources from time to time...

Do we collectively suffer from "tunnel vision"?

We stayed nailed to what is in front of us for so long that we have created our reality around what we can see just in our nearby proximity. Our distorted reality shaped our hopeless beliefs that nothing can be changed and that the only tool we have left is to endlessly complain about the unfairness of our lives.

It's similar to the stories about people dying of thirst at the sea — being surrounded by water entire time. Yes, I know it is salty, but it is still water; how complicated can it be to create a mini reverse osmosis pump!?

Isn't it, in a way, ironic that we live on a finite planet where we have to struggle for things, but at the same time we live inside of infinite space with an infinite amount of resources?

The only thing we need to do is to ask ourselves a few simple "how to" questions:

- How to build better tools
- How to get there
- How to best use those resources

With enough effort, and with time, after numerous failures and things we are going to learn, we will get there.

For most of us, currently, our horizon is limited by buildings or by the blueness of the sky. What would happen, if we change that perspective?

Don't get me wrong: there is nothing bad about our blue sky and I agree it is beautiful. But, even the most beautiful bird cage, made of gold and diamonds, is still just a cage — a prison.

Every egg goes through the same process: it goes through the embryo phase and infancy, and then, the chick hatches, in order to become something more; otherwise, if the bird stays inside of the egg longer than it should – it will die.

From time to time, when sky is clear, raise your eyes up from the horizon and gaze into the starry night. There is our future. That is the horizon we should strive for, unlimited places with unlimited possibilities, where there is enough room for everyone, and enough resources for every possible dream you can imagine.

Og Mandino once wrote the following: "Is it not better to aim my spear at the moon and strike only an eagle than to aim my spear at the eagle and strike only a rock?" [164] American motivation speaker Les Brown [165] said something we can relate to even more: "Shoot for the moon. Even if you miss, you'll land among the stars."

We should not limit our dreams; we should strive toward infinity; and one day, we will become one with it.

Control by design

When we talk about controlling human behavior, what we usually have in mind are rules and laws. On a day-to-day basis, there is a control going on that is largely not described as such and mostly goes unnoticed: it is **control imposed by design**.

Our body, physical reality, and everything around us shape our internal world. The way we behave, act, and think largely is due to the things that are around us. By learning to use them, they have changed us.

Think about any object you are using frequently and ask yourself: Could this look differently, and what would happen if it did?

Take, for instance, a spoon. It precisely controls the size of the liquid you can take; if you try to take more, it will not let you. How you handle the spoon is also inbuilt; most of us learned to use it at a very young age.

Unlike the rules and laws, there is no arguing about physical reality. You can argue with a fire as much as you like, but, if you extend your finger toward it, it will bite you. With fire, there is no negotiation; it is just there, it does not understand, and it does not think. It just does its thing.

Everything we learn, in some peculiar way, changes us. We are becoming slaves to it. You and I, we are slaves to letters and grammar. If you want to convey a message to another person, and if you want to be understood, you have to shape your mind and your will to bend around established system and use it the way others, you are trying to communicate, do.

Language and writing systems do make up a large portion of who we are, but what about those other, smaller things you are not even noticing? Take, as example, widely-adopted Internet platforms. Each of them created a niche market by creating their own unique product. And you, you have bent around that product. That product has changed you and your life.

Take Twitter, for instance, and its famous limit of 140 characters. The company was formed in 2006; at the time, smartphones, as we know them today, did not exist. The idea to send a short message you can later review on a web portal was interesting, and the 140-character limit was set largely due to SMS compatibility reasons. Although the first smartphones arrived one year later, with the ability to connect to WiFi, Bluetooth, or mobile Internet, the 140-character limit has remained as the product's unique feature and has not changed since.

Now, the question is what has that done for you — or rather, to you — or to people who are widely using it?

Some researchers are saying that our sentences became shorter and that many rules of grammar and spelling often are avoided, in order to satisfy the 140-character limit. Although many have become more creative with this needless skill, at the same time, their writing skills declined as a result of frequent usage.

Think about it: the 140-character limit was the limit of some antiquated technology; back then, we did not have the technological capability to transfer more. Now, it is just an arbitrary number, a limit without any justifiable reason. But, some people would rather "die" protecting this rule than accept the possibility of change. It seems we would rather change the way we speak, create sentences, and form our grammar rules than change an arbitrary rule that was designed because of technical limit.

Similar things are all around us. Most of the keyboards in the world are QWERTY. The interesting about it is that, at the time typing machines were invented, the typing speed of some machines was causing frequent jamming of some letters, such as "A" letter. In order to fix this issue, typewriter manufacturers decided to put the letter "A" to correspond to our little finger, which is physically not as responsive as the index finger. Although there is no any possible reason to keep this rule, we are still doing it, and most of our computer keyboards have the same key alignment.

In a political and economic sense, at one point, we said that GDP is the main indicator for how well one country provides for its citizens, and someone else added that growth is the most important. We adjusted our game around this principle, and we indulged everything to that idea, but the effects are far from desired. We have seen detrimental effects on the environment, we have seen countless issues with infinite growth, and we have seen economic crises as the direct result of this rule, but people keep preaching how important the concept of economic growth is.

Now, what does this mean?

Does this mean that every type of control by design will always have negative effects?

Well, there are no negative or positive effects, there are just effects and side effects, and it is largely determined by how we design our tools and systems.

It is possible to design things with equally good and bad influence on us.

Take the bed, for instance: every human being will spend at least 1/3 of his life sleeping, and as it is that much, we care to have the most comfortable feeling we can get. So, the real important change in bed design has happened with raising beds off the ground to avoid drafts, dirt, and pests. This also had an impact on how we get up from the bed, because many are now at knee height; it is significantly easier to get up. But, easier does not always mean better. Researchers have discovered that people who exercise more and move more live longer. In Japan, where the aging population is on the rise, they are redesigning houses to be uncomfortable; each movement is an additional workout and requires bit of effort, forcing elderly people to exercise while carrying out simple, daily household tasks. Having traditional Japanese mattresses, instead of a bed — makes people exercise, a bit more than they would usually do. Researchers found that this change is enough to make people healthier and improve their well-being.

We are bad with tasks that require discipline in the long-term. So, instead of changing ourselves, it is possible to change our environment in such a way that will "nudge" us to a positive action. By accepting that people are bad at certain things, we are left with the option of solving problems without the need to ask people to change their behavior.

Just as we have the understanding that it is not very smart to walk in the middle of the highway, we can also build a system which will create constant reminders by its design. Any web or mobile application does the same, it gives you a user-friendly environment that is easy and enjoyable to use, but you can do only things the creators provided for you. Despite the fact that you cannot do everything you may desire, you will still use it and be happy about it.

A good example is speeding while driving. We know that many humans generally have bad driving skills, often driving faster than it is allowed in certain road sections, without any awareness that they are doing it. Instead of forcing people to stop speeding with rules, laws, tickets, and punishment, we could avoid this entire issue by creating a network of traffic stations that would communicate with cars and limit speeds without human intervention. Humans will still have the ability to steer the wheel, to brake until the car stops, or choose to drive slower or faster, but they could only reach the maximum speed that is limited by that particular road section.

With a few additional precautions, for those who would like to block or disable their speed-limiting devices, this approach would work much better than any law or policing available.

Why don't we see any similar system in the real world?

Although it is very simple and technologically easy to build, for someone those fines are a source of income, and they do not want to give up that source of income. This leads to the conclusion that most of the issues we face on a global scale have the same cause: we still think in terms of money, instead in the terms of solving real issues.

For one person to change his or her negative habits, it takes a lot of time and also requires a big change in attitude and personality. Changing the habits of large populations by preaching or advising is an almost impossible task, although, sometimes, that is exactly what we need.

Take, for instance, the excessive consumption of red meat: one person could change this habit by experiencing a need for significant change but, for most people, changing habits would require a different approach.

To change the behavior of the population, we would need to change the system and incorporate change by design.

By creating production caps and import caps on certain products, and also significantly increasing the prices of those products, we could combat our daily habits.

It is also interesting to mention that, when people are scared, they will eagerly change their habits. In a few occasions of salmonella, swine flu, and mad-cow disease, for instance, this lead to notable drop in meat consumption. Although I am not in favor of producing those effects deliberately or artificially, I must notice that the effects, from sociological perspective, are indeed very interesting.

There are many examples of solutions by design, and how — by changing small things — it is possible to change the system. For instance in the city of Milan they conducted a study where they use a schema for paying people to cycle to work in order to fight traffic congestions and air pollution *[166]; in Sweden, they solved the congestion problem by taxing people who drive during peak hours.*[167] And recently, in Washington, DC, they decided to try out a new schema where they pay criminals to avoid crime. The results are largely speculative and are yet to be seen.

The current system is largely governed by money, profit and the way how and where money flows; if that would change the game would change as well.

Redefining the system toward quality, instead of arbitrary economic growth numbers, would require a significant shift in thinking. Imagine world where everyone would compete to make our lives better. Redefining goals toward a world where all people have decent homes, clean water, and healthy food (without usage of GMO or dangerous pesticides and herbicides) may look like a far fetch dream, but, if we put our minds to work, there are no goals we cannot reach.

We need to constantly remind ourselves that what is good for nature is also good for us, and what is good for our current economy is not overly important. In the sense that if we lose the planet's biosphere, the economy, as we know it, will vanish along with us.

If we want to make changes in large and complex social systems, bearing in mind that any system has a tendency to resist change, we will need to make a shift from traditional thinking in terms of laws and policies — toward control and management established by design.

Control by design – examples

The fundamental issue with trying to change human behavior by rules and laws is that it is not effective, simply because laws and regulations are currently so big that even those who study law do not know them all by heart. Regarding the rest of us, there is a high probability that we will never read any law book during our lifetimes, even if there were a significantly smaller number of these laws. A good example is the Bible: although many people will claim that they are Christians, there is a high percent among them which does not know what the 10 commandments are, and an even higher percent of those who never read the Bible — especially not all of it.

Additionally, the issue is that, even when we know what the laws are and what the punitive measures are for not obeying the law, a certain percent of people will still disobey. The reason can be as simple as believing you can get away with breaking the law, or, maybe, the circumstances of their lives are such that, despite being aware of the consequences, they are simply forced to commit a crime.

The reason why laws and rules do not work to the desired extent is because the relation between human beings, laws, and punishment is not organic enough. Humans have to spend time reading, learning, remembering, and recalling laws in any instance; it all requires mental effort. For most people, major rules are interwoven in their thoughts from an early age through their upbringing, when the sense of right and wrong is imprinted in the core of a person's being, and feelings of justice, fairness, love, and fear of punishment can push those rules into a higher level of mind we call "conscience," which lingers above all our thoughts, weighing all of our actions and determining what is right or wrong.

The issue is that there is a huge number of people on the planet, and we do not have the same upbringing, and, even if we had, there is no possible way we can all know or remember the content of those huge law books.

In order to impact or change human behavior in a positive way, there is a better approach: by shaping our world in such a way that the surroundings will impact our behavior and we will learn organically, without noticing or investing any significant effort. By repeating something multiple times, a habit will form and stay with us for a very long time.

The best way to show behavioral control by design is to give a few examples:

Spoon

Imagine that someone has an issue of eating soup with large gulps, and that we, out of safety and health reasons, need to teach the person to take smaller "bites." If someone tries to ask/tell/order the person to take smaller bites, depending on personality, that approach will probably fail, even when the "command" has been repeated several times. Furthermore, this process will risk frustration and annoyance on both sides equally.

A more effective solution would be just to give the person a smaller spoon, and the spoon size will regulate the maximum amount of liquid one can take with one sweep.

There is that joke: "If you want someone to lose weight, instead of a fork, give him chopsticks. If you want him to lose weight quickly, give him just one chopstick."

However, using a smaller spoon can cause the person to start grabbing food faster!

If that happens, a more advanced approach can be used: it would be possible to create an electronic spoon that will do the opposite of that "Smart Parkinson Spoon" *[168] — shaking and spilling the contents, if a person tries to eat too fast. In time, the person will learn to eat slower.

Doors

In the office where I worked once, there was a particular door where people went in and out, often forgetting to close the door behind them. The outside noise was affecting work performance and annoying those near the door. During winter days, this was additionally uncomfortable for those sitting at the desks near the door, as the cold breeze flowed over their legs.

People near the door started complaining, and, not long after, everything was raised to the manager's level. The manager, in his wisdom, sent an email to all of the employees, requesting everyone to be mindful about closing the doors. For the first few days, everything was working ok, except for the office guests, who did not know about the rule. After a few weeks, people started forgetting again, returning to old habits.

So, without the desired success, people next to the door decided to put a sign on both sides of the door: "PLEASE CLOSE THE DOOR." They tried experimenting with different red and yellow combinations of text and paper, but, at the end of the day, people were distracted, didn't notice, or didn't care.

At one point, the entire thing got so heated that people started arguing and shouting at each other. The janitor overheard, calmly went outside, and, within half an hour, came back with his toolbox and a door-closer-spring. After a few minutes, everything was installed, and the problem was gone forever, leaving the now somewhat confusing message "PLEASE CLOSE THE DOOR" where it was. On the other hand, the office people, in their surprise, were left thinking about how they spent so much time arguing over nothing.

Pavement

The goal of every park is to provide green surfaces we can enjoy, but, at the same time, allow us to move by paths that will be secure, dry, and clean (mud free) for our shoes during rainy or winter days.

Almost every park has lawns with paved paths crossing it, and yet, there are usually footpaths across the grass, trying to shorten distances, avoid obstacles, or simply create paths that are more comfortable or safer than the one offered by the existing pavement.

Usually, these cow paths (footpaths) are a sign of poor design or, ignorance of user needs.

Some advise that the best way to lay the pavements would be to first wait for pedestrians to create footpaths and then just pave over those in exactly the same place. But, builders often do not follow this advice.

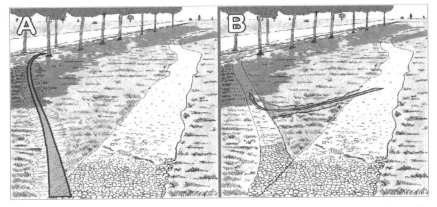

Sometimes, following that approach of building pavement over footpaths works, but often it does not. A few weeks after one pavement is laid down over the footpath, a new footpath will appear, creating a shortcut between two pavements. (B)

So, when design fails, people will try with laws, rules, commands, and polite messages, but that rarely works.

One of the ideas to prevent pedestrians walking over green surfaces would be to create a fence. A fence, high enough to create additional effort that feels like a jumping over, is a larger effort than staying on the track. At the same time, the fence must discourage attempts to sit on it, but a fence in a park must not have any type of spikes or open bars that could cause accidental injuries. Its only reason for existence is to prevent a majority of "users" from jumping over and making footpaths by constantly walking over the same path.

The fence must be adjusted for the type of user; what may pose an extra effort for the walker may not represent any significant obstacle for the runner. Runners, because they experience an additional stress on joints, usually prefer grass/dirt over concrete surfaces. So, a fence height above the knees may suffice for walkers, but, for runners, the fence needs to be raised to chest level or above. Keeping that in mind, at some point, there will be a gate/passage in the fence, and runners will use that passage, over time creating a footpath and destroying the grass in the process, as can be seen in the following image. Therefore, a fence is not a good solution, either.

Similar to runners, cyclists have specific needs that can impact green surfaces.

In the first image below, you can see the pavement with the gate installed on it. In order to avoid accidents on a potentially dangerous intersection with the main road, the designer built a gate, in order to slow down cyclists while making them more aware of traffic. But, a few months after, annoyed by the excessively difficult approach, cyclists created an alternative road, avoiding the obstacle completely.

In the third image, while building pavement for pedestrians, the road designers forgot to create slopes and gradients for cyclists. In the below example, the natural land fall was not too steep, so, an organic "footpath" was created, in order to avoid stairs, which would otherwise compel a cyclist to get off the bike and carry it, wherever stairs are erected.

By now, you have got the picture: a task that seemed very simple at the beginning now looks like a fairly complex piece of work.

In order to layout the pavement, the designer must take into account the following:

- What are the main goals?
- How much money is secured for the project?
- Who are the users? Pedestrians, runners, cyclists, and who else? We need to think about different age groups and how they behave. Children will not behave in the park in the same way as old people, for instance.
- What is the configuration of the terrain? Is it dirt or rock? Is the terrain flat or with hills and gradients? If the terrain is bumpy and hilly, how steep are those surfaces?
- What does the surrounding area look like? Are there any major roads? Is the park in the middle of the town or at the edge?
- What about weather conditions? What can appear to someone as a beautiful, marble surface on summer days can become a slippery "death trap" on winter days.
- Are there any other conditions that can impact structure? Earthquakes, land acidity, landslides...

At this point, you probably are thinking, "Wait a minute. Isn't that a bit too much? We are not building pyramids here; we are building simple pavement."

That is the point: if you want to create a good solution, even when what you are designing (in its appearance) looks like a very simple thing; it may possess a challenge equal to some proportionally much larger project.

Over time, we have built technology that, generally speaking, does not cooperate very well with nature, and, as we simplify the problems too much, we usually end up with solutions that do not work or are not fit for many user groups.

If we go back to the original requirements, we can see that the end goal is to allow nature (grass) to coexist with people during the entire year. Nature requires land, water, sun, and a stress-free environment. Humans enjoy being in nature, but they also require commodity.

In the above photos, you can see that it is possible to make concrete pavement in such a way that it would have patches of grass inside. In that way, the total amount of grass would be increased by almost half over surfaces where, otherwise, there would be a single sheet of concrete, tiles, bricks, or bitumen.

As we need to take into account cyclists and runners next to this road, a porous, rubber-coated concrete should be put in place.*[169] The rubber coating would have a positive impact on runners' joints, and the porosity of material and material inertia would allow for a dry road and pleasant usage. At the same time, the water collected could be used for irrigation of plants, trees, and grass in the park.

When a solution is designed in a way that fits most of the users' needs, everyone will conform to the desired behavior without any additional external input, rules, or laws, in order to protect the green surfaces.

Designing an appropriate solution like this comes with a price, in the form of mental effort necessary to find the solution, and it can come with bit higher price tag, but that is not a rule; sometimes, "behavioral control by design" solutions can come in very simple and yet effective forms.

After a cost analysis study of building and maintaining park pavements, a nearby council decided that the best option for the time being would be to actually remove existing, worn out pavements and put a layer of sand and new grass above. Over time, people will create new footpaths, and then they will just pave the gravel over it in places where mud usually forms. They concluded that, sometimes, the optimal solution is just to leave things as they are and act upon "problems" as they arise.

I personally may not agree with their decision, but, in some way, this resembles a traffic experiment conducted in the German town of Bohmte *[170] and Portishead *[171], a coastal town in England. The highway code has been abolished, in order to create a common code for car drivers, cyclists, and pedestrians. This type of urban design is called "Shared Space" *[172] and aims to minimize the segregation of pedestrians and vehicles by removing features such as curbs, road surface markings, traffic signs, and traffic lights. As the follow-up study showed, although it looks chaotic, this schema actually significantly improved safety on the roads.

Cars

Humans are terrible drivers, not just because of the huge number of car accidents and yearly deaths as result, but also because human overall driving skills are very poor: short attention span and slow reaction time, combined with intersections, can quickly lead to dis-coordination and traffic jams. Even when we have decent driving skills, our social driving skills and how we behave in relation to other drivers are at a very low level, frequently causing combined traffic effects like jams, gridlocks, phantom intersections, and traffic snakes.

This urban traffic congestion, in return, is causing stress, accidents, traffic delays, and, above all, increased consumption of petrol; therefore, they add to cars' inefficiency and global warming.

Most of these issues are caused simply because the cars in front suddenly brake for no apparent reason. This type of behavior can cause traffic jams that are sometimes several miles long and can be caused just by one person braking too hard.

Usually, the underlying cause of this is travelling too close to the vehicle in front or driving much slower or faster than everyone else.*[173]

What could be a fix for this type of problem?

It would be possible to make traffic jams less likely, if drivers would change the way they drive. The goal for each driver would be to stay the same distance from the car ahead as from the car behind at all times. Now, somehow, we would need to inform each driver about this and also make them all aware, educate them, and, in the end, as it is a question of changing human behavior on a grand scale, it would probably fail.

If we do not have any type of systematic approach that would reinforce the learning process, this type of solution is destined to fail.

What other options do we have?

We could create sensors that will warn us whenever we tailgate the vehicle in front of us, or the car behind us gets to close. And we could make a law that would demand that each car install these sensors, but, at the end of day, it is again on how humans drive and what is their awareness, attention span, and reaction time.

So, what is the final solution?

The best solution would be to use control by design, removing the problem at its root, and that is where self-driving cars come in, removing the root cause of this problem: human drivers.

Without drivers, there would not be traffic jams; if machines would take over; they would drive more precisely, they could keep perfect distance, they would talk to each other, and they would not need traffic lights.
They could slow down and accelerate precisely, navigate to accommodate optimal routes, and do all that in order to satisfy the best interest of the collective. More self-driving cars there on the road, means the more efficient those roads will be.

Self-driving robot cars also never get tired, they do not get sleepy, they do not have emotional problems, they do not lose attention over SMS messages or phone calls, they do not get drunk or do drugs — all that plus more makes them more secure and a better choice for traffic solutions than any of the human beings will ever be.

Or, as author of the CGP Grey video "The Simple Solution to Traffic" says as a conclusion of his funny but serious video, "So, the real, simple solution to traffic is no more monkeys driving cars." *[174]

Although it is not as simple as they say, because the self-driving car solution still have many technical challenges, recent progress in this technology shows that those challenges are nothing we cannot overcome.

Economy

The last example is a thought experiment; you will need to think about the questions below and what impact each has on you or on the society around you:

- Is credit borrowing a good or bad thing?
- What would happen, if there was no interest on borrowed money?
- Banks charge almost double the amount of money you borrow, but the bank does not pay you anywhere near this amount of interest for the money you keep in the bank; would it be possible to do this differently?
- Is it possible to regulate this to be better for common people, and, if so, how?
- What would happen if there was no requirement to pay equal mortgage installments each month?
- What would happen if houses were not taken away, when people miss a few installments?
- Can you imagine a different mortgage system that is fairer?
- What would happen if there was no inflation?

How to build a new game

In order to end repetition of the cycle, we need a new type of game.

Saying that "history repeats itself" is not completely true, at least not in one specific segment; every cycle we experience is stronger, more advanced and potentially more damaging. That is also the reason we need a new type of game more than ever before. Otherwise, the next cycle may lack players.

So, the question is: How do we make this new type of game?

First, we need to set a goal. Let's ask ourselves what will be the main goal from which majority of people will benefit.

- The majority of people must be winners.

How will players know they are winning?

- It is similar to the idea that when you are healthy you do not think about it. Only when you get sick you realize what being healthy means.
- The best answer here is that if people die happy with a sense of purpose and with peace in their hearts, they have won.

How will they get to the winning stage?

- As in any game, players will need to complete secondary goals.

What will the secondary goals be?

- Protect and spread life
- Help others
- Learn why playing
- Learn while playing
- Resolve obstacles

What will the obstacles in the new game be? What are typical obstacles in this world?

- Lack of energy, food, love, compassion, fun, etc.
- Emerging diseases, imbalances in nature, overpopulation
- Pollution, dying species
- And so on

Who will be the losers?

- Those who decide to play against themselves

How long will this game last?

- Maybe an entire lifetime, maybe generations or maybe it won't end; after all, we are trying to escape the 'chains of cycles'.

What will be the main winning strategies?

- Networking
- Cooperation
- Development of intelligent but ethical solutions
- Sharing
- Socializing
- Helping others
- ... and maybe you know something else you think it will work?

Although I refer to the word 'winning', this can be understood purely as an abstract concept. The concept of winning exists because we still think in terms of the knowledge imprinted in us.

The concept of this new game is more in terms of a thriving tree, which spreads its branches and explores the world. Winning, in this context, is just a word used to explain the tree's fruitful life and its ability to fulfill its purpose, which it already does all the time.

In order to build a new game or change the old one, we have to understand the internal physics and the problems of the system we have now, and then design a system or an upgrade that will tackle as many as possible of the problems we currently have.

The Qin Shi Huang or the First Emperor of Qin (China in 227 BC), in one scene of what are probably imaginary events depicted in the movie Hero [x] [175], comes to a realization on what is the true meaning behind the scroll created by the villain Broken Sword. As he explains, the scroll says that in the first stage of a skillful warrior, man and sword become one with each other. There, even a

---

[x]   Interesting thing is that in Chinese word "hero" is written with two words "Ying xiong" which can be literally translated into "should endure (bare)," meaning that their understanding is not just that hero "is not person that should be admired for their courage and outstanding achievements," but the ability to endure and overcome suffering.

blade of grass can be used as a lethal weapon. In the next stage, the sword resides not in the hand, but in the heart. Even without a weapon, the warrior can slay his enemy from a hundred paces. But, the ultimate ideal is when the sword disappears altogether. **The warrior embraces all around him. The desire to kill no longer exists.** Only peace remains. Therefore, a warrior's ultimate act is to lay down his sword.

In the same way, relative to our system, when we achieve enough wisdom, we will see that everything around us is there to help us, and that we can indeed use it in order to live in peace with one another.

In the very beginning of this book, I mentioned the Sheikh's riddle "The Slowest Race," where a wise man, by saying the simple advice to "change horses" completely changed their (human) behavior from crawling to racing their "new" horses – is the leitmotif of this book. It is a notation that – instead of spending huge amounts of time forcing, educating, psychologically indoctrinating, and brainwashing people's minds to change their behavior – we can simply change the system in such way that people will not even notice a change but will start racing for a better environment and better life on and beyond this planet.

Basic Tax Control has the same goal: to change human behavior in a positive way by **changing the system first**, and, if the system is designed in correct way, being naturally adaptive, people will adapt to new circumstances for the better without noticing that they behave in a different way.

Both Basic Tax Control and Universal Basic Income are envisioned as systems that should fit all, regardless of age, race, gander, wealth, or position in society. These are the systems that will help us get out of the psychological cage we have created, and help us overcome our "work necessity" fixation by letting go and allowing us time to adjust to new circumstances, so we can find a new purpose/meaning in life.

Living in a transition time will not be without issues; just as our current society is not without issues, the future, moneyless society will not be without issues, but we have to learn to live with them and deal with them as they arise, the same we have always done.

Potential issues should not stop us from trying, as, without trying, we will never know what could be the issues or potential gains. Only by designing and implementing a new game will we be able to create a road map that could be reused later.

By using everything and everyone available, applying what we have learned to this point and allowing people to self-organize, we can create a better, much fairer game.

In today's circumstances, is it possible to design a "new game"?

Imagine the world as a randomly scattered image of pixels with different colors. The image on its own has some complexity, and, also, each color has a value, but we have the ability to reorder them as we like. We can leave them as they are or align them in gradients and groups of colors, or we could align them in, for us, more meaningful pictures of mountain ranges, portraits, or mandalas. What is apparently a chaos of colorful pixels hides unlimited numbers of hidden images, and we are the ones to decide what kind of picture we are going to create from that randomness; we are the ones who can find harmony in that complexity. Everything is already there, we just need to align the pieces in the desired way.

Just as we can decide what we want to build from random pixels, we can decide what we want from our future. In every moment, we have the power to create something, make things even more chaotic, or simply leave things as they are.

And yes, it is true: despite all the good things, some people may be against a moneyless society that would provide resources without any attachments. Also, it is possible that the same people, by any means, may try to stop the efforts of the majority to get to that stage of development. And maybe it is the truth that they could start a new war, like many wars that have been already fought over oil or other resources.

So, it is necessary to constantly remind ourselves, rich or poor, president or peasant, that, if we start another World War, regardless of how safe and deep someone may think his underground bunker is, it will not protect him.

Regarding the future society, we do not have many options to choose from — just one, and that is this: either we will learn to live together as brothers, or we will perish together as fools. *[176]

Part IV
Visualizing the future

Robots and work

The new industrial revolution – where machines, artificial intelligence, and automation are creating a huge disruption in the job market – is filling news sites with headlines that spread fears and worries about the uncertain future of work.

Robots and algorithms will make many occupations obsolete, leaving millions of people without jobs. For the first time in history, industry is not creating near enough new jobs to meet the number of jobs that will be lost. As a result, a huge number of people will be pushed into poverty, causing massive unrest.

Recent developments in narrow AI (artificial intelligence),*[177] especially in healthcare *[178] and transport industries, *[179] threaten millions of jobs.

Is this a problem?

It all depends on perspective. Two stories that follow are fictional representations of what can be our world in the not-so-distant future. Each story will have a different outcome, and, although many concepts in those stories are simplified, we are not very far from either of those societies.

"Was" village

In some faraway world, there was a small village, a home for a population of around a hundred people, situated on the hill near a beautiful valley with a small river lazily passing though its center. It looks at a valley gently tucked in by the surrounding woods — a home for abundant wild life.

The entire village made their living growing their own apples and everything else those trees could offer.

One day, one villager got a very clever idea. Instead of growing apples in the villagers' individual gardens, why not plant a community apple orchard in the nearby valley? This would be more efficient and they could grow more apples by working less. However, he kept his idea for himself.

Instead, he formed a company and said, "Come and work for me. You will work less and take more apples home."

He did not lie. Jobs became more specialized. Every apple tree needed care; watering, soil tilling and raking, pruning, and when ripe — apple picking. Then, when trees were dead or old and needed cutting, there was a job for that. Each job had dedicated people who knew how to do their jobs better than anyone else. No single person had to do everything as they had when they were working for themselves.

Working on their own, no single person could produce more than 100 apples, but with this setup they were producing 170 apples each. As promised, the owner gave them 150 apples each, and kept only 20 apples for himself from each person's yield. Everyone was happy since they were taking home so much more. After each harvest, the owner invested all of his apples into buying land from his workers, with the ultimate goal of extending his orchard and increasing production.

After expanding his land and planting new trees, the owner said to himself, "I could probably do even more." And he spent a lot of time planning how to do it. One day, during his hunting trip through the surrounding woods, he got an idea. "All this land is covered with wild woods. They do not have any fruits, so they are useless. If I chop them down I can expand my orchards." Soon after, the surrounding woods began shrinking due to the collective efforts of all the wood cutters.

While the owner extended his land as much as he could, the land where the wild woods once proudly stood was not as fertile as the one in the valley, so many parts of the now naked land could not grow apple trees, and as land eroded, it could not regrow the wild woods either.

The owner was not bothered by this too much. However, slightly distracted by this setback, he turned his mind toward optimizing production, as he knew things could always be done faster.

At this time, none of villagers owned their own land anymore, but they were happy since the owner had increased their "salaries" by giving every person 250 apples to take home after each harvest. Even though the company was producing 350 apples per each worker, no one was complaining and everyone was happy.

But now there was one problem. When the villagers had owned their own land and apple trees, for they would use the old ones for firewood. Now that they did not own any land or trees, and they need wood for the winter, so they asked their boss for advice. He said, "This is what we will do. Every time you need firewood, you will give me one of your apples back, and I will give you the firewood." And again they were happy. They could not spend as much as before, but after firewood costs, they were still earning an amazing 230 apples, so they were still happy.

While everyone was working, the owner had lots of free time on his hands, so he would invent lots of new things: apple pies, pickled apples, jams, marmalades, apple baskets, chandeliers, comfy seats and many other goodies. Other people wanted to try these new products and the owner simply said, "Same rule applies." Whenever they wanted one of the new products, they gave up more of their take-home apples.

But soon, the owner realized that even with all his free time, he could not meet the demand of the new products, so he created a small factory for more workers to be in charge of making his inventions. It was an amazing success.

After a few years the company was so productive that it was yielding 2700 apples per person. The workers remained happy, because all had their salaries had increased to a staggering 310 apples. That was three times as many they could ever produce on their own, although at this point they were working bit longer than before in order to keep up with the demand for all of the new inventions being produced at the factory. And being so successful, the factory grew.

And people were spending their earned apples to buy other products: pies, firewood, trunks, furniture...

The village grew, and people were happy, so they started their own families and many children were born. Many families had five or six children. The owner was happy too, since he knew that every newborn baby in the village would one day be a new worker in his orchard or factory too.

No one noticed the subtle change. While the owner's opportunities continued to grow, the villagers had less than a few. The first person to realize this was Ned, who was discharged because of few mistakes he made. Unable to afford anything, he soon found himself homeless — scavenging for any food he could get from whatever was left of the once wild woods. He could not find any other job as there were none on this side of the world. None of other villagers understood Ned; in fact they blamed him for his circumstances, saying that everything was probably his fault, and that hardship he was going through was an appropriate punishment for the mistakes he made.

Meanwhile, the owner was wondering about new ways to make even more. One day he got an idea. Why couldn't all of his workers live under the same roof? It would be more efficient, and they could spend more time providing work and less time traveling to work.

He liked that idea, so he convinced people that it would be cheaper if they lived together, since it would save them living expenses. The idea seemed reasonable, so they sold their houses and started renting flats from the building owned by their boss. Since their salaries were now 400 apples and rent was only 40, they were happy.

In the mean time, the boss employed some very smart kids and paid them double than any other worker. Their only task was to invent the most amazing things they could in order to increase apple production.

One day, one of the smart kids came to the owner with a plan to build a machine that could replace workers for apple picking. The boss thought about it. He knew that apple picking was a tough job to do, and he approved it. The machine was built, and soon, it turned out it was better than people. After the initial testing phase, the machine was approved, and almost all apple pickers were fired since they were not needed any more ... just a handful were left to take care of the machine.

For the discharged apple pickers everything that happened was too sudden. They wanted to work and do something else, but there weren't any other jobs. There was only one company in the village. After a few months, they were forced to live on the street as they no longer had any apples with which to pay the rent. Other workers, meeting former apple pickers on the street looking all tired and dirty, looked upon them with repulsion and disgust in their eyes, not willing to sympathize with their misfortune. They had little understanding that just in a few months, the same fate could strike them all.

Many of jobless, faced with starvation, turned to foraging, but food was quite scarce. Others turned to different means... Covered by the darkness of the night they started stealing from the orchard, and the most desperate turned to haphazard robberies, attacking those who still had their jobs.

After a while this became a serious problem, so the owner chose the strongest of his workers to protect his property and the workers. He gave them the power to use any means to stop those "evil beasts."

In time, new machines were introduced. New jobs were created and some of them were destroyed. But slowly, one by one, all jobs were obsolete, and most people were left out of jobs. Apple orchards were richer and fuller than ever before, but there was almost no one to use their products, and after initial storage, production came almost completely to a halt.

The only workers left in the company were the smartest kids and guards. On one side, there was excessive wealth for a few, while on other side, there was poverty and suffering. Everyone believed that no one should get anything for free, and in order to live, one should work. The boss didn't want to give them food without work and people didn't want his apples without working for him.

For few years, there was real struggle between guards and a huge mass of people who demanded that they had rights. Afraid of riots and angry masses, the smartest kids built machines to protect company from anyone not employed there. Unlike guards, machines haven't had harts, and unlike guards they haven't had sympathy or understanding for the suffering of the people. Above all, sentry machines were ruthless to perpetrators.

At this point, machines were taking care about everything, about orchard, about factory, even about themselves, they recorded everything and watched over everything. Small number of people that has left inside, became obsolete after one unfortunate glitch in programming. By forcing their masters out on the street, machines remained alone.

After a few months, those in need had spent all they had. The only option they had left was to scavenge garbage. But, that was not enough for everyone. Many of them went to what was left of the surrounding forest, but the forest could not save them, either, and, when winter came, this story was brought to an end.

"Can be" village

On the other side of the world, across the sea, there is another village. About one hundred people live there. They are a somewhat lazy bunch of folks, but they are a smart kind of lazy — while they do not like to work, they know that some work has to be done. They know they are lazy and they believe that being lazy is good thing, and are quite proud of their laziness. They know there is no shame in being lazy, but they also know there is no shame in doing any work.

In the beginning they all owned apple trees, but one day, one lazy but very smart kid came up with idea to join forces and to combine resources into one collectively owned apple orchard. He calculated that in this way, they would save time they used working, which meant more free time to enjoy their laziness. He decided to share his idea with others.

The first time the kid revealed his idea at one of the village meetings, villagers were, to say the least, confused. Slowly, after many questions, they began getting it, understanding the idea and what it meant for the village's productivity. Unanimously, they decided to give it a go, agreeing that they should share everything. They succeeded in creating a set of rules good enough for everyone, to ensure they would not fight about who was working when and how much. Every member was valued for his or her own merits and rightfully rewarded.

Because everyone had more free time, they started inventing new creative things in order to make their life easier and more comfortable — apple pies, marmalades, house furniture, toys... With every new thing they invented, they needed to either create a new job or teach other people how to do or make those same things on their own. They shared their knowledge without any cost; however, those who had knowledge were a bit annoyed at the fact that they were giving up their own free lazy time teaching others.

They all knew that they needed to contribute, but would occasionally have an argument when some of their laziest members did not want to contribute, and instead only wanted to enjoy.

People were not arguing and fighting much, but their usual reason for a fight or an argument was a boring or labor-intensive task like apple picking. So, one day, another very smart kid, who liked to learn and play, was so fed up with all the fights that he decided to make a machine to pick apples. He just wanted to end all those annoying fights so that he could get on with reading his books.

This kid was determined to succeed. He studied hard and worked with gadgets he invented to perfect his skills. After many hours spent in his garage and countless failures, he'd done it. He built the machine, and his apple picking machine worked beautifully.

When people saw that the machine was working, they were over their heads. They were so excited that they threw a huge party to celebrate the kid and his marvelous apple picking machine. For years, the machine was working flawlessly. Now and then, it needed a few repairs, but that was very rare.

Sadly, the kid, who was not a kid anymore, got very sick, and he could not maintain his machine anymore. Eventually, the machine stopped working. On that day, something important happened. People understood that one day the apple-picker maker would be gone, in the same way that everyone in the village would one day be. They got really worried and wondered who was going to fix his machine then.

Someone got an idea: why not ask the inventor to teach them everything he knew? While the inventor was still in his bed, they visited him and asked him if he would be willing to teach them. He was thrilled. The interest and enthusiasm shown by his fellow townspeople actually helped him to overcome his illness faster. As soon as he was on his feet again, he prepared a room with a few chairs and tables to teach whoever was interested in learning his craft. And that is the way the first school was born.

In this way, a new generation of inventors was created. They invented many new machines, even machines to fix the other machines. They were enjoying building machines; in fact, they had so much fun with it, they called it play. They never even considered that what they were doing was work.

Villagers realized that knowledge is important. They also realized something far more important — deep down inside, it was not the laziness they wanted the most, as laziness can quickly lead to boredom. Instead, what they wanted was a fun and exciting life, and in order to have more fun, you have to learn new things and open your horizons and explore.

The more time they could free up, the more time there was for everyone to learn, play and explore.

Understanding the difference between lazy and fun made a huge difference. They learned that people who were very lazy, were really just lacking fun in their lives, which slowly drifted to boredom. Most of the time, afraid to do new things, troubled by their emotions, blamed their environment and gradually became bored-sick. Boredom in the village was treated as a mental condition,*[180] an illness that needed to be overcome so that that person could live their life to their full potential. However, the only caveat was that the person needed to ask for the help first. They believe that any sentient being must have the right to express its own free will, unless that "will" jeopardizes other sentient beings. So, if someone deliberately wants to suffer, they let him be.

This realization, and many others, strengthened the emotional bonds between all the people of village, and they began to think of each other as the cells of one big organism. Even the small, occasional amount of work they needed to do, as machines were doing almost all the work now, was not difficult anymore. From that time forth, they believe that they can have fun with anything they do. Every action can be a reason for challenge, play and having fun. In everything they did, they realized, they could enjoy.

To this day, if one of the villagers has to do something repetitive, hard or boring (or in other words, "not fun"), but something that still needs to be done, they will think about inventing a new machine to do that work for them.

Nowadays, machines in the village are doing nearly all of the work, and villagers have more time to enjoy life in a different way. They spend their lives learning, exploring, having fun, and deciding what they are going to do in the future.

The distinguished members of society have a few more benefits than others, but the difference is not huge. Education is a large part of what allowed them to become who they are. Most of the time people chose on their own what they want to learn, although from time to time they may have been advised to pursue complementary courses of study in order to expand their points of view. After higher education, only an hour a day is organized, and after, they are free to do whatever else they want — on their own. More or less the education process is largely gamified, where people are entirely immersed in a learning environment and exposed to experiences that are very hard to forget.

Recent advances in technology and science allowed them to achieve miraculous things. Even learning is not hard anymore, especially for those who had issues with learning before. Thanks to nanobiology memory enhancers, which sped up the learning process, now in a single hour they can learn more than they could in thousands of hours before.

While machines took over their jobs, the villagers largely used their free time to explore all corners of their world. During one of these explorations, they stumbled across a strange country, where everything was rich and full and handled by machines. It was very much like their own corner of the world, but no one was there — no one except machines. The chronicles they found revealed that the last person who died was the richest of them all. They left the place as it was, to be a testimony for future generations for how things can go the wrong way with just a few bad decisions and attitudes.

At this very moment, as they have largely extended their lives to thousands of years, just for fun they exploring the unlimited wonders of the universe, and in its vastness they never get bored.

Moneyless world

By analyzing historical patterns and future trends, with confidence, we can conclude that, regardless of what many want to believe, soon, we will have a modern society without money. When I say no money, I mean that there won't be any type of credit calculation or quid pro quo merchandise exchange. This is not just a personal, intuitive hunch, but also a natural, logical, evolutionary step in our society that is unavoidable.

We are at tipping point, and it is almost certain that, with the pace at which we are going, we will live in either a "utopian" or dystopian society. Although I do not know whether it will turn into a world of abundance for all or a sadistic dream for a few and hell for everyone else, I can say that it will happen as a natural consequence of the technological advancement we are currently experiencing.

Think about it: one day, when everything we could possibly imagine gets produced by machines and tended to by machines, increasingly better than it could be ever possible by any human being, why would, in all that abundance, we need to have money at all?

One of the earliest thoughts about similar systems can be found in ideas about Technocracy, Sociocracy, and Cybersocialism,*[181] where computers were used to calculate how much work is necessary to satisfy the need for a certain commodity. In those systems, the central figure is still a human being. Without the need for human beings to carry out the work, money will disappear — along with all financial structures we have crated, in order to manage our economy efficiently.

Some of the people and ideas worth exploring are Robert Owens's idea of labor notes (labor vouchers) that suspend the usual means of exchange and the need for middlemen; Salvador Allende and his "Project Cybersyn;" Leonid

Kantorovich and his mathematical solution on how to best use equipment in the plant; and Sergey Lebedev's ideas advocating for cybernetic socialism.

Similar ideas are also almost stealthily woven inside of the "Star Trek" TV franchise, where earthlings of the future use replicators to satisfy all their material needs. Instead of seeking material wealth, global civilization has shifted its goals toward seeking new discoveries and new space frontiers, exploring the vastness of the unknown.

It seems, we are at a point in time where all futures coexist at the same time, and all of them are equally possible. At the same time, we are facing possible extinction, due to global climate change or nuclear annihilation, but also, at the same time, we are at the point where we can see future people living thousands of years, traveling through the vastness of space, and where machines do all manual and significant portions of intellectual jobs.

Currently we do not have many good ideas about how to organize our social structures in a society without money, being heavily addicted to life and society as we know it. In the meantime, until we, as society, psychologically mature for the change, we can try phasing out money slowly, by trying to learn how to live without it.

Basic Tax Control and Universal Basic Income may help us to bridge that gap, by creating structures where we would slowly adapt to a new system and transfer to a new society in the same way one would adopt a new piece of electronic equipment, changing while learning.

Setting the goal

The first step toward the new society is to imagine it. We collectively and each person on his or her own have to imagine a new way of life — life where money will not rule our world and navigate our daily decisions.

To get somewhere, first, you must imagine where you want to be, or, where you do not want to be. Although the latter will bring you somewhere, it is not certain where that will be.

Let's say you desire to travel somewhere; for instance, you would like to visit the France, and, while there, you would like to taste different wines and cheeses. It is very likely you will visit a few shops, wine cellars, or exquisite restaurants that serve those. Also, there are chances that you will see other things, but it is very likely, if you have not planned those, that you will miss the chance to see them. If you are following a trail of wines through Pays de la Loire, Centre, and Burgundy, there are good chances that, on your trip, you will not see Paris and the Eiffel Tower, for instance.

That being said, if you currently live in a country or a neighborhood where you are experiencing hardship, and you are trying to escape from those conditions, there are equal chances that, if you do not know where you are going, you may end up in equally bad or worse conditions. It is like the story about the Japanese man Tsutomu Yamaguchi, who survived the Hiroshima bombing and then decided to flee and take cover with his cousin at Nagasaki. Officially, he is recognized by the government of Japan as a survivor of both explosions. *[182]

Now, Mr. Yamaguchi, even with the best plan, could not predict what would happen at Nagasaki, and his story tells us that, sometime, regardless of what we decide, and regardless of how well we plan, the future can be uncertain. Of course, the fear of uncertainty should never stop us from dreaming, fighting for, or doing what is good.

Imagination, on its own, is not good enough; we need to visualize how we want to live. We need to see it in our minds so vividly that we can almost touch our dreams. Visualization is something that prepares us for what will come; it plasters (sets) the goal. It defines our aim.

Psychologist Alan Richardson has found that, in the case of free throws in basketball, visualization is almost equally good as *[183] practicing it. Although, in order to work, you have to distinguish that visualization is not daydreaming; it is not like watching a movie, where you get instant pleasure from a theatrical show. Visualization is like a time machine that prepares your body and mind for something that may happen in the future by saying, "You may become this, but only if you do what is necessary." Visualization makes you more aware, so, when the opportunity arises, you will have the ability to recognize it more easily.

Ask yourself: what is the place you would like to live in, if there were no money anymore?

Maybe, in your dream you will play more and work less. Maybe you will travel constantly or maybe something else. Try to imagine such a world, where you have all, and you do not need to work for it — a world where everyone can choose freely whatever he or she wants.

Would you still go to school? Would you fight hard for your dreams? Would you still serve in the army and go to war? What about relationships — would anyone look for a "rich" partner, if all were equal? Would you travel around the world? Would you be more tolerant of other people? What about jealousy and envy?

In multiple occasions, while meeting with different people, I asked them a simple question: "What would you do, if you did not need money to live?" There were no rules, and they could ask me as many additional questions as they liked. I was astonished to learn that many cannot imagine a different way of life than just bare survival. They were so long in the game that they forgot how to dream. The game crushed them so much that, like that gorilla who spent too long in the cage, they lost ability to see when the door was open.

To think about uncharted lands requires a dreamer; to follow that dream and take on that journey requires courage, strength, endurance, and effort. Ready or not, soon, we all will need to become all of that.

The first thing to do on that path is to ask yourself a key question: how would you live in a world where you have everything and the world does not require you to work, compete, and show off?

Work and laziness

Part of the many Universal Basic Income discussions is the nature of work. The central question is: will the people who were given all the basic needs to survive lose interest in striving toward higher things and not live their lives to their full potential, by just watching TV, playing games, browsing internet and doing nothing?

If the major fear is about "losing interest for striving toward higher goals," we need to remind ourselves that, even now, many (being caught in a survival cycle) won't live up to their full potential, simply because they spend most of their time working just to survive. As we cannot predict which person will potentially be the new Virginia Wolf or Fyodor Dostoyevsky, and we do not know what circumstances create exceptional talents, along with not knowing how many of those potential talents we have lost during the course of history, it follows that the worst thing that could happen is that nothing will really change.

Those who are born with the urge to learn or express themselves in art and science will continue doing so, regardless of the conditions of the world in which they may have born or live. When you are born with a craving for learning and knowledge, you will do it, despite your circumstances, and regardless of whether they are bad or good.

On the other hand, the complaint that you will become lazy, if money were given to you, usually comes from rich people and from their own self-reflections. It is the same type of complaint given by parents who punish their children for becoming, behaving, and looking like them. Hating themselves, they cannot stand the constant reminder in the form of their children, as they see their own reflections looking back at them.

What is the relation between work and laziness and what work and laziness mean?

From the Oxford dictionary definitions:

- **Work** (wəːk): an activity involving mental or physical effort done in order to achieve a result.
- **Laziness** ('leɪzɪnəs): the quality of being unwilling to work or use energy; idleness.

A more broad definition of work, which is hardwired into our system, is directly related to a job and the need to earn money. We work to get money, so that we can use it for our daily needs and to buy goods.

Since we were kids, we were taught different types of skills, skills that will help us in the future. By giving us chores, tasks, and different lessons we needed to master at home and in school, we were prepared to be independent; we were trained to survive.

Those survival skills are not the same for everyone; they largely vary in relation to time and civilization development. Tribes from Africa would probably not understand what office work means, and, if they could watch office people from a distance, they would probably think that as office people are lacking in basic survival skills, they are destined to die from starvation. The bushman could hardly survive in a modern city on his own, just as the office person would fail to survive in wild savannas or jungles.

For some, work may mean hunting or gathering, but, for someone else, it may mean breeding cattle, working in a factory, or being behind a desk, crunching numbers using a computer. Work can also have a creative nature: producing paintings, songs, novels, scientific discoveries, and inventions.

In one way, the nature of work is the physical or intellectual effort that will provide us with commodities, but it also has the nature of optimizing both the processes and the work itself, making it less difficult to carry out. In that sense, the improvement of civilization is nothing but discovering new ways to make our survival much easier in the long run.

Our greatest misunderstanding about the nature of work lies in our inability to predict what that "effort" will look like in the future. Just as there is a civilization discrepancy between "lost tribes" and modern civilizations in their understanding of work, there can be a misunderstanding between generations that are just few decades apart.

When accumulated knowledge is exponentially growing, the ability to predict future can be increasingly difficult. Effectively, the blue collar working class will struggle to understand why some kid with a computer may earn more in a few weeks than they will earn during their entire lives by working physically-demanding jobs. In the same way, today's office generation may struggle to understand why future people may be provided with resources for free for seemingly not doing anything.

Furthermore, this discrepancy in understanding different technological capabilities in human generations can cause the older generation (because they are missing the frame of reference) to confuse the already-optimized process for laziness.

For a physical worker, mental work can be considered laziness; however, for the intellectual worker, Buddhist monks in the middle of mediation, transcending mortal toils, can be also labeled as lazy.

So, is "laziness" an issue?

Our desire for laziness is the best thing that could happen to us; for all our health, long life, comfort, and technological progress, we can be largely grateful to laziness. The desire to be lazy and have more free time, where we can enjoy and play, has created everything we have today. In the beginning, we needed to work very hard, in order to survive. Back then, to enjoy more in life we had two options: to go to war for looting/pillaging or to work harder.

With time, we gathered the knowledge of how to hunt, grow food, make fire, cook, and improve on tools, which made life easier. With every invention, we freed a bit more time for fun and leisure. Our laziness made our brains work better, shifting our efforts from the physical plane to the mental plane. All that, so we could find a way to be in our natural state of being: to wonder, to be amazed, and to play. Without that desire to be lazy, we would probably be satisfied with what we could find on the trees or could scatter on the open fields.

On the other hand, laziness, by definition, is an impossibility. The definition says that laziness is "unwillingness to use work (physical or mental) or use energy." Just by being human, we use energy, and, even if we decide to lay and do nothing, we will think and use mental energy. Even the best-trained monks in states of deep meditation or people in a coma (a state of deep unconsciousness) will still spend some mental and physical energy.

We should embrace laziness, and, when we work, we should work in line with it. We do not like menial, boring, and repetitive jobs. Why else would we invent so many shortcuts? Food processing, the transportation industry, computer applications, automation, and mobile technology — everything ever invented is to make our lives easier. There is no need to consider laziness as a bad thing. We should accept it as a part of who we are and work in line with it, not against it.

The real issue about laziness is not the type of effort we are providing; our issue with laziness comes from the idea that those who are not giving any social contribution are taking more resources than they are providing. If you aren't working, building, growing food, paying taxes... you don't deserve to receive anything from what society has produced. That's the idea most people hold.

We have created a belief system which says that, in order to live, we have to work, and, in some cases, people are convinced that we have to work hard, so we will contribute more for our families and for our society.

As the consequence of working hard, working also means having less time for play and fun. In order to support such a belief system, the "work" always needed a lot of advertisement. Over time, as the "work hard" idea prevailed, an entire indoctrination training system was created. Usually, it starts at a very young age, when people are trained to stay seated in one place for a certain number of hours. Later in life, that time will gradually increase. Everyone will preach how important it is to do this or that, how to behave, what to do, and how to succeed at work and life. Often, the system will use the carrot and the stick approach: on one side, trying to scare people with what will happen from not working hard, and, on the other end, the celebrities and wealthy people enjoying all the riches of a material life, presented as a prize for those who work hard.

Every single piece of this illusion is carefully constructed, and most people will follow the same path, lured by the carrot on one end and scared by the stick on the other. The paradox is that those who were presented as a "carrot" rarely ever got there by working hard to achieve the successes they are enjoying, and most of those people who worked really hard for their entire lives never got to the point of enjoying the riches by which they were lured.

That entire construction was created for the sake of advertising the same system of values that was supposed to keep the engine running indefinitely.

The best things in the world do not require any marketing: nature, air, water, food, sex... You know those are good; they do not need any advertisements. You know, as your life depends on those. It is imprinted in your DNA.

When we enjoy something, we are willing to engage. It is in our nature to be curious, to explore, to learn, and to play. Doing hard, boring, and repetitive things is not.

Long time ago, in order to make things happen, ruling classes were compelled to create some kind of incentive that would push the working class to do the work that was necessary at the time. That incentive was created in the form of a system where you won't be able to survive without working hard.

The system also created a false image, in which we all have the freedom to choose, improve, and work in the way we desire, reassuring us that "with enough effort, anyone can succeed." But, that was not and is not true. In reality, a pyramidal system does not allow everyone to succeed. Furthermore, those who are beginning from the bottom have significantly less numbers of choices than those on the top. Those in poverty do not have the same access to clean water, quality food, sanitation, health care, education, or other privileges wealthy people enjoy.

Because of the system, the meanings of work and laziness have changed. Now — when we are technologically so advanced that soon there will be no need for any types of manual work, and there will be no need for many types of intellectual work — we need to go back to our roots and rethink work and its purpose — and change the system and its rules.

Increasing automation is only a problem when it is considered through the prism of the existing system, where only the rich elite has the privilege of enjoying resources. But, if we consider it as a tool of achieving the goal of laziness for everyone, then, instead of being a problem, the same tools become the solution. The first industrial revolution can be considered the beginning of automation. Industrial machines removed the need for labor-intensive, repetitive actions while creating significantly more goods and, therefore, more wealth.

Swami Prabhupada was preaching that: "First class-man is lazy intelligent. He knows the value of life. He's thinking soberly. Just like, you will find, all our great saintly persons. They were living in the forest, (performing) meditation, tapasya (austerity), and writing books." *[184]

The goal of human beings from the beginning was to become lazy, and not just any kind of lazy. A person's goal should be to become lazy-intelligent: one who spends his time on Earth exploring higher things, intellectually engaging himself in affairs that other animals cannot do.

The concept of what we consider lazy has changed over time, and it will significantly change in the future. Increasing levels of automation is not a bad thing, and we should embrace it, as it will help us to do much more than it would be possible by standard means.

Bill Gates once said "I choose a lazy person to do a hard job. Because a lazy person will find an easy way to do it."

One day, thanks to our natural strive to be lazy, and our ever-advancing technology, we may have the ability to terraform planets (transform so that it can support human life), spreading life across the universe. Without technology, just by considering the sheer scale of the work involved, that would be an impossible task for humans – regardless of their number. For self-replicating, automatic machines, in contrast, it would be just as easy as wondering about it.

One day, all manual work will be gone – and probably even many of those jobs we now consider intellectual and that is the price we will need to pay for our technological advancement.

Somehow, along the way, we accepted work as our purpose, equalizing the means of survival and comfort with the purpose of life. One day, when work disappears, we will need to find the answer to the philosophical question of what will be our next purpose of existence.

How much money is enough for happiness?

Richard A. Easterlin in his paper "Economics of Happiness," *[185] wrote that when people were asked in surveys the question "Does more money make people happier?" the most of them gave confirmative answer, although there is a twist. When asked how much more money they would need to be completely happy, people typically named a figure 20% greater than their current income.

Later named the Easterlin Paradox,*[186] it states the following:
Within a society, rich people tend to be much happier than poor people.
But, rich societies tend not to be happier than poor societies (or not by much).
As countries get richer, they do not get happier.

Easterlin argued that, although the result confirms the economists' assumption that more money makes you happier, the life cycle result contradicts it.

The paradox is arising from our psychological tendency to compare ourselves with those with whom we come in closest contact. As life progresses, our contacts are limited to those with similar income, and our happiness level remains unchanged.

Professor Paul Bloom, in his lecture on "The Good Life: Happiness," *[187] says the following:

So, the first moral of the science of happiness is that your happiness is actually rather fixed. It's fixed, in part, genetically, and it's fixed, in part, because what happens in your life you'll get used to, to a large extent.

The second one is: happiness is relative. As long as your country – as long as you're not starving to death, it kind of doesn't matter how rich your country is for how happy you are.

If you're desperately poor, no matter where you are, no matter who's around you, you're not going to be happy. But, beyond that, your happiness depends on your relative circumstance. And this is an old insight. H.L. Mencken wrote, "A wealthy man is one who earns a hundred dollars more than his wife's sister's husband." The idea is what matters isn't how much you make. What matters is how much you make relative to the people around you.

And they've asked people following question.

What option would you prefer more, bearing in mind that your current salary is $70,000?

To make...
In case A:
$70,000, if everyone else in your office was making $65,000 or
$75,000, if everyone else in your office was making $80,000
In case B:
$70,000, if everyone else in your office was making $65,000 or
$70,000, if everyone else in your office was making $75,000
In case C:
$70,000, if everyone else in your office was making $65,000 or
$65,000, if everyone else in your office was making $70,000

Does it matter how much money you bring home, or does it matter how much money you make relative to other people?

They prefer to be making less, if they're making more than the people around them. It turns out that there's research on British social servants and their happiness and their health and the quality of their relationships and how they love their lives doesn't depend on how much money they make. It depends on where they are relative to everybody else.

Easterlin also explains that we decide on how to use our time based on a "money illusion": the belief that more money will make us happier, failing to see that we will never meet these expectations, as they will rise with time in regards to our own income and the income of our contacts.

Because of the money illusion, we are running in an endless treadmill, allocating an excessive amount of time to monetary goals at the expense of time that could really make us happy such as — **family life and health**.

Although we cannot do much about our genetics or personality, all of us have the potential for managing our lives more efficiently to produce greater happiness.

The pursuit of money is an inbuilt property of the current system — that is advertised as the point of the game. That is what the system thought, trained, and prepared us to do. It is no wonder that, later in our lives, most of us just do exactly what is expected of us.

If we would change the rules, would that change the present state to a better one?

We are definitely shifting toward a moneyless society, and that train is not stopping for anyone. Automation will take over most jobs, and the biggest challenge for the majority will be what to do in a society which does not require us to work and, more importantly, how are we going to manage access to resources in such a society.

At this point, it would be interesting to find out how people would answer the above surveys, if they were selected from those who already receive Universal Basic Income.

Would the outcome change if those questioned were chosen from a group of people who love the jobs they do?

Would the results change, or would they compete for money in the same way, trying to be "above" their co-workers?

These are important questions for a future "economics of happiness" study, and considering the pace at which we are moving, we won't need to wait for very long.

Quantity or quality

Things will change when we shift our focus from the things we cannot afford or do not need to those small things and moments that do not require any money but we still enjoy the most.

In Buddhist philosophy, the Three Poisons (lobha, dvesha, and moha) are the source of all "evil" — Sanskrit words usually translated as "greed," "hate," and "ignorance." Everything begins with ignorance, ignorance leads to greed and hate, which, as a consequence, leads to suffering.

According to Buddhism, to reach peace and happiness, one needs to acquire wisdom about world attachments and then free himself or herself from those attachments. Attachment is the emotional dependence we put on things, animals, or people. The delusion in which we mistakenly see ourselves as separate from everything else to which we are "attached" is the deepest cause of our unhappiness.

We continuously buy things we think we need to make us happy, and we usually lose interest not very long after obtaining them. We may see a shirt we think we must have, despite having a closet full of perfectly good shirts. If we buy the desired shirt, we may enjoy it for a while, but, soon enough, we will forget it and want something else.

Greed grows the economy, but, as we have seen from the financial crisis, greed also can destroy it.

Corporations spend huge amounts of money developing new products and hypnotic advertisements, playing with consumer feelings, convincing them that they must buy those new products — like their existence depends on it.

In the current system, we have put rich people on a pedestal, and material possessions are encouraged. We teach this kids in school, using advertisements, creating TV shows, and showing rich people as role models — conveying the message that luxury is something worth striving and living for.

Let's put Buddhism aside, as I am not trying to convert you to Buddhism or urge you to seek enlightenment, although some of you may do that; here, I am trying to propose a moderate approach by using reason and logic.

Beyond religious philosophies, thinking in simple, physical terms, any material possession we own will create a trap, sucking up our time, the same way like a leach would suck our blood — too many of those, and your life will be gone, without you noticing that you ever lived.

Imagine buying a new gadget — a mobile phone, for instance. First, you will need to spend time working for the money to buy it, and then you will spend time using it, cleaning it, and maintaining it. Each time you buy something new, it will require the dedication of your time.

What about a house — probably the biggest investment for the largest portion of the population? The bigger a house is, the more time it will consume. How many people do you know who lost houses, because they bought something they could not afford? How many people do you know imprisoned in a half-built property, unable to finish it, due to a lack of funds? They bought a house that is just a little bit bigger than their neighbor or friend has, and they became trapped. How many people do you know who live alone and constantly worry about what may happen (fire, burglary, storm damage) while they are away? What about taxes and insurance or bills — electricity, heating, water? A bigger house means more time for cleaning and more time for maintenance, which, again, leads to more money wasted.

Money is equal to time — time spent in some office or industrial floor, working for it. If you do not waste your money, you will waste someone else's; maybe you will waste the money of the people who work for you.

In 1900, the average world life expectancy for humans was around 31 years. While that number has more than doubled to 68 years, we are still more than eager to lock ourselves in mortgages and loans for which we will need 35 years of our lives to pay off. Where is reason in that?

The rich person is not the one who earns a lot but the one who has low expenses. If you are earning $2 million a year, and you spend equal amount or more, it is obvious that you will be in the same rat race, like everyone else is, just trying to earn more and more.

To be liberated, to be free, means to have time. If the things we are attached to spend all of our time, we are not free — we are just slaves in some other form. Life will pass in front of our eyes, and we won't live; instead, we will barely exist.

The difference between existing and being alive is feeling things around you, feeling those small moments and people, experiencing equally good and bad things, as they are part of our life.

If you want to put down roots in one place, that is perfectly fine, but do not become a slave to it. Do not buy a house with 7 rooms when, in reality, you need just one. Buy cheaper than what you can afford, and create a nest out of it — something that will have your creative touch, something built with beauty and precision — instead of a simple desire to have "larger" and "more expensive."

Why pay $5000 or more for a luxury, designer bed, if you can buy a perfectly comfortable, and even more functional, bed for $300? Are the looks and brand during the day more important than actual comfort while spending those 8 hours sleeping during the night?

If you have money to spare, you like art, and you have empty walls you would like to decorate, do not buy expensive paintings of well-known, long-dead artists. Try, for a change, doing something on your own, or buy cheap paintings from your talented friends; rarely will they come with high price tag. Buy art, not because someone else says it is good, but because it means something to you. And, if you still like to see those famous paintings, just go to a museum or gallery; they were meant to be seen by other people and not hidden away in some luxury home or underground bunker. They were created, so we could appreciate beauty, spark ideas, or initiate critical thinking. Cathedrals, public halls, and churches were ancient Pinterest or Imgur — places where artists would have the ability to "post" their creations, so that anyone could see them, "comment" about them, and express their feelings about the work.

The movement that calls themselves Minimalist *[188] is advocating a type of life that, as a goal, has the removal of all things in our homes we do not use. In that way, our space becomes less cluttered, and we start living life with less stress, anxiety, and financial debt by not spending on things we do not need. The end goal is to live a happier life by removing attachment to things we do not need or do not use.

Personally, I do not have anything against material things, and I am not saying that the minimalist type of life is for everyone, but, between having 50 pair of shoes and having only one, there is a wide range of choices, and, if we can keep that choice in the realm of one digit, I think we will have more freedom in our lives. Think about it: how much time will you spend every time you go out, deciding what to wear, if you have 50 pairs of shoes? What if you have only one?

Choose the path where things you possess serve you, instead of you serving them.

One thing is obvious: in a moneyless society, it won't be possible to have an infinite number of clothing pieces or unlimited space we could use for our houses. Taking into account current the human population number, it is understandable that, even with machines working on everything, it would be detrimental from the perspective of energy and resource consumption.

However, science has shown that it has ability to surprise us, so it is possible that, in the future, we will have shape-shifting second skin. That second skin will have the ability to take on any shape we desire; it will morph, it will clean itself, and it will clean your body in the process. Even without taking a shower, we will feel and be clean and fresh, regardless of how long we run or what kind of work we do, and, regardless of the weather outside, we will always feel dry, appropriately cooled or warmed.

Until then, it is more likely that, in a moneyless society, we will have access to everything, but we will not possess anything.

This shift will happen gradually; first, companies will turn to a sharing economy, where the transport industry will be turned from a "private ownership model" into the "service sharing model," significantly reducing the number of cars on the road — something like the Uber and Lyft are trying to do now. This change will transform the mental image of a car as from an item of pride and prestige into a form of service where the only purpose of the vehicle will be to bridge the gap between point A and point B in the least time-consuming, most energy-efficient, safest, and most enjoyable way.

Similar things may happen with housing, clothing, entertainment, and many other industries.

In order to understand the reason why this shift will happen, we need to grasp the future — not only through the lenses of the one, single advancement, but as a combination of all of them.

Among other things, people of the future will put significant efforts into reducing the risk of accidental and premature deaths. By nearing the point of time where we will be able to cure all diseases, and significantly increase our lifespan, protection from accidents will become imperative.

This is not science-fiction — this is science reality, and many of these things are on the horizon. Some of them are just 10 to 20 years away from reality.

Some scientists say that there will be no obstacles to living even 1000 years; how long we could live with all perfect technologies, no one really knows, and we can only speculate that it may be 10,000 years, or even more. No one can really know at this point. Now, if someone could live 1,000 years, it is very likely that he/she would like to reduce the unnecessary risk of losing life by going into fights, conflicts, or driving cars.

Probably, if we still have the desire for risk and have a need for an adrenalin rush from time to time, we will move that risk into an immersive Virtual Reality environment, where we will be able to possess a collection of a large number of items, own castles, climb high mountains, or be part of a car race and die multiple times trying dangerous sports, while still remaining completely safe in our physical world.

In previous eras, humans were inspired by religious beliefs that, one day, they will end up in paradise, yet differences between beliefs created more conflict, hatred, and deaths than anyone could imagine.

In this day and age, we could try to be inspired by the mutual goal of good health, life, and longevity for everyone, valuing each life as unique and dealing with it with kindness and respect.

In order to get into that future, we will need to start living like we are already there — to avoid conflicts and wars, reduce our carbon footprint that affects climate change, eat healthy and exercise, reduce stress, and do all other things that will rule out, as much as possible, the risk of dying before we get there.

In terms of the global economy, we will need to tackle the issue that actually drives this entire need for more: the idea which says that, in order to win, we need growth. Currently, our idea of growth means creating more things and more money. So, we concentrate our power and resources, frequently investing huge amounts of time, just to produce new shiny gadgets, so we can achieve constant growth. To supposedly measure the level of our success, we created the GDP number, usually using it to compare with other countries in the global market.

In reality, we are far from winning; while producing endless piles of things we do not need, we are missing the fact that, by killing nature, we are cutting the branch we are sitting on. While we are apparently growing, we are actually living in debt, taking credit from future generations, and using up their natural resources without asking for permission.

If we could focus on what really matters, by putting our efforts into solving real problems and creating a society that is both environmentally and socially safer, healthier, and more enjoyable, we could create a future that will have good outcome for all of us.

Part V
How to succeed with your project

Lodestar

This part is not a "how to" manual and it will not give you instructions how to use the Basic Tax Control portal or how to navigate through its user interface, create projects, or start democratic debates.

Although instructions will be available on the platform after you (along with your community) get access to it, there are good chances that you will not need them at all. The aim is to build an online platform that will have an intuitive, user-friendly, self-explanatory interface that will be easy to use — especially for those who already have experience with similar, already-existing Internet portals and social network platforms.

The goal of this part of the book is not to give you a step-by-step recipe on how to run your business and succeed with it. Many influential writers and very successful business people have already written a formidable number of books dealing with that subject. This chapter is more of a pep talk, stressing the most important things that can certainly help to build the right attitude and hopefully give you enough courage to start your own project.

Hopefully, some of the following stories will help you to deal with moments when you are low on steam, or when procrastination takes over in such a way that even the simplest of tasks look like Herculean challenge. Those general rules and life attitudes should help you in your own pursuit to make your dreams come true.

Delayed Gratification

For those of you who have never heard about the marshmallow experiment,[*189] it is a psychology test in which children were offered a choice between one marshmallow immediately or two marshmallows if they waited for a short period of time (approximately 15 minutes). The tester would leave the room at the beginning of the experiment and then return after the time expired. If the child has not eaten the first marshmallow after the tester has returned, the tester will give a child another marshmallow.

For a child to wait for 15 minutes when sweets are in front of him is a very long time. In comparison, for a child to wait that long is similar to an adult addicted to coffee waiting 2 hours for his or her morning coffee.

The researchers did a follow-up study after 10 years, assessing the same children who were part of the initial experiment, and they found that children who were able to wait longer for the higher rewards tended to have better life outcomes; they were generally more successful, they had better health and better scores in school, and many other things.

Basically what this mean is that **delayed gratification**,[*190] or the ability to resist the temptation of an immediate reward and wait for a later reward, can have a significant impact on someone's life.

Research also points out that delaying gratification is a skill that can be learned, especially during early childhood. But there is a catch to this: in order for a child or an adult to learn this skill, **the environment has to be reliable.**

In 2012, the University of Rochester did a study in which they did the same experiment but divided the children into two groups: the unreliable tester group, where the testers gave broken promises, and the reliable tester group. They found that the reliable tester group waited up to four times longer (12 minutes) than the unreliable tester group for the second marshmallow to appear.

This is the point we will do a small thought experiment. Imagine all possible things researchers have not thought about and have not included in the marshmallow experiment, but that could have happened and that are happening in our world on a daily basis.

The basic setup is this: a room, a tester, a child, a reward, a promise of double reward.

The following are some of my questions:

- Will hunger impact the outcome of test and by how much?
- What if the child is under stress during an experiment or was stressed before an experiment?
- What impact does the child's background have on the test? Do children from poor families perform the same as children from rich families?
- What would happen if the child were left to wait indefinitely?
- What if we just measure the time of the breaking point, when the child eventually cannot wait anymore and eats the marshmallow, which is followed by the tester going in, causing the effect of "I am so unlucky, if I just waited for few seconds more I would have got second marshmallow"?
- At what point of time will the child stop being distracted by the reward and look for a parent?
- What if the child has to go to the toilet? Will the child go to the toilet and leave the marshmallow or just bring the marshmallow with him? If he/she left the marshmallow, what would be his/her reaction if the marshmallow were not there anymore when he/she comes back from the toilet?
- What would happen if another person, different from first tester, rushed in and asked for the marshmallow for another child who is very hungry?
- What would happen in the case of an emergency, such as an alarm being set off and everyone having to "abandon posts" because there is a fire in the building? Will the child take the marshmallow or leave it on the plate?
- What if halfway through the waiting time, some other person rushes in and takes the marshmallow from the child?
- What if another person tries to bribe the child with a replacement (chocolate) for a marshmallow?
- What if another person tries to bribe the child with a promise that contradicts the original promise, saying "if you eat that marshmallow now I will give you two or three more?"
- What if the same tester, after the waiting time, goes in but does not fulfill the promise, and also takes the marshmallow the child had all that time in front of him?
- And at the end, how would any of the previous scenarios impact subsequent tests with the same child?

You have probably already guessed where I am heading with all these questions: the original marshmallow experiment relies solely on strictly predefined conditions.

The issue lies in the word "**promise**," which, according to Merriam-Webster, is "a statement telling someone that you will definitely do something or that something will definitely happen in the future."

When we work on something — for instance, digging a hole — according to the rules of reality, after some time we should have a hole. So, the **expectation** is that removing dirt, layer by layer, will create a round, hollow space, and that is the reality of it, so, if we put our **effort** into the task of digging a hole, eventually, a hole will appear. On the other hand, if someone makes us a promise that he will dig a hole on our behalf, there is always some **uncertainty** whether, at the end of the expected time, we will get exactly what we need. It is not just that this person's behavior can be unreliable, but the environment can impact the person in multiple ways, preventing him/her from finishing the promised task.

The difference between an expectation when we are doing something on our own and when we expect something from someone else is **feedback**. When we do something on our own, we have thousands of pieces of feedback information, and we may not be even aware of it; we will not be disappointed, because we accurately know what has gone wrong, if something happens. If we get a phone call, or the soil erodes, or the ground is wet while we dig, at every moment, we will know. In contrast, when we expect something from someone else, that feedback **information** is almost always **delayed** or inaccessible.

In order to be successful in life, we have to learn certain skills. The expression of these skills will be determined by how accurately we've judged the situation and the people around us.

Knowing how beneficial the delayed gratification can be, instead of just relying on a majority of people to learn on their own, a better approach would be to actively and consciously train people.

Is that possible?

Delayed gratification is largely influenced by upbringing, but research has shown that conscious teaching can give a much better result. A team led by B. J. Casey, of Cornell University,*[191] showed that, if kids were taught a simple visualization technique, where they would imagine that the marshmallow was a cloud or just a picture of a marshmallow, instead of an actual, edible treat, they could withstand waiting for a much longer time.

Additionally, our environment and events in the environment will have a huge impact on delayed gratification. In an unreliable environment, where it is highly likely that what is agreed will not be respected, delayed gratification can have the opposite effect. So, it is unlikely that there will be many individuals who will decide to play against the well-established rules of the game (just like growing up in gang environment is more likely to create another gang member than a well-educated person).

In order to create a prosperous society with a greater number of successful people, we have to **change the environment**, making it more **reliable** and less uncertain.

By creating a fully transparent Basic Tax Control platform, the idea is to give enough real-time feedback, creating an environment that can potentially prevent possible fraudulent activities, encouraging people or/and companies to trust one another.

Eating an elephant

Every project, regardless of its size, has some kind of issues. Those issues can emerge because of the project size or/and its complexity, making it difficult to begin and even harder to run afterwards. The common thing for all projects is that, in order to avoid further technical debt and possible project failure, issues need to be addressed as soon as possible.

Someone said: "if you need to swallow a bunch of big, fat and ugly frogs, the best way to do it is to start with the largest one first." Although I agree with that approach, I would first chop it into very small pieces, so, that at the moment I start eating, I would not even notice that a frog was there in the first place.

You have probably heard the following quotes before:
- **"A journey of a thousand miles begins with a single step."** *[192] — Chinese philosopher Laozi (c 604 BC – c 531 BC), or
- "Build your castle one brick at a time."

or the following two:
- "How do you eat an elephant? One bite at a time."
- **"When eating an elephant, take one bite at a time."** *[193] — United States Army general - Creighton Abrams.

All above metaphors give instructions on how to tackle difficult projects or tasks. But, recently, I stumbled on one more unique approach that jokingly starts with the politically correct command, "Stop Eating the Elephant," *[194] opposing what was previously said. The basic concept of the article is that we use the wrong metaphor, and that our projects are rarely things we disassemble but, in reality, are things we grow. So, instead of eating the elephant, we should start growing our elephant by feeding it one small meal at a time.

Speaking of which, even that metaphor is wrong. Interestingly enough, because our brain uses images for the most part; we like to tell colorful stories in order to easier remember things, rules or morals that are important to us. Therefore, we use metaphors to imprint something in our brains. The shorter and more colorful the metaphor, the more likely it will be remembered. But, therein lies the issue; metaphors depend on our cognitive context. We all have different cognitive contexts, so to each person, the same metaphor can have a different meaning or even be completely wrong.

Difficult tasks and projects, except if your project is not a real, full-size living being, are usually the products of design and imagination.

Regardless of what your project is – book, hardware, software, song, painting or something else – it will rarely come as a finished thing. Usually, it will be a vague representation of what you need to do.

Living beings already have everything inside them; they have the seed of hardware and also physical "software" in the form of DNA, telling each part where to go and how to grow and assemble.

In our case, for our projects, we are the ones who are creating that DNA and also executing the process, and most of the time we do not know, or rather, we cannot predict or envision what the end product will look like. You can start with one melody for the song but at the end, you may discover a much better fit if you replace the fifth, eighth and fourteenth cord. Equivalently, for our baby elephant, that would mean a replacement of the hip, trunk and the left ear, and that does not sounds like an example of very good parenting, especially if we do it as frequently as our clients require from us.

For every difficult problem we have to solve, there are two parts; the first is **knowledge** and the other is **action** (realization).

Our knowledge is indeed like that baby elephant, and it will grow if you feed it regularly with appropriate food. That is because we already have a seed of knowledge; we all have hardware that was already there at the time of our birth.

On the other hand, realization is a sequential process, and although you can have a blueprint, you will draw that blueprint one stroke at a time. When you start assembling things, you will do it one action at a time. Parts can change with time, and a project can grow and become more complex. Regardless of how difficult the things look like on the blueprint, focusing on small parts will relieve you of the psychological pressure, and you will eventually get things done.

Even more importantly, your happiness level will grow during the entire process, as completing every small task will have a meaning of achievement; a small success that will be added up to a bigger pile.

And if you need a metaphor, take this as your picture mnemonic:

Baby elephant (your knowledge) is assembling or taking apart a robot (your project or problem), with the books (things you need to learn) and plan (vision you are trying to complete) alongside. Whatever it does, if done in small steps, baby elephant will be happy during and at end of the process.

Minimum Viable Product

Minimum viable product (MVP) *[195] is a lean startup technique, where the **goal is to develop a product that will only have a minimum core of features essential for product deployment and nothing more**. In this way waste of money and time is avoided by potentially building a product that no one wants to use or pay for.

MVP is also known as the product with the highest return on investment versus risk. The MVP term was first created by Frank Robinson, and later popularized by Steve Blank and Eric Ries.

The first time Eric Ries used the term, he described it in the following way:

"A Minimum Viable Product is that version of a new product which allows a team to collect the maximum amount of validated learning about customers with the least effort."

The following illustration is maybe the best way to describe what is the proper way to create MVP:

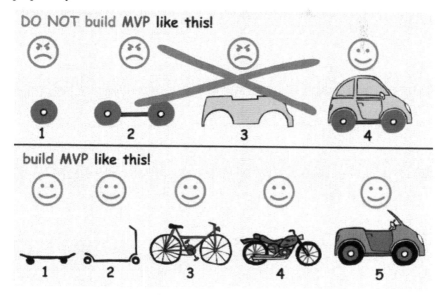

A similar image to this was shown for the first time by Henrik Kniberg,*[196] the Agile & Lean coach, and also the author of several books; by many testimonies, it still represents the truest and simplest explanation of what MVP is all about.

Notice, that at the bottom of the image – on the part that describes "how to build an MVP" – all the faces are smiling. That part usually varies from one author to another, and it also depends on whom you are talking to. Whether you are talking to clients or you have your own product and you are doing personal introspection. In that sense, level of happiness (size of the smile) people experience while working with MVP hugely depends on the outcome, or whether the minimum viable product will be success or failure.

Most of the time, the very first idea we get, along the way, will significantly diverge from the original, and many of its parts will be replaced. In order to minimize risks and get the necessary satisfaction to keep us and our project on the track when times are hard, it is beneficial to have those multiple incremental steps in order to get to the final product. Having those multiple steps with multiple finished products or versions of products will, similar to the checkpoints in video games, keep us entertained and prolong our stay in the "game."

Cooking a frog

The story about the frog that will be cooked to death by being placed in cold water that is slowly heated is often used as a metaphorical example of the inability or unwillingness of people to react to or be aware of threats that occurs gradually.*[197]

Some scientists say that this story is true and other dispute this experiment. Nevertheless, as a metaphor, it is very applicable to many types of human behaviors. Examples such as smoking, overeating, global warming, pollution and overpopulation are very good evidence of this metaphor. Also, this effect has been often used as a tool of oppressive governments limiting personal freedoms, and gradually pushing people into an Orwellian dictatorship type of government.

But can we do better than that?

If this method can be used in a negative way, we can probably harness it for positive things as well. There are already many examples of this: emerging technologies, green energy, social co-housing, crowd funding, open governments, food growing and many more, they all use similar method to gain mass interest.

As part of our nature, we resist to a certain degree any change, good or bad. We may resist changes or adopting new things for many reasons but the most common are fear of the unknown, mistrust, loss of control, bad timing and an individual's predisposition toward change.*[198]

But, by applying the boiling frog "principle", change can happen. Slowly, over time, a stream of water can erode entire mountains and the hardest of rocks. Take the Grand Canyon,*[199] for example: if you give it enough time, it will do wonders. And the softer the rock is, the more significant the change will be.

This does not say that you should act passively. No, you have to be active. You have to roll those small pebbles on the river bed. Every single day you have to scratch that granite a little bit. And it will crack eventually. Every single day you have to do it, no exception, and no rest; with **constant** and **persistent** pressure, regardless of how small it is. And, change will happen.

Rarely can any habit be changed overnight, and hardly any skill can be learned to perfection instantly. Rookie drivers usually cannot handle fast cars very well. Before you learn to run, you have to learn how to stand, how to move your limbs, to walk, and then, by improving, you will manage to run. And, if you continue, you will run as fast as you body's limitations allow you.

The same goes for businesses. Without certain knowledge, people do not know how to handle large amount of money. An excellent example of this, are people who won the lottery; rarely does anyone of them succeed to maintain any significant amount after just one year. Frequently, they end up even more broke than before. *12

The same thing also goes for the systems that are rooted for a very long time in our minds and society. Change requires willingness, persistence and time, and if something is good it will stick. Political change must happen gradually. History has shown that revolutions do not always fulfill a promise of expected change.

In order to make change, we need to know what it is that we are trying to do, and where is it that we are trying to go. When we know these, we just need to move slowly toward it, one step at the time, allowing everyone to adjust to new things.

Therefore, the recipe to cook a frog goes like this: First, try to identify and understand what it is that you want to cook and what frog you are going to pick from the lot. Learn as much about the frog but also about the specific ingredients you will include. Find out more about who will consume your meal, and how that can impact them (maybe they are allergic to "frog legs"). Eventually, you must find out why they might refuse your cooking, as maybe it is not the meal they do not like, but rather the way how it is being served. (*198)

Getting the Dinner Done

Setting goals too high mixed with an unrealistic desire to achieve those goals can burn down the enthusiasm prematurely. If we set before ourselves goals that are very high, we may give up even before we start. This does not mean you should give up; it only means you need to learn how to do it.

Making our dreams come true is very similar to cooking a meal.

Dreams (the things we want or wish for — the objects of our desire) are food, and they are limited by the size of the pot. The flame by which you cook the meal is your enthusiasm, and the strength of the flame represents the strength of your will to get things done.

If the flame is large enough, a dish will be cooked quickly, as influenced by that flame, everything necessary will be done in the shortest possible time. But you have to be cautious; too powerful a flame also means that you can easily burn the meal completely, or it will be well done outside but undercooked inside.

On the other hand, sometimes it happens that a flame is very small but the meal is very big. This is similar to using a lighter to boil a large saucepan full of water.

But even when the flame is small, there is a way to cook the food. We just have to use a **pressure cooker**.

We all often have an urge or need to talk about things we are trying to cook in our heads. Talking is very analogous to opening the lid on the pot while we cook. Each time the lid is off, its container, pressure and the energy are released and the food gets colder. So, in order to cook the food, the flame must be either big enough or the lid must be kept closed most of the time.

Sometimes the conditions are such that many external influences go against our cooking, and they put down our flame or temperature inside of the cooker: winds, frostbites, snow and rain. In those circumstances, keep in mind to shield the cooker and to use pressure cooking as much as possible. If we persist in

235

keeping the meal hermetically closed, the cooker will give us a sign — a steam release sigh sound — telling us that the meal is done.

All that is left is to savor your effort and enjoy the fruits of your work.

...

Have you ever had people around you tell you that you'll never succeed, it will never work, and you'll never make it?

How many times have you had a nice dream but everything was against you?

Just hold those dreams inside and let them boil. Work on your dreams secretly, and do not share them until they are ready, especially not with those that might distract you from what you intend to do. Unless they are willing to help you, so you can join your flames together and enjoy the fruits of your labor with true friends.

World is full of talented actors, singers, scientists and sportsmen who never used their talents. A long time ago, someone said to them that they wouldn't succeed, that they would fail to get what they want and, unfortunately, they believed them.

Do not let anyone convince you that you cannot accomplish what you believe in, and that dreams are just for fools. The simple truth is that deep down we all know even thou we are not aware of it — we all are infinite beings of unlimited potential.

Goals to(o) High

We often get excited about things like political injustice, environment, health, self-improvement... and yet somehow, so many of us fail to achieve even modest progress.

The pattern is well known, regardless of the topic. We will read a book or two, an article, or maybe watch a documentary or online course about our favorite topic and something will click in our brains. We will get really pumped up about it, but then just at the time it is necessary to take action, either very little or nothing happens. All the will, desire and excitement will diminish about the time we are turning that last page of the book we just read.

It's like our inflated bubble of dreams suddenly burst under the pressure of actual work we have to carry out, in order to get to the object we have set as our goal.

There is nothing wrong with a bubble metaphor, or inflating our dream bubble, the only issue is that at the beginning surface of our bubble is neither starchy nor strong enough to withstand the pressure we are putting on it, which will cause the bubble to deflate or suddenly burst.

In the best case, the enthusiasm will last through the next day and then everything gets forgotten, as if the "Men in Black" were in the room just few moments ago. It's very much like a good movie, after which we say to ourselves, "That was just a movie, let's wake up – it's time to get back to reality", forgetting that we are the ones who create our own reality each day.

So, how do we achieve the things we would like to accomplish and avoid our dreams being shattered into a million pieces by our daily reality? Should we dream smaller dreams? Should we settle for something smaller and more realistic, something that is achievable?

If we want to run a marathon, should we set the goal for just one mile? No, we should dream even bigger than our goals. If you want to run a marathon, set the goal even farther and dream about the day you will run 50 miles.

Q: That is completely opposite of what we've learned to this point, isn't that going to crush our will even sooner?

Well, there is a difference. We should understand that dreams are exactly that, dreams — an almost unachievable construction, though structured in such a way as to cause us to start obsessing about them. In the back of our brains we know that maybe we will never get there, but if we keep moving forward each passing day, the dream will be closer and, in one moment, we will pass the marathon line that was our actual goal.

Q: So, we have set our goal, what is next?

The important to realize that adventure is not only about the end point, but more about the path; how the journey is going to shape us and the way we will take to get there. Now, when we dream dreams grandioso, we should not attempt to make them come true immediately, as that will probably fail because we won't be up to challenge. If we ever succeed at the beginning, there is a high probability that our dreams were not big enough.

Q: How to get there?

It is said that "every journey begins with the first step." So, we have to start moving toward the goal we've set in our minds. The steps do not need to be huge ones; even baby steps will do the trick.

Bear in mind that in order to achieve the goal we have envisioned, it is important to maintain a certain level of energy necessary to take those steps and give us a push to continue going in the same direction. The easiest way to achieve this is by dividing one big task into very small pieces. The smaller the pieces - the better; not too small to be insignificant and not too large they will crush us, but just big enough to make us feel comfortable and at the same time a little bit challenged. Each small success will give us back our energy and all of them combined will create a much larger picture, which will tell the story of our struggle and our success.

Each day, just a little bit more than what we did the previous day.

If we want to run a marathon and we have already set the dream that we will one day run a double marathon, but at this very moment we cannot run even one mile, we will first ask ourselves, "What is the longest distance we can run now? Is it 1000 yards?"

On the first day, we will run only 1000 yards. The next day, we will push ourselves to run just a bit more, just an additional 50 yards. Each following day, another 50 yards more than the previous day. After one year, we will be in very good shape to run a half-marathon and probably even more.

There are many approaches to finishing something within a foreseeable time. One of the most frequently used is to create a time frame within which something has to be finished and then put our best efforts into finishing it on time. This approach can cause stress, and make us miserable if we do not meet the deadline.

Instead of using fixed times and deadlines, another approach would be to set the velocity at which we need to move every day. If we do not meet the velocity we have set, we can always decrease it to something that feels more comfortable. The only thing we have to fulfill is that each day we have to do a bit more than the previous day, regardless of how small that is.

In stories, we usually portray victors as especially talented people and we tend to see them through the glass of success. We glorify their success and in the process, we tend to overlook and neglect the effort they have invested - the mental and physical toil through which they have gone.

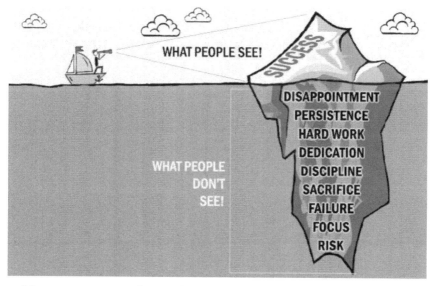

No one wants to watch a movie where a basketball player shoots a thousand times through the hoop each day, every day, for ten years or more in a row. First, it would be a very long movie and secondly it would be a very boring movie. We like romantic, caffeinated versions, where one scene shows our hero as a young student fooling around with his friends, spending time as any other kid, then a few moments later he is already in the NBA, earning huge amounts of money and fooling around with his new posh friends.

Our mind knows everything about us, so to achieve something, we must believe we can. When you think you can**not** do something, your own subconscious mind will undermine your efforts to fulfill your dreams. This effect is so powerful that even when the opportunity is presented on a silver platter, we are unable to see it; we simple dismiss it as bogus. With this in mind, there is one bigger danger, if we try to do the opposite; we may fall into the trap of scammers, who lure those who are eager to cut corners and search for the schemes that will "fulfill" their dreams overnight. There are not too many shortcuts in life, only the paths we choose to follow.

Human beings are capable of achieving remarkable things that are much bigger than they are, but the rule is always the same - you have to put in the effort, in order to achieve something.

Do not be afraid you have set your dreams too high. The best dreams are bigger than us. And, regardless how big your dreams are, follow them! Follow them with such passion that even God would say "Wow. That was pretty amazing...!"

So then, what are your dreams and what are you waiting for?

Part VI
Final words

Waiting for a savior

Not so rare, we as civilization hope that, for all our troubles, in the end, something will happen, and we will be saved. Somehow, we will cope; we will find a way out. While this may have been true historically, now I have a reason to believe that if we do not change something, this time, it won't be the case, as any lucky streak eventually comes to its end.

Many believers wait for a messiah to show up and lead the way, some expect help will come directly from God and others think that aliens will come and solve all of our issues. Many believe that scientists or governments should solve all of our problems.

Some people are waiting, and others completely ignore the problem — like everything that's going on around us is just someone else's job, and it was never our problem to begin with. Climate change, wars, poverty, species extinction... you name it. Don't wait any longer; no one will come!

Why would they?

At the very beginning of the Bible, in the Book Genesis, it is written:
Then God said, "And now we will make human beings; they will be like us and resemble us."...
"I am putting you in charge of the fish, the birds, and all the wild animals."

Now, if you are a believer, please stop there for a minute and think. Imagine you gave a few of your friends your house to take care of while you were gone. When you came back, you have found most of the furniture demolished, all your pets are dead, the kitchen burned to the ground, and most of the walls are knocked down. Would you give those "friends" one more chance to take care of your second house?

If you think aliens will come and help us... why would they? Why would they help someone who does not know how to take care of their own planet? Why would they help someone who is capable of killing members of their own species for small quantities of metal ore? And what about other species? What about all those animals, bugs, plants, and other beings we've caused to go extinct?

Do not wait for aliens or God to help us. We have not deserved the help. We were left to take care of the planet like stewards, but we behave like hooligans.

All the issues we have are not things that appeared suddenly, surprising us. It was not a nearby supernova, black hole, or raging Sun that has happened to us. "We" have happened to us.

This is not a "car crash" by accident, where we are at the mercy of those who are passing by, hopping for help. This is more like road rage, driving under the influence of drugs and alcohol, having two loaded guns shooting around, all while the car trunk is full of dynamite. It was a disaster waiting to happen all along.

Whenever you think about praying for help to God or aliens, just go back to the above sentence.

Ask yourself, if they exist, why should they help us?

On the other end, there are those who fervently comfort themselves with claims that, if nature wanted, it would have gotten rid of us long ago. Adding anthropomorphic properties to nature, and by giving it a will to decide or think as a conscious being is just another of the broad range of our excuses. Expecting nature to take care of itself and us at the same time is like expecting wildfire to put itself out. Yes, it will do that, when all fuel is consumed, when the last tree is devoured by its flames, yes it will — it will stop, like any other chemical process.

In the meantime, we could use our brains and hands to stop that fire much earlier. We could, but that does not mean we will.

Nature does not have a brain to suddenly change its decisions or mood. Nature is not our enemy, seeking to wipe us out. Regardless of what you believe, it is not, but it is not our friend, either. Nature just IS.

We are the ones with brains; we are the ones who can think. We are the ones who can change our minds in a split second. So, instead finding excuses, why don't we take some responsibility and try to fix the things we have broken?

Do not wait for some divine entity. We can only help each other. When I say "we," I mean — me and you.

Wasn't that the entire point all this time — to be like, to behave like, and to resemble gods?

No more excuses, no more whining, and no more waiting.

Sober up, put away all of your weapons, roll up your sleeves, and let's do some work.

Difficult Subjects

"Hope is being able to see that there is light,
despite all of the darkness."
– Desmond Tutu

Regardless of the subject being AI, robots disrupting jobs, the Middle East crises, a cure for aging,*[200] the future system, the possibility of nuclear war, overpopulation or climate change, more and more statements use the phrase "This is something that requires public discussion" or "This is something we need to talk about," "We have to talk," followed by what can be described as close to nothing.

Everyone is agreeing that these subjects are difficult to discuss but rarely anyone does something worth mentioning. Even when we have discussions, they are just scratching the surface, constantly repeating the one same question.

Most of the time, we do not need to hear the same question over and over again, what we need are solutions. What we need is the brainstorming of ideas and the framework that will allow us to quickly validate those ideas.

But, it seems that we are more concerned with what is going on with the rear end of some completely unimportant celebrity persona than what represents a real life-and-death situation.

Maybe the issue is with the media as they do not know how to properly address things and are more centered on scandals and celebrity gossip than what really matters. Maybe by chasing sensationalistic stories to boost their ratings and profit, they forgot what journalism really is.

News reporting should be about a few short questions: Who, What, When, Where, Why, and How. Although journalism nowadays does reflect those questions, these questions being so short usually leave lots of space for misinterpretation. We do not have enough journalists with a good understanding of science, and instead have too many of those who are capable of copy paste journalism.

The main purpose of journalism should be to increase awareness in order for readers to take the necessary action that will lead to positive change. Or, as American Press Institute described it: "The foremost value of news is as a utility to empower the informed. The purpose of journalism is thus to provide citizens with the information they need to make the best possible decisions about their lives, their communities, their societies, and their governments." *[201]

Now, what we currently have resembles more the Nazi Germany propaganda machinery during the Second World War than what modern democracy news broadcasting should look like. And, this is not limited to our country; it looks like the entire world is infected by the same virus.

Maybe the issue is with the platforms and the concepts of likes, comments, and algorithmic timelines. Maybe what really matters is struggling to reach the surface but is buried with daily jokes, sensationalistic news, images of kittens, endless advertisements, and deliberate algorithmic censorship.

An old saying tells us that "a bad workman blames his tools," but on the other hand there is a question why would you drill a hole with the axe? I am not saying that it is not possible, but it is definitely inaccurate and inefficient. Think about it, if technology allows you to make a distance call and connect with someone by video, would you want to use telegraph or smoke signals if the circumstances did not require you to do so?

Every job that needs to be done has its own most efficient set of tools. The better and the more specific the tools are, the faster and more accurate the job will be finished.

Or maybe issue is with us. We have become used to multitasking, constantly seeking new sources of information, similar to junkies desperately seeking their next drug dose. Now, whenever a difficult subject arises, requiring more attention and more concentration, we just procrastinate. It is similar to students who need to study for an exam, but the fear of failure gets the best of them; fear is so disturbing that they tend to do everything else, except what is needed to increase their chances of passing that exam.

We have shaped our technology, and in turn our technology has changed us. Similar to the blacksmith hardening his muscles by pounding on the hot metal, with every swing, the metal will take the shape he has envisioned. However, the metal he is trying to change will untraceably shape his arms, shoulders, bones and muscles.

We cannot blame the man for what he has become, as same as we cannot blame water for taking shape of the bowl. We have become what we have built. We've taken the shape of our surroundings.

If we are unsatisfied with marketing and leisure, with money-centered bullying media, we will not stop it by complaining. The only way to stop it is to build something better so people can migrate toward it.

People, unlike water, have the ability to choose. But that choice is limited to things that already exist. Most people do not have the will strong enough to swim their entire life against the stream — and this is something we have to take into consideration.

To create change in people it isn't enough to expect that only people have to change, for a long lasting change we have to change our tools, platforms, and systems.

Imagine first what we want to become, and then create systems that will mould us in the way we need to change, to become what we imagined.

If we create an environment where bullying is discouraged, where every idea is praised and celebrated, maybe people will not be afraid to speak and share their ideas openly, and then maybe "difficult subjects" will not be difficult anymore.

Then, it will be easier to speak about those difficult subjects in a timely manner. In the meanwhile, we have to do what we can with what we have. And we should not forget that we are the ones who need to build new tools, as there will be no one else to help us or guide us.

"Do not wait; the time will never be 'just right.'
Start where you stand, and work with whatever
tools you may have at your command,
and better tools will be found as you go along."
- George Herbert

Tale of two wolves

In ancient times, when we did not have a written language, one way to transfer our knowledge was by passing metaphors from one generation to another. Usually packaged inside of colorful stories, they helped us remember what is truly important.

Instead of an epilogue, I would like to remind you of a legend whose origins can be traced back to the Native American Cherokee Indians. In a slightly modified form of a somewhat newer date, the same story can be found in the book "The Holy Spirit: Activating God's Power in Your Life," by Billy Graham (1978) and also in "Experiencing the Soul: Before Birth, During Life, After Death" by Eliot Rosen and Ellen Burstyn (1997) and, most recently, in the movie Tomorrowland (2015), where the tale of two wolves is actually its leitmotif.

> An old Cherokee is teaching his grandson about life.
> "A fight is going on inside me," he said to the boy.
> "It is a terrible fight, and it is between two wolves.
> One is evil—he is anger, envy, sorrow, regret, greed, arrogance, self-pity, guilt, resentment, inferiority, lies, false pride, superiority, and ego."
> He continued, "The other is good—he is joy, peace, love, hope, serenity, humility, kindness, benevolence, empathy, generosity, truth, compassion, and faith.
> The same fight is going on inside you—and inside every other person, too."
> The grandson thought about it for a minute and then asked his grandfather, "Which wolf will win?"
> The old Cherokee simply replied, "The one you feed."

In the end, all our choices are down to the individual level — the stuff we are made of and the relation between the system and the person. In the same way as a bowl shapes the water, each person is shaped by the system. The majority of people behave just like water, accepting the shape of the system; some of them are like clay and need more time to conform. Only a small number behave like rocks, unable to take the shape without breaking the bowl or being broken — for better or worse, always staying true to themselves. If we want to change the "shape" of the water, we will need to change the bowl.

The outcome of the problems we are facing solely lies in what we believe is possible and what we are willing to try. If we want peace and understanding, a decent life for everyone, a clean planet with nature thriving, or to travel to other stars, and we believe we can, we will find the way.

It is simply a matter of feeding the right wolf.

And do not forget that feeding the right wolf is a habit. You will need to learn how to do it every single day, until it becomes a part of who you are — an impulse, an instinctive reaction you will not need to think about. It will become part of your character.

> "If you really want to do something, you'll find a way.
> If you don't, you'll find an excuse." *[202]
> — Jim Rohn

Now, go back and read the part with **solutions** again, and everything will be much clearer and conceivable.

Wish to help?

If you liked the book, or you care about the same things and think that we could change the system to meet the challenges of the future, please send us your comments, positive or negative — it will help us to improve future versions of the book.

Our plan for the future is to build a Basic Tax Control platform and make trial runs in small places/communities that are around 5,000 people. In order to get conclusive data, we would need to run those trials for at least one year; if successful, later on, the schema could be applied to an entire country.

Solutions in this book do not have, as a goal fixing climate change or the economy on its own; instead, the goal is to propose a possible foundation that will allow those things to happen faster. When we show that the platform can be successful — real experiences will create easily-replicable "war stories." Those experiences will be open sourced and shared with the global community.

Predominantly, the aim of this book is changing the system; by changing the system, those who already have solutions for climate change will have easier access to funds and the ability to bring them to the surface, creating valuable business that will build a foundation for a future moneyless society.

This is a huge task, and we would appreciate if you can help us to make things better. We would like to share this journey with you. Please share the story, and help us build a community. If you think that Basic Tax Control may work, please tell others, so we can gain more traction and more funds, so we could make things happen faster.

Contact us via email, follow us on Twitter (https://twitter.com/grisanik) and Facebook (https://www.facebook.com/grisanik), support us on Patreon, (https://www.patreon.com/grisanik), and help us build a community.

Visit our official websites www.basictaxcontrol.org and www.grisanik.com or become a member of our group www.facebook.com/groups/basictaxcontrol/ . There, you will find more information on what to do, if you wish to help make things come true faster.

At the end, I would like to thank you for buying this book and/or supporting us on Patreon. All earnings will go toward developing the BTC platform, fighting climate change, and other difficult issues that pester our society.

Appendix

Glossary of terms

AI	– Artificial Intelligence
BTC	– Basic Tax Control
Catch 22	– a dilemma or difficult circumstance from which there is no escape because of mutually conflicting or dependent conditions
CH4	– Methane
CO2	– Carbon Dioxide
EMP	– Electro Magnetic Pulse
EPA	– U.S.A. Environmental Protection Agency
GDP	– Gross Domestic Products
MAD	– Mutually Assured Destruction
Megaton	– million ton
MVP	– Minimum viable product
NASA	– National Aeronautics and Space Administration
NOAA	– National Oceanic and Atmospheric Administration
permafrost	– soil, rock, or sediment that is frozen for more than two consecutive years.
ppm	– parts per million
singularity	– a point at which a function takes an infinite value, especially in space–time when matter is infinitely dense, such as at the centre of a black hole
terraform	– transform (a planet) so as to resemble the earth, especially so that it can support human life.
TNT	– trinitrotoluene (explosive)
UBI	– Universal Basic Income

Endnotes

[1] Wise man words were **"Switch horses."**
The king said whoever's "horse" crossed the finish line last would win. Therefore, by riding the other person's "horse", they would want to cross first, as their horse would then cross last.

[2] Official website for Basic Tax Control
https://www.BasicTaxControl.org

[3] Demography of the United Kingdom – Age structure
https://en.wikipedia.org/wiki/Demography_of_the_United_Kingdom#Age_structure

[4] UK dementia statistics
http://www.alzheimers-support.com/en-GB/alzheimers-stats-uk.html

Learning disability
http://www.improvinghealthandlives.org.uk/securefiles/160228_1447//IHAL2012-04PWLD2011.pdf

[5] A survey of the UK tax system: 2014 – 2015 Tax collection Forecast (page 5)
http://www.ifs.org.uk/bns/bn09.pdf

[6] Which costs more: benefit fraud or tax avoidance?
http://www.theweek.co.uk/62461/which-costs-more-benefit-fraud-or-tax-avoidance

[7] Former Presidents Act
https://en.wikipedia.org/wiki/Former_Presidents_Act

[8] Basic income
https://en.wikipedia.org/wiki/Basic_income

[9] History of Basic Income
http://www.basicincome.org/basic-income/history/

[10] One Man and His Bike: A Life-Changing Journey All the Way Around the Coast of Britain by Mike Carter
https://books.google.co.uk/books?id=0KMbVY0jjEUC&printsec=frontcover&source=gbs_ge_summary_r&cad=0#v=onepage&q&f=false

[11] Are we naturally good or bad?
http://www.bbc.com/future/story/20130114-are-we-naturally-good-or-bad

Social evaluation by preverbal infants
http://www.nature.com/nature/journal/v450/n7169/full/nature06288.html

[12] 21 lottery winners who blew it all
http://uk.businessinsider.com/lottery-winners-who-lost-everything-2015-2

[13] Direct democracy
https://en.wikipedia.org/wiki/Direct_democracy

[14] United Kingdom population mid-year estimate
https://www.ons.gov.uk/peoplepopulationandcommunity/populationandmigration/populationestimates/timeseries/ukpop

[15] Gross Domestic Product: chained volume measures: Seasonally adjusted £m
https://www.ons.gov.uk/economy/grossdomesticproductgdp/timeseries/abmi

[16] How public spending was calculated in your tax summary
https://www.gov.uk/government/publications/how-public-spending-was-calculated-in-your-tax-summary/how-public-spending-was-calculated-in-your-tax-summary

[17] Creative citizen, creative state: the principled and pragmatic case for a Universal Basic Income by Anthony Painter and Chris Thoung (December 2015)
https://www.thersa.org/discover/publications-and-articles/reports/basic-income/Download
https://medium.com/@thersa/creative-citizen-creative-state-a3cef3f25775

[18] "Universal Basic Income: An idea whose time has come?" by Howard Reed and Stewart Lansley (May 2016)
http://www.compassonline.org.uk/wp-content/uploads/2016/05/UniversalBasicIncomeByCompass-Spreads.pdf

[19] Public Expenditure Statistical Analyses 2015
https://www.gov.uk/government/uploads/system/uploads/attachment_data/file/446716/50600_PES
A_2015_PRINT.pdf

[20]Income Tax rates and Personal Allowances
https://www.gov.uk/income-tax-rates/current-rates-and-allowances

[21] Prozac Nation: Use of antidepressants in the UK has soared by 500% in the past 20 years
http://www.dailymail.co.uk/health/article-2356902/Prozac-Nation-Use-antidepressants-UK-soared-
500-past-20-years.html

[22] Total healthcare expenditure in the UK
http://www.ons.gov.uk/peoplepopulationandcommunity/healthandsocialcare/healthcaresystem/articles
/expenditureonhealthcareintheuk/2015-03-26

[23] Is the World Ready for a Guaranteed Basic Income?
http://freakonomics.com/podcast/mincome/

[24] Basic Income Grants Alleviate Poverty in Namibia
http://www.policyinnovations.org/ideas/briefings/data/000163

[25] The Fourth Industrial Revolution: what it means, how to respond
https://www.weforum.org/agenda/2016/01/the-fourth-industrial-revolution-what-it-means-and-how-
to-respond/

[26] Hans Rosling: Global population growth, box by box
https://www.ted.com/talks/hans_rosling_on_global_population_growth?language=en

[27] How public spending was calculated in your tax summary
https://www.gov.uk/government/publications/how-public-spending-was-calculated-in-your-tax-
summary/how-public-spending-was-calculated-in-your-tax-summary

How your taxes are REALLY spent
http://www.dailymail.co.uk/news/article-2596059/Where-taxes-REALLY-spent-24million-workers-
sent-statements-showing-22-goes-benefits.html

[28] Wealth Inequality in America
https://youtu.be/QPKKQnijnsM?t=2m19s

[29] Cost of Scottish independence referendum to exceed £16m
http://www.heraldscotland.com/news/13195426.Cost_of_Scottish_independence_referendum_to_exce
ed___16m/

[30] Direct Democracy
https://en.wikipedia.org/wiki/Direct_democracy
https://en.wikipedia.org/wiki/E-democracy
https://en.wikipedia.org/wiki/Collaborative_e-democracy
https://en.wikipedia.org/wiki/Demoex

[31] List of ruling political parties by country
https://en.wikipedia.org/wiki/List_of_ruling_political_parties_by_country

[32] Totalitarian democracy
https://en.wikipedia.org/wiki/Totalitarian_democracy

[33] Middle Way
https://en.wikipedia.org/wiki/Middle_Way

Movie: Little Buddha (1993)
http://www.imdb.com/title/tt0107426/

[34] Poem "The Eyes" by Mika Antic
www.infinitesouljourney.com/wisdom/poems/eyes

[35] Richard Nixon
http://en.wikipedia.org/wiki/Richard_Nixon

Watergate scandal
http://en.wikipedia.org/wiki/Watergate_scandal

[36] Blood cell Analogy by Lauren Watson
https://prezi.com/j53zefki6plr/blood-cell-analogy/

[37] The three minds of the body
http://www.nariphaltan.org/gut.pdf

[38] Your Gut Has Taste Receptors
http://www.sciencedaily.com/releases/2007/08/070820175426.htm

[39] Self-fulfilling prophecy
https://en.wikipedia.org/wiki/Self-fulfilling_prophecy

[40] Ancient Rome
https://en.wikipedia.org/wiki/Bread_and_circuses
https://en.wikipedia.org/wiki/History_of_games

[41] Competitive dance
http://en.wikipedia.org/wiki/Dancesport#History

[42] Movie "Groundhog Day" (1993) by Harold Ramis
http://www.imdb.com/title/tt0107048/

[43] Monopoly (game)
http://en.wikipedia.org/wiki/Monopoly_%28game%29

Goal of monopoly
http://www.chacha.com/question/what-is-the-goal-of-monopoly

[44] Kevin O'Leary Quotes
http://quotes.lifehack.org/quote/kevin-oleary/i-want-to-go-to-bed-richer/

Talking to Dragons (2:24)
http://toromagazine.com/features/talking-to/toro-tv/20121016/talking-to-dragons

Kevin O'Leary says 3.5 billion people living in poverty is 'fantastic news'
https://www.youtube.com/watch?v=U79DoiC49r0

[45] Animals can tell right from wrong
http://www.telegraph.co.uk/news/earth/wildlife/5373379/Animals-can-tell-right-from-wrong.html

[46] IQ Percentile and Rarity Chart
http://www.iqcomparisonsite.com/iqtable.aspx

[47] "Robots Will Steal Your Job, But That's OK" - Federico Pistono
http://robotswillstealyourjob.com

[48] America Lost $10.2 Trillion In 2008
http://www.businessinsider.com/2009/2/america-lost-102-trillion-of-wealth-in-2008?IR=T

Trillions for the Bankers, Debts for the People
https://papermacheworld.wordpress.com/trillions-for-the-bankers-debts-for-the-people/

[49] Thomas Paine
https://en.wikipedia.org/wiki/Thomas_Paine
https://www.youtube.com/watch?v=sJbGgZowCcA
https://en.wikipedia.org/wiki/Common_Sense_%28pamphlet%29

[50] Estate tax in the United States
https://en.wikipedia.org/wiki/Estate_tax_in_the_United_States

[51] Billionaire Tetra Pak heir Hans Rausing tells inquest he hid wife Eva's body
http://www.dailymail.co.uk/news/article-2248047/Eva-Rausing-death-Billionaire-Tetra-Pak-heir-tells-inquest-hid-wifes-body-12-layers-clothes.html

[52] Abraham Maslow
https://en.wikipedia.org/wiki/Abraham_Maslow

[53] Autogenocide
https://en.wikipedia.org/wiki/Cambodian_genocide#Autogenocide

[54] Milgram experiment
https://en.wikipedia.org/wiki/Milgram_experiment

[55] 10,000-year-old massacre suggests hunter-gatherers went to war
http://www.sciencemag.org/news/2016/01/10000-year-old-massacre-suggests-hunter-gatherers-went-war

56 US nearly detonated atomic bomb over North Carolina – secret document
https://www.theguardian.com/world/2013/sep/20/usaf-atomic-bomb-north-carolina-1961

57 NWO Plans To Depopulate The Earth
http://rense.com/general64/pordc.htm

58 Turkey's downing of Russian warplane - what we know
http://www.bbc.co.uk/news/world-middle-east-34912581

59 The nine countries that have nuclear weapons
http://www.independent.co.uk/news/world/politics/the-nine-countries-that-have-nuclear-weapons-a6798756.html

60 Nuclear power by country
https://en.wikipedia.org/wiki/Nuclear_power_by_country

61 Comparison of Chernobyl and other radioactivity releases
https://en.wikipedia.org/wiki/Comparison_of_Chernobyl_and_other_radioactivity_releases

62 Nuclear Power in the World Today
http://www.world-nuclear.org/information-library/current-and-future-generation/nuclear-power-in-the-world-today.aspx

63 Radioactive Waste Management
http://www.world-nuclear.org/information-library/nuclear-fuel-cycle/nuclear-wastes/radioactive-waste-management.aspx

64 United States Has Enough Operational Nuclear Weapons to Destroy Itself Four Times
http://www.telesurtv.net/english/news/United-States-Has-Enough-Operational-Nuclear-Weapons-to-Destroy-Itself-Four-Times-20140914-0033.html
http://www.nucleardarkness.org/include/nucleardarkness/files/global_nuclear_arsenal_in_number_2009.pdf

65 Genghis Khan the GREEN: Invader killed so many people that carbon levels plummeted
http://www.dailymail.co.uk/sciencetech/article-1350272/Genghis-Khan-killed-people-forests-grew-carbon-levels-dropped.html

66 Stanislav Petrov: The man who may have saved the world
http://www.bbc.co.uk/news/world-europe-24280831

67 2016 set to be world's hottest year on record, says UN
https://www.theguardian.com/environment/2016/jul/21/2016-worlds-hottest-year-on-record-un-wmo

68 We just broke the record for hottest year, nine straight times
https://www.theguardian.com/environment/climate-consensus-97-per-cent/2016/jul/11/we-just-broke-the-record-for-hottest-year-9-straight-times

69 NASA Analysis Finds July 2016 is Warmest on Record
http://data.giss.nasa.gov/gistemp/news/20160816/
http://data.giss.nasa.gov/gistemp/news/20161017/gistemp_seas_sep16.gif

Global Annual Mean Surface Air Temperature Change
http://data.giss.nasa.gov/gistemp/graphs/

70 Antarctic Ice Shelf in Last Throes of Collapse
http://www.livescience.com/50850-antarctica-larsen-ice-shelf-collapsing.html

71 'Next year or the year after, the Arctic will be free of ice'
https://www.theguardian.com/environment/2016/aug/21/arctic-will-be-ice-free-in-summer-next-year

72 Ice
https://en.wikipedia.org/wiki/Ice

73 Risks of Global Warming : Land Ice Melting and Rising Sea Levels
https://www.youtube.com/watch?v=XjjZzAwkRNw

74 Church, J. A. and N.J. White (2006), A 20th century acceleration in global sea level rise, Geophysical Research Letters, 33, L01602, doi:10.1029/2005GL024826.
The global sea level estimate described in this work can be downloaded from the CSIRO website.

75 Heated Water Expanding
https://www.youtube.com/watch?v=R8QsllztZ68

[76] Great Barrier Reef: 93% of reefs hit by coral bleaching
https://www.theguardian.com/environment/2016/apr/19/great-barrier-reef-93-of-reefs-hit-by-coral-bleaching

[77] Antarctic CO2 hits 400ppm for first time in 4m years
https://www.theguardian.com/environment/2016/jun/16/antarctic-co2-hits-400ppm-for-first-time-in-4m-years

[78] The Last Time CO2 Was This High, Humans Didn't Exist
http://www.climatecentral.org/news/the-last-time-co2-was-this-high-humans-didnt-exist-15938

[79] NASA scientists react to 400 ppm carbon milestone
http://climate.nasa.gov/400ppmquotes/

[80] Direct evidence for positive feedback in climate change: Global warming itself will likely accelerate warming
https://www.sciencedaily.com/releases/2015/03/150330122439.htm

[81] Global carbon dioxide levels break 400ppm milestone
https://www.theguardian.com/environment/2015/may/06/global-carbon-dioxide-levels-break-400ppm-milestone

[82] 4. Methane clathrate
https://en.wikipedia.org/wiki/Methane_clathrate

[83] Methane Hydrates - Extended Interview Extracts With Natalia Shakhova
https://www.youtube.com/watch?v=kx1Jxk6kjbQ

[84] Giant holes are bursting open in Siberia, and you can hear the explosions from 60 miles away
http://www.techinsider.io/russian-exploding-permafrost-methane-craters-global-warming-2016-6

[85] Arctic Death Spiral and the Methane Time Bomb : Melting Methane clathrate
https://youtu.be/OoztduCa1uw?t=59m36s

[86] A degree by degree explanation of what will happen when the earth warms
http://globalwarming.berrens.nl/globalwarming.htm

[87] Are the Effects of Global Warming Really that Bad?
https://www.nrdc.org/stories/are-effects-global-warming-really-bad

[88] Tsar Bomba
https://en.wikipedia.org/wiki/Tsar_Bomba

[89] Global Greenhouse Gas Emissions Data
https://www.epa.gov/ghgemissions/global-greenhouse-gas-emissions-data

[90] Carbon Dioxide Emissions
https://www.epa.gov/ghgemissions/overview-greenhouse-gases#carbon-dioxide

[9191] Methane Emissions
https://www.epa.gov/ghgemissions/overview-greenhouse-gases#methane

[92] Ranking of the world's countries by 2013 total CO2 emissions
http://cdiac.ornl.gov/trends/emis/top2013.tot

[93] How many Earths do we need?
http://www.bbc.co.uk/news/magazine-33133712

[94] Earth is now in overdraft for this year: We've used up the planet's resources for 2016 in less than eight months
http://www.dailymail.co.uk/sciencetech/article-3729127/Earth-overdraft-ve-used-planet-s-resources-year-EIGHT-months.html

[95] Planned obsolescence
https://en.wikipedia.org/wiki/Planned_obsolescence

[96] Global Initiative on Food Loss and Waste Reduction
http://www.fao.org/save-food/resources/keyfindings/en/

[97] Key facts on food loss and waste you should know!
http://www.fao.org/save-food/resources/keyfindings/en/

[98] Nearly one-third of the world's population is obese or overweight, new data show
http://www.healthdata.org/news-release/nearly-one-third-world%E2%80%99s-population-obese-or-overweight-new-data-show

[99] Hunger Statistics
https://www.wfp.org/hunger/stats

[100] Estimated U.S. energy Consumption in 2015
https://flowcharts.llnl.gov/content/assets/images/energy/us/Energy_US_2015.png

[101] Global Carbon Budget 2015
http://cdiac.ornl.gov/ftp/Global_Carbon_Project/Global_Carbon_Budget_2015_v1.1.xlsx

[102] The Beyond Burger - Beyond Meat
http://beyondmeat.com/products/view/beyond-burger

[103] World's first lab-grown burger is eaten in London
http://www.bbc.co.uk/news/science-environment-23576143

[104] Do Cow Farts Really Significantly Contribute to Global Warming?
http://www.todayifoundout.com/index.php/2014/04/cow-farts-really-significantly-contribute-global-warming/

[105] Project Clean Cow
http://www.dsm.com/corporate/science/competences/chemical-sciences/project-clean-cow.html

[106] Airlines turn to alcohol as potential jet fuel replacement
https://www.flightglobal.com/news/articles/in-focus-airlines-turn-to-alcohol-as-potential-jet-fuel-368555/

[107] 20 Ways To Transform A Piece of Fabric Into A Shirt, Skirt, & Dress!
https://www.youtube.com/watch?v=Kn1yLZUPN7g

How To Make a DIY Travel Infinity Scarf and Wear it 25 Ways
https://www.youtube.com/watch?v=hkjR7Qm54II

[108] Earthships
http://earthship.com/

[109] Converting Plastics to Oil
http://www.ecology.com/2013/08/07/converting-plastics-to-oil/

[110] Watermill
https://en.wikipedia.org/wiki/Watermill

[111] Archimedes' screw
https://en.wikipedia.org/wiki/Archimedes%27_screw

[112] Weaving
https://en.wikipedia.org/wiki/Weaving#Industrial_Revolution

[113] Robots Will Steal Your Job, But That's OK - Chapter 9: Unemployment Tomorrow
http://www.robotswillstealyourjob.com/read/part1/ch9-unemployment-tomorrow

[114] Elon Musk Hints That Tesla Updates Will Soon Lead To Level 4 Autonomy
http://futurism.com/elon-musk-hints-that-tesla-updates-will-soon-lead-to-level-4-autonomy/

[115] Autonomous car – Classification
https://en.wikipedia.org/wiki/Autonomous_car#Classification

[116] Uber's test track almost ready still no official word on when self-driving cars will roll out
http://www.post-gazette.com/business/development/2016/09/03/Uber-s-test-track-almost-ready-still-no-official-word-on-when-self-driving-cars-will-roll-out/stories/201609020144

[117] The first self-driving car you see may be an Uber truck on the highway
http://www.recode.net/2016/9/4/12791186/self-driving-truck-otto-uber

[118] Self-driving buses are roaming the streets of Helsinki
http://money.cnn.com/2016/08/18/technology/self-driving-bus-helsinki-finland/

[119] Watch a Driverless Bus Putter Through the Streets
http://news.nationalgeographic.com/2016/03/160325-self-driving-bus-automation-video/

120 A self-driving bus has hit the road in Australia
http://uk.businessinsider.com/a-self-driving-bus-has-hit-the-road-in-australia-2016-9/

121 Self driving trucks set to take to American roads by the end of the year
http://www.dailymail.co.uk/sciencetech/article-3725859/Self-driving-trucks-American-roads-end-year.html

122 Uber Self-Driving Truck Packed With Budweiser Makes First Delivery in Colorado
https://www.bloomberg.com/news/articles/2016-10-25/uber-self-driving-truck-packed-with-budweiser-makes-first-delivery-in-colorado

123 Watch These Self-Driving Drone Tractors Redefine Farming
https://www.yahoo.com/news/watch-self-driving-drone-tractors-154658185.html

124 Amazon warehouse robots
https://www.youtube.com/watch?v=quWFjS3Ci7A

30,000 robots now work at Amazon; competing systems emerging
https://www.therobotreport.com/news/amazon-has-30000-kiva-robots-at-work-alternatives-begin-to-compete

125 No Sailors Needed: Robot Sailboats Scour the Oceans for Data
http://www.nytimes.com/2016/09/05/technology/no-sailors-needed-robot-sailboats-scour-the-oceans-for-data.html

126 Ship Operators Explore Autonomous Sailing
http://www.wsj.com/articles/ship-operators-explore-autonomous-sailing-1472635800

127 DeepSee - Automated theft detection with deep learning.
https://www.youtube.com/watch?v=WAC5iutVsZM

128 New McDonald's In Phoenix Run Entirely By Robots
http://newsexaminer.net/food/mcdonalds-to-open-restaurant-run-by-robots/

129 The automated Japanese restaurant without waiters
http://www.bbc.co.uk/news/technology-24525541

Japanese fully automated restaurant
https://www.youtube.com/watch?v=yICVmyySHmE

130 Foxconn replaces '60,000 factory workers with robots'
http://www.bbc.co.uk/news/technology-36376966

131 3D Printed Concrete Castle
https://www.youtube.com/watch?v=DQ5Elbvvr1M

Thai Company SCG Develops Custom 3D Printable Cement for 3D Printing Houses and Structures
https://3dprint.com/131560/scg-3d-printable-cement/

132 Houston invention: Artificial Intelligence to read mammograms
http://www.houstonchronicle.com/local/prognosis/article/Houston-researchers-develop-artificial-9226237.php

133 Robot Radiologists Will Soon Analyze Your X-Rays
http://www.wired.com/2015/10/robot-radiologists-are-going-to-start-analyzing-x-rays/

In Radiology, Man Versus Machine
http://www.diagnosticimaging.com/pacs-and-informatics/radiology-man-versus-machine

134 Another AI start-up wants to replace hedge funds
http://www.recode.net/2016/8/7/12391180/artificial-intelligence-emma-hedge-fund

135 Legal firms unleash office automatons
http://www.ft.com/cms/s/0/19807d3e-1765-11e6-9d98-00386a18e39d.html

The world's first artificially intelligent lawyer was just hired at a law firm
http://www.techinsider.io/the-worlds-first-artificially-intelligent-lawyer-gets-hired-2016-5

Artificial Intelligence and the legal profession
http://www.lawcareers.net/Information/BurningQuestion/Olswang-LLP-Artificial-Intelligence-and-the-legal-profession

136 Robo-journalism: How a computer describes a sports match
http://www.bbc.co.uk/news/technology-34204052

The journalists who never sleep
https://www.theguardian.com/technology/2014/sep/12/artificial-intelligence-data-journalism-media

[137] Moore's law
https://en.wikipedia.org/wiki/Moore%27s_law

[138] Go and mathematics
https://en.wikipedia.org/wiki/Go_and_mathematics

[139] Google says its quantum computer is 100 million times faster than PC
http://www.theregister.co.uk/2015/12/09/googles_quantum_computer/

[140] Will you be replaced by a robot? We reveal the 100 occupations judged most and least at risk of automation
http://www.thisismoney.co.uk/money/news/article-2642880/Table-700-jobs-reveals-professions-likely-replaced-robots.html

[141] Expert warns sex with robots could be dangerously good
http://nypost.com/2016/09/04/sex-with-robots-will-be-so-good-researcher-warns-of-addiction/

[142] What Will the Future Be Like? Information Age, Economy, Finance (1995)
https://www.youtube.com/watch?v=MgwVlsHxdWY

[143] Why do Greek statues have such small penises?
http://qz.com/689617/why-do-greek-statues-have-such-small-penises/

[144] Giant house-building robot lay 1,000 bricks per hour
http://www.digitaltrends.com/cool-tech/fastbrick-robotics-bricklayer-robot-hadrian-x/

[145] Harry Cleaver
https://en.wikipedia.org/wiki/Harry_Cleaver

[146] Economics 304L "Introduction to Macroeconomics" by Harry Cleaver
Chapter 4: The Great Depression and the Keynesian Solution
https://la.utexas.edu/users/hcleaver/304L/304Lrise.html

[147] The Town That Took on the Taxman
http://www.bbc.co.uk/iplayer/episode/b06ygl19/the-town-that-took-on-the-taxman

[148] Global gross domestic product (GDP) at current prices from 2010 to 2020 (in billion U.S. dollars)
www.statista.com/statistics/268750/global-gross-domestic-product-gdp/

[149] List of largest companies by revenue
https://en.wikipedia.org/wiki/List_of_largest_companies_by_revenue

[150] The Story of Stuff Project's Official Web Site
http://storyofstuff.org/

[151] The Story of Solutions
https://www.youtube.com/watch?v=cpkRvc-sOKk

[152] Thriving since 1960, my garden in a bottle: Seedling sealed in its own ecosystem and watered just once in 53 years
http://www.dailymail.co.uk/sciencetech/article-2267504/The-sealed-bottle-garden-thriving-40-years-fresh-air-water.html

[153] Governing Dynamics – "Ignore the Blond" - A Beautiful Mind
https://www.youtube.com/watch?v=ic2JRy1SYqA

[154] De-extinction
https://en.wikipedia.org/wiki/De-extinction

[155] Thomas Robert Malthus
https://en.wikipedia.org/wiki/Thomas_Robert_Malthus
https://en.wikipedia.org/wiki/Malthusian_trap
https://en.wikipedia.org/wiki/Malthusianism

[156] Hawthorne effect
https://en.wikipedia.org/wiki/Hawthorne_effect

[157] Everything We Think We Know About Addiction Is Wrong
https://www.youtube.com/watch?v=ao8L-0nSYzg
https://en.wikipedia.org/wiki/Bruce_K._Alexander#Rat_Park

[158] Utopia (Book) - Thomas More
https://en.wikipedia.org/wiki/Utopia_%28book%29
https://librivox.org/utopia-by-thomas-more/

[159] Wars of the Roses
https://en.wikipedia.org/wiki/Wars_of_the_Roses

[160] Henry VIII of England
https://en.wikipedia.org/wiki/Henry_VIII_of_England

[161] Star Trek
https://en.wikipedia.org/wiki/Star_Trek

[162] Kardashev scale
https://en.wikipedia.org/wiki/Kardashev_scale

[163] Researchers found a way to enable mind communication
http://www.dailydot.com/technology/brain-to-brain-interface/

[164] The Greatest Salesman in the World – Og Mandino
https://en.wikipedia.org/wiki/The_Greatest_Salesman_in_the_World

[165] Les Brown (speaker)
https://en.wikipedia.org/wiki/Les_Brown_(speaker)

[166] Cash for cycling? Polluted Milan wants to pay commuters to bike to work
http://www.theguardian.com/cities/2016/feb/29/cash-cycling-polluted-milan-italy-pay-commuters-bike-to-work

[167] Stockholm congestion tax
https://en.wikipedia.org/wiki/Stockholm_congestion_tax

Stockholm Congestion Tax - It must be perfect from day one
https://www.youtube.com/watch?v=cvIv2PXzLRc
https://www.youtube.com/watch?v=wRS_urfujmw

[168] 'Smart' Spoon Allows Parkinson's Sufferers to Feed Themselves
http://www.voanews.com/content/smart-spoon-allows-parkinsons-sufferers-to-feed-themselves/1830217.html

[169] New 'thirsty' concrete absorbs water
https://www.youtube.com/watch?v=LWiq0NbJmaw

[170] No code on German roads
https://www.youtube.com/watch?v=Sf-O5o4aqcs

[171] "Naked Streets" Without Traffic Lights Improve Flow and Safety
http://thecityfix.com/blog/naked-streets-without-traffic-lights-improve-flow-and-safety/

[172] Shared space
https://en.wikipedia.org/wiki/Shared_space

[173] What causes traffic jams?
http://mocktheorytest.com/resources/what-causes-traffic-jams/

[174] The Simple Solution to Traffic
https://www.youtube.com/watch?v=iHzzSao6ypE

[175] Hero (Ying xiong) (2002) Director: Yimou Zhang
http://www.imdb.com/title/tt0299977/

[176] Martin Luther King, Jr Quote
http://richmondvale.org/35-best-martin-luther-king-quotes/

[177] DeepMind AI Computer Dominate Old Atari Games
http://observer.com/2015/01/watch-googles-deepmind-ai-computer-dominate-old-atari-games/

Google's 16,000 CPU neural network can identify a cat
http://hexus.net/tech/news/software/41537-googles-16000-cpu-neural-network-can-identify-cat/

IBM's Watson Computer Beats the Superstars of Jeopardy
http://bigthink.com/dr-kakus-universe/ibms-watson-computer-beats-the-superstars-of-jeopardy-but-what-does-it-mean

[178] Robot Radiologists Will Soon Analyze Your X-Rays
http://www.wired.com/2015/10/robot-radiologists-are-going-to-start-analyzing-x-rays/

[179] Self-driving trucks and 8.7 million US trucking-related jobs
https://medium.com/basic-income/self-driving-trucks-are-going-to-hit-us-like-a-human-driven-truck-b8507d9c5961

[180] The root cause of boredom
http://www.health24.com/Mental-Health/News/The-root-cause-of-boredom-20130210

[181] Technocracy / Sociocracy
https://en.wikipedia.org/wiki/Technocracy
https://en.wikipedia.org/wiki/Sociocracy
https://en.wikipedia.org/wiki/Leonid_Kantorovich
https://en.wikipedia.org/wiki/Kantorovich_theorem
http://www.nobelprize.org/nobel_prizes/economic-sciences/laureates/1975/kantorovich-autobio.html
https://en.wikipedia.org/wiki/Robert_Owen
https://en.wikipedia.org/wiki/Gennady_Lebedev
https://en.wikipedia.org/wiki/Sergey_Lebedev_%28scientist%29

[182] Tsutomu Yamaguchi
https://en.wikipedia.org/wiki/Tsutomu_Yamaguchi

[183] Sports Visualizations
http://www.llewellyn.com/encyclopedia/article/244
http://expertenough.com/1898/visualization-works

[184] Working Hard?
https://sites.google.com/site/bodhihangout/simple-living/workinghard

[185] The Economics of Happiness by Richard A. Easterlin
http://www-bcf.usc.edu/~easterl/papers/Happiness.pdf

[186] Easterlin paradox
https://en.wikipedia.org/wiki/Easterlin_paradox

[187] Introduction to Psychology: Lecture 20 - The Good Life: Happiness by Professor Paul Bloom
http://oyc.yale.edu/psychology/psyc-110/lecture-20
http://oyc.yale.edu/psychology/psyc-110#sessions
http://openmedia.yale.edu/projects/iphone/departments/psyc/psyc110/transcript20.html

[188] How to Become a Minimalist
https://www.youtube.com/watch?v=VFieLnWZDJ8

In pictures: Less is more, minimalism in Japan
http://www.bbc.co.uk/news/in-pictures-36574697

A rich life with less stuff | The Minimalists | TEDxWhitefish
https://www.youtube.com/watch?v=GgBpyNsS-jU

[189] Marshmallow experiment
https://en.wikipedia.org/wiki/Stanford_marshmallow_experiment
http://www.ted.com/talks/joachim_de_posada_says_don_t_eat_the_marshmallow_yet#t-6399
https://www.youtube.com/watch?v=amsqeYOk--w

[190] Delayed gratification
https://en.wikipedia.org/wiki/Delayed_gratification

[191] Behavioral and neural correlates of delay of gratification 40 years later
http://www.pnas.org/content/108/36/14998.full

[192] "A journey of a thousand miles begins with a single step" – etymology
https://en.wiktionary.org/wiki/a_journey_of_a_thousand_miles_begins_with_a_single_step

[193] Creighton Abrams
https://simple.wikiquote.org/wiki/Creighton_Abrams

[194] Stop Eating the Elephant
http://www.therobertd.com/stop-eating-the-elephant/
http://achievethegreenberetway.com/dont-eat-the-elephant-one-bite-at-a-time/

[195] Minimum viable product (MVP)
https://en.wikipedia.org/wiki/Minimum_viable_product

[196] Henrik Kniberg
http://blog.crisp.se/author/henrikkniberg
http://www.amazon.com/Henrik-Kniberg/e/B007AK6OT4

[197] Boiling frog
https://en.wikipedia.org/wiki/Boiling_frog

Boiling Frog Experiment (no animals were hurt in the making of that video)
https://www.youtube.com/watch?v=APxGubAkOz0

[198] Overcome The 5 Main Reasons People Resist Change
http://www.forbes.com/sites/lisaquast/2012/11/26/overcome-the-5-main-reasons-people-resist-change/

[199] Grand Canyon
https://en.wikipedia.org/wiki/Grand_Canyon

[200] WHO Soon To Classify Aging As A Disease, Opening The Flood Gates For New Pharmaceuticals
http://tapnewswire.com/2015/11/who-soon-to-classify-aging-as-a-disease-opening-the-flood-gates-for-new-pharmaceuticals/

[201] What is the purpose of journalism?
http://www.americanpressinstitute.org/journalism-essentials/what-is-journalism/purpose-journalism/

[202] Jim Rohn - Quote origin
http://www.barrypopik.com/index.php/new_york_city/entry/if_its_important_to_you_youll_find_a_way_if_not_youll_find_an_excuse

Printed in Great
Britain
by Amazon